CUSTER
VINDICATED

CUSTER VINDICATED

JACK L. PENNINGTON

iUniverse, Inc.
New York Lincoln Shanghai

CUSTER VINDICATED

iUniverse books may be ordered through booksellers or by contacting:

iUniverse
2021 Pine Lake Road, Suite 100
Lincoln, NE 68512
www.iuniverse.com
1-800-Authors (1-800-288-4677)

Because of the dynamic nature of the Internet, any Web addresses or links contained in this book may have changed since publication and may no longer be valid.

ISBN: 978-0-595-45542-3 (pbk)
ISBN: 978-0-595-89851-0 (ebk)

Printed in the United States of America

Contents

PREFACE. vii

OVERVIEW xiii

CRITIQUE: Vanishing Victory, by Bruce Liddic *1*

CHAPTER 1   COVER-UPS 3

CHAPTER 2   TIMING DIFFERENCES 13

CHAPTER 3   THE TIME GAP 26

CHAPTER 4   CUSTER'S ATTACK PLAN 31

CHAPTER 5   CUSTER'S ORDERS TO RENO AND
BENTEEN 40

CHAPTER 6   RENO IN THE VALLEY. 59

CHAPTER 7   CUSTER'S TRIP TO MEDICINE TAIL
COULEE 78

CHAPTER 8   CUSTER IN MEDICINE TAIL COULEE . . . 107

CHAPTER 9   BENTEEN JOINS RENO 128

CHAPTER 10   THE FINAL STAGE 141

CRITIQUE: Custer's Last Fight: The Story of The Little Big Horn, By David C. Evans. *153*

CRITIQUE: The Little Big Horn, By Robert Nightengale *167*

CONCLUSION 185

SUMMARY 191

APPENDIX A   EXAMINING A TIME ANALYSIS 199

APPENDIX B   THE MEANING OF BENTEEN'S ORDERS. 205

APPENDIX C   CUSTER'S ORDERS ACCORDING TO DAVERN AND MARTIN 211

Map I 215

Map II. 217

Map III 219

PREFACE

In the books and articles I have written on the Battle of the Little Big Horn, I have brought out questions that have not been asked let alone answered. I have strong differences of opinion with writers that are recognized authorities on the battle. My main premise is that Lt. Colonel Custer was a competent commander, and his decisions and actions until he reached Medicine Tail Coulee were militarily sound. The fact that Custer has been blamed for the defeat of his five companies is a result of the Reno Court of Inquiry, the desire of the court to prevent further investigations, and the 7th Cavalry officers' attempt to keep Major Reno from being court-martialed and Captain Benteen indicted.

I believe the underlying views of the battle are wrong, and have been for a hundred and twenty eight years. They depict Lt. Colonel George Armstrong Custer as being incompetent.

In this manuscript I will be presenting reasons which should prove Custer was not at fault for the loss of his five companies or the defeat suffered by the 7th Cavalry. I will critique three well known writers' views of Lt. Colonel Custer, the Little Big Horn Battle, and the Reno Court of Inquiry. They are writers that are not biased against Custer, but have failed to ask the questions they should have, and by not doing so have inadvertently placed the blame for the defeat on Custer.

An excellent example of what I refer to as the "accepted" version of the battle is Bruce Liddic's book, *Vanishing Victory*. I will use Liddic's book as my main critique. I will then exam David C. Evans' book, *Custer's Last Fight*. Evans' book follows the accepted version with variations on time and Custer's final defensive movements. My third review will be the book, *Little Big Horn*, by Robert Nightengale. Nightengale takes a more extreme position in that he places the blame for the wiping out of Custer's five companies squarely on Major Reno's and Captain Benteen's actions during the battle. Nightengale then attempts to levy charges against the Reno Court of Inquiry which he hopes the Army Board will examine, and will then reverse the Court's decision. He believes Custer's actions have been blamed for the defeat because of the cover-ups at the Reno Court by Major Reno, Captain Benteen, officers, and the Court's own bias. Nightengale wants the Army Board to exonerate Custer, and place the blame for the defeat on Major Reno and Captain Benteen. Nightengale goes along with the accepted version until Major Reno and Captain Benteen move to Weir Point. There he has them seeing, or realizing, that Custer's five companies have not gone into action, but instead of going to support them they retreat back to Reno Hill.

All three of the writers recognize the partiality displayed by the Reno Court, and the cover-up by officers, and yet they fail to connect them to what I consider quintessential details. However, their overall coverage of the battle, along with sources and background material that they bring out is superb. All three of these books should be required reading for anyone interested in either Custer or the Battle of the Little Big Horn.

A good example of my main criticism of these and other writers can be seen in their support of the Custer maxim, but their failure to explain why it was never applied by Custer. The maxim brings out that to Custer attack and victory were synonymous. However, these writers fail to show where Custer with his five companies ever launched an attack against the Indians.

Since I continually use the term the "accepted" version, I should explain what I mean. The following is what I refer to as the "accepted" version which provides the basic structure found in practically all writings. Writers have added minor variations, but have stayed within the accepted framework, which is:

1. At the conference held on the steamboat the Far West on June 21st, Custer ignored warnings of the strength of the Indians because he believed his 7th Cavalry could defeat any number of Indians. As the 7th traveled down the Rosebud, Custer dismissed or failed to recognize the significance of the Indian signs, or the warnings issued by his scouts.

2. Custer, when at the Crow's Nest, failed to accept the scouts' sightings of the Indian encampment, and so the division of his command was only a precautionary move. Custer sends Captain Benteen to the bluffs on his left to either check for Indians or because of Benteen's enmity he wants to "take him down a notch." Custer then proceeds down Reno Creek, but since he has not accepted his scouts' sighting of the Indian village, writers refer to the move as a "reconnaissance in force."

3. As Custer nears the Little Big Horn they pass the Lone Tepee, and note some Indians fleeing. He then sends Reno after these Indians, or to attack the Indian village. He allows his five companies to water, and plans to then follow Reno. He hasn't heard from Benteen, but still doesn't believe it is necessary to send him any messages that would indicate his plans.

4. Custer hears from both Reno and Girard, the Ree interpreter, that the Indians are "strong" and moving against Reno. Custer then decides to flank the Indians, so he moves to the bluffs on the east side of the river. Reno has moved down the valley and is about to set up his skirmish line. Custer sends Sgt. Kanipe to have Captain McDougall hurry the packs. Custer decides to keep his five companies hidden from the Indians so they go down Cedar Coulee.

5. Custer goes to Medicine Tail Coulee and then to Luce Ridge, from where he is able to observe Ford B and the Indian village. Reno is firing on the village. Custer sends two companies to the ford to demonstrate in order to draw the warriors away from Reno. Custer hears that Benteen is back on the main trail and sends Trumpeter Martin with a message for him to come to his aid and "be quick."

6. Custer decides to wait for Benteen before attacking. However, the Indians have now forced the two companies at the ford to retreat. Custer decides to instigate an offense by moving to the north in order to cut off the noncombatants, or to envelop the Indian villages.

7. You now find a number of hypothesis with the same final result. Custer and his five companies are defeated by an overwhelming number of Indians, after a valiant but futile effort.

Although the three writers I critique recognize that the officers' testimony at the Reno Court differs with their prior statements, these writers fail to apply or connect the cover-ups to the actions or lack of action by the major participants. There were three major cover-ups. The first and most important being the orders Custer gave. The second was a time change, and the third was the sighting of Custer on the ridge by Reno's troops and Ree scouts as they moved down the valley.

The generally accepted basis for establishing the time of events or action is based on time given at the Reno Court by Lieutenant Wallace for when Custer divided the command. A time-motion analysis has then been used in determining comparative locations of the command and Indians, rather than comparing and analyzing position statements. A time-motion analysis is exemplified by John S. Gray in his book, *Centennial Campaign,* which David Evans also uses in formulating his determination of the related positions of the major participants and their actions. Such time-motion analysis are inaccurate because they are based not only on Lt. Wallace's initial time cover-up but also on faulty premises. A time-motion analysis should not be used in determining the relation between the various military units. It has therefore been misleading and the basis for errors by Gray, Evans, and most of the other major writers.

In other words, time should not be measured by your assumption of gaits, distance, and terrain covered, but instead by relative positions as reported by the major players. The actual time of the day is not important for determining relative positions, although it certainly is useful in other analysis. Probably the best example of the importance of relative positions, but where the actual time is a secondary consideration, is the position of Reno's troops in relation to Custer's. The accepted version has Reno's move down the valley ahead of Custer arriving on the ridge. In fact most writers have Reno already establishing his skirmish line. This has been accomplished by a time-motion analysis. However, these same writers will describe how Custer sees a napping village, and how Curley says Mitch Bouyer wonders were the warriors have gone. This creates a paradox that cannot be logically explained, so it is ignored, or brushed off by giving a simple unrealistic excuse or using a time-motion analysis. If you connect the dots by examining conflicting accounts, you find testimony that Reno's troops reported seeing Custer on the ridge when reforming after crossing Ford A, and while moving down the valley. Logic and common sense would then indicate that there is no sound explanation as to how Custer can see a "napping" village, or how one can possibly wonder where the warriors have gone at a time when Reno has already set up his skirmish line and fired on the village. Indian reports show the village erupting after the initial gunfire by Reno's troops, so the village would be in a state of bedlam. This state of bedlam would have lasted for some time. This is a quintessential time relation. What this actually means is that Custer was on the ridge and undoubtedly moving toward Medicine Tail Coulee as Reno moved down the valley. This can be substantiated by an analysis of Lieutenant Varnum's statement that Reno was establishing his skirmish line when Custer was on his way to Medicine Tail Coulee. Although one should consider that Varnum may have been attempting to justify Reno's flight to the ridge, time-wise "E" Company could have been in the process of leaving the Weir Point vicinity.

This is an essential analysis that these writers ignore, brush-off, or simply fail to see why it is important. In other words Custer knew where the Indian village was, he had plans on how to attack it, and he wasn't planning on following Reno across Ford A. These plans (as the orderlies' testimony substantiates) would have been known by Major Reno and Captain Benteen. Custer would have reached Ford B while Reno was still fighting in the valley, and by putting time statements together (connecting the dots) one should know Reno's troops were fleeing to the ridge at the time Custer's troops had or were still retreating from Ford B.

Bruce Liddic's latest book, *Vanishing Victory*, fits the case study role which exemplifies the framework scenario or what I refer to as "the accepted version" of the Battle of the Little Big Horn. Writers have brought out additional information and sources, but their portrayal of Custer's actions stays within the same outline created by the Reno Court cover-ups. Liddic, as do the other two writers that I critique, realize that there were cover-ups at the Reno Court by Major Reno and Captain Benteen, which officers complied with. However, there is a failure to then connect the cover-ups with the actions Reno and Benteen accuse Custer of doing. These actions make Custer out to be an incompetent commander.

My critique of Liddic's book will cover those premises that are essential for an understanding as to who or what was at fault for the debacle that occurred. I will show that by accepting the cover-ups presented at the Reno Court writers have allowed a distorted perception of Custer to emerge. In contrast to my other two critiques, I will utilize Liddic's overall coverage of the battle in an attempt to show how writers fail to connect the cover-ups to the action that took place.

In doing so I will bring out that from the time Custer left the meeting on the steamboat Far West with General Terry, Colonel Gibbon, and others, he expected to encounter a large force of Indians. And he knows that those Indians most likely would be found along the Little Big Horn. The Indian signs that they saw along the Rosebud would have only substantiated those views. I will explain the part that the sighting at the Crow's Nest played in the essential cover-up, how it has affected the view of the writers, and how the term a "reconnaissance in force" was adopted by these writers in order to support their unsound scenarios. I will show that Custer formulated orders at the division of the command that would be expected from any competent commander, and how they were out of necessity covered-up. It will become clear that there can be no objective way to refute that the time of events was changed in order to prevent the court-martial of Major Reno. It will also become apparent that Indian accounts have been twisted to support the accepted views rather than connecting them to create a rational conclusion. And I will explain how Custer's move to Ford B has been distorted or ignored, and why something must have happened to the commander of the 7th Cavalry while crossing Ford B.

I am not an authority on courts of inquiry or court-martials that have taken place in our history, but I am aware of many of the official lies, distortions, and cover-ups that have taken place. Today there is a myriad of these examples, so to merely say, as Colonel Graham said to Captain Carter, that all these officers wouldn't have lied at Reno's Court of Inquiry,[1] misses the point of *why* they would have lied or said they were not in a position to have known the answer. Liddic, and others, reveal the many "whitewashes" officers made at the Court, but fail to either recognize or connect them to the major premises necessary to accurately assess the battle. They fail to note the lack of questions that show the Court was a massive cover-up. These are the questions I will deal with along with the reasons why the Court failed to ask them.

I think any of us become biased, and I want to emphasize that I am biased. I believe Custer was a competent, attack-minded, courageous commander. He was able to process a situation quickly and accurately, as stated by General McClellan, and again by General Pleasonton in recommending Custer to the rank of General during the Civil War.[2] The purpose of this manuscript is to counter the arguments used by those who have portrayed Custer over the years as an incompetent commander. If my arguments are not sound, hopefully those writers will take the time to objectively refute them.

SOURCES

1. Graham, *The Custer Myth*, 207.

2. Urwin, *Custer Victorious*, 80, 81.

OVERVIEW

I will not spend time on the background of the campaign since this has been covered thoroughly from many angles by practically all the writers of the battle. That is not the purpose of this book.

Briefly: The campaign was to force the Indians back on the reservations. The action became known as "The 1876 Indian War." The Army decided on a three pronged operation into the Powder River country where they realized the Indians would be found. General George Crook was to lead a command from the south, while Brigadier General Alfred Terry would be over-all commander of a force moving against the Indians from the north. Terry's command was divided into two components, one being called the Dakota Column made up of the 7th Cavalry under control of Lt. Colonel George Armstrong Custer, and the other the Montana Column under Colonel John Gibbon. General Crook's command was stopped at the Battle of the Rosebud, just over a week before the ill-fated defeat of Custer at the Battle of the Little Big Horn.

There was a meeting on the 21st of June between General Terry and his commanders. The plan devised was for Colonel Custer to take the 7th Cavalry and move down the Rosebud, making sure the Indians wouldn't scatter to the south. However, it was left to Custer's discretion, once the Indians were found, whether to attack or wait for Colonel Gibbon and his primarily infantry column which would march from the Yellowstone down the Big Horn River to the Little Big Horn, hopefully arriving on the 26th. Note their assumption that the Indians would be found along the Little Big Horn, and they could expect to find between 1500 to 3000 warriors.[1]

Custer, as he traveled down the Rosebud, noticed the growing number of recent Indian signs. If there were any questions as to their meaning, either the Ree scouts or Mitch Bouyer and the Crow scouts would have informed Custer. The Crow scouts and Mitch Bouyer were well-versed in both the Lacotah signs and the topography. Custer's three white scouts, Girard, Reynolds, and Herendeen, were also familiar with the Indians. Girard was interpreter for the Rees, and Mitch Bouyer for the Crows. There is no reason to believe, as some have, that Custer would have ignored the signs.

SOURCES

1. Willert, *Little Big Horn Diary,* 193.

CRITIQUE:

Vanishing Victory, by Bruce Liddic

1

COVER-UPS

In his official report following the battle, Major Reno said that the regiment encamped on the night of the 24th and waited for information from the scouts. About 9 p.m. Custer called a meeting in which he informed the officers that beyond a doubt the village was in the valley of the Little Big Horn.[1] In order to reach it, it was necessary to cross the divide between the Rosebud and the Little Big Horn, and it would be impossible to do so in the daytime without the Indians discovering their march. Custer said they should be prepared to march by 11:20 p.m.[2] Custer informed them that they could expect to meet 1000 to 1500 warriors. Prior to this they compared watches to be sure everyone had the official time.[3] Like Custer's attack maxim, these elements are important to remember. One should also recognize that Custer had stopped and was waiting for the scouts' report, and he had enough respect for that report to believe the Indians would be found along the Little Big Horn. The authorities should connect Custer's acceptance of scouting reports with accusations made against Custer.

An interesting timing cover-up can already be seen in comparing Reno's report from right after the battle with that of General Godfrey's revised 1908 *Narrative*. Major Reno's report made July 5, 1876, said that they came to a halt after the scouts told Custer he would not be able to cross the divide before daylight (again, a decision made because of the scouts' report). The time was about 2 a.m. of the 25th.[4] Godfrey's report also said 2 a.m., but Reno's report indicated that they moved out after about three hours which would make it roughly 5 a.m.,[5] whereas Godfrey didn't have them moving out until 8 a.m.[6] This was earlier than many other reports by the authorities. (Throughout my manuscript I will be referring to the "authorities," "writers," and "coterie" as those historians who have accepted the basic findings from the Reno Court.) The Reno Court time was 8:45 a.m.[7] One should already be able to see that a timing cover-up was being made, which can be traced back to the Reno Court

In his account of the night march and when they came to a halt, Benteen put the time at about 2:30 a.m.[8] This halt became known as Halt 1. Benteen said they rested for about an hour and a half; Reno said 3 hours.[9] I have used the longer period and said the command moved out by 5 a.m. One doesn't mistake 5 a.m. in the morning with 8 a.m. or 8:45 a.m. or later. Since the two officers who benefited from the later time gave the earlier hours (before subsequently changing them), I think it is safe to say the regiment moved out by 5 a.m. We should also remember that Custer had already left for the Crow's Nest. How far was the Crow's Nest from Halt 1 along Davis Creek? According to Gray's accepted estimate it was roughly 4 3/4 miles.[10]

Colonel Godfrey wrote to Cyrus Townshend Brady disputing a portion of an article printed in a semiofficial account entitled "Record of Engagements with Hostile Indians in the Division of the Missouri, from 1868 to 1882," it was being reprinted in the United States Cavalry Journal, Fort Leavenworth, Kansas, and said:

> "About two o'clock in the morning of July 25th, the column halted for about three hours, made coffee, and then resumed the march, crossed the divide, and by eight o'clock were in the valley of one of the branches of the Little Big Horn.[11]

Colonel Godfrey wrote "This is misleading and not altogether true. We halted about two a.m., til 8 a.m., then marched till ten a.m., halted, and it was not until nearly noon that we crossed the divide."[12]

What Godfrey's statement brings out is that once the officers testified at the Reno Court they were going to stick by what they said. It was better to "let sleeping dogs lie" then to stir up a "hornets nest." This is evident in Benteen's reference to his comments at the Reno Court concerning Reno,[13] and also in Judge Goldin's remarks that Lt. Hare would never even discuss the battle.[14] When you have such extremely different accounts, whether they have to do with time, orders, or actions, then you need to look for underlying motives. In this example—Godfrey's, Hare's, and Benteen's are apparent, but what is the reason that earlier times were stated, and on official documents? In your search for motive take it a step further: Why the difference not only in timing, but in orders between those stated by officers, and those by orderlies and enlisted men? There is only one answer that I have came up with and that is in order to protect Reno, Benteen, and the image of the 7th Cavalry, as well as the army, the officers needed to cover-up both Custer's orders, and the time gap that existed after Benteen joined Reno and before they moved to aid Custer. The earlier time and the orders stated by those other than officers, were made and they were not involved in the cover-ups, and so they reported the time and orders as they remembered them. To substantiate the earlier times one only has to look at Indian accounts. There is no way that officers, after the trial, were going to make public statements changing their court testimony.

On the night of the twenty fourth the scouts had informed Custer that in the early morning they would be able to see whether the Indian camps were along the Little Big Horn or not. Lt. Varnum, as Chief of Scouts, went with the scouts to what the Indians called the Crow's Nest. Custer told Varnum he thought he would be at the divide by daylight, and that they would be leaving by eleven that night. Varnum wanted another white man to go with him, and asked for Charlie Reynolds. Varnum said they left about 9 p.m.[15] We should recognize that the times, until the next morning, are accepted times, so why are there extreme variances found in the times used the next day?

As I said before, there should be no question that the times given right after the battle by the two major figures, Reno and Benteen, as to when the regiment moved from Halt 1 should be taken as correct, if for no other reason than they were the ones who benefited by using later times, and by the time of the Reno Court needed to and did change their stories.

There are several things that have made an analysis of the battle difficult. The nationwide curiosity and concern, along with the criticism leveled particularly at Major Reno caused him to call the Court of Inquiry. In order to protect not only Reno but Benteen, other officers, the image of the 7th Cavalry, and the army, it meant the officers had to make the Reno Court a cover-up of court martial offenses. Then if the enlisted men's', the civilians', and Indians' statements didn't correlate with the officers they would be discarded or discredited. The officers' testimony would be the correct version of events.

Let's look at the erroneous times used by Liddic and most writers. Liddic times are similar to those created by John Gray.

I will be using the sun times established by Gray. The following are the ones we are concerned with: Nautical twilight began at 2:44 a.m.—this is when full darkness ends; civil twilight began at 3:34 a.m.; and the sun rose at 4:13 a.m.[16]

In my other books and articles I tried to be diplomatic when referring to timing cover-ups, and have presented them in what I consider to be non prejudicial manner, but this time I am biased. To me the timing cover-ups are so apparent and abjectly illogical that I will state them as such.

We should know and accept the following: At nautical twilight several of the scouts, most likely two Crows or Mitch Bouyer, and at least one of the Crows, go to a lookout area on the Crow's Nest. Shortly afterwards they see smoke rising from the Indian village. This is still during Nautical twilight. They then awaken Varnum, who went to the lookout as daylight began to appear.[17] This is not 4 a.m. when Liddic has Varnum being awakened, but closer to 3 a.m. Varnum is not able to see what the Indians indicate are horses and smoke from the village. However, Varnum was certainly not going to spend a lot of time looking, since this was the information Custer had been waiting to hear. Although he was not able to see what the scouts were pointing out, Varnum knew that he had to assume they were correct. He would have wasted no time in sending Red Star and Bull to Custer. We should keep in mind that Reno and Benteen have the regiment moving from Halt 1 by at least 5 a.m., and Custer has already left for the Crow's Nest. But Gray, Liddic, and others don't have Custer receiving the message from Red Star until 7:30 a.m.[18] Benteen at Halt 1 said Custer passed him on horseback as it was just getting light.[19] Michael Reynolds, the son of the Crow agent, was with his father and the three Crow scouts, White Man Runs Him, Hairy Moccasin, and Goes Ahead, when they took Edward Curtis, General Woodruff, and others over Custer's route. Michael said Custer was at the Crow's Nest by 4 a.m.,[20] and White Man Runs HIm said 6 a.m.[21] During this time Custer would have reached the Crow's Nest lookout. These times correspond to Reno's and Benteen's, which have the regiment moving from Halt 1 by 5 a.m. Benteen said that they went a mile or so and then halted (Halt 2).[22] Let's keep in mind that by cavalry horse time a mile at a walk could be covered in twenty minutes. Custer met them after having been to the lookout, and told them the scouts had seen the smoke from the Indian village on the west side of the Little Big Horn, but the village couldn't be seen because of the bluffs. Red Star said Custer at first didn't see the horses or the village, but after receiving glasses from Reynolds he nodded that he did.[23] Benteen acted as if Custer had not seen the Indian encampment and didn't even believe there was one.[24] This was one of several outright lies that Benteen gave at the Reno Court. Whether you use deductive reason or simply common sense to realize that Red Star had no reason to distort the truth about what Custer saw, it boils down to the fact that Benteen lied. If we need to use logic to come to that conclusion, it doesn't take a great mind to realize that Custer stated that the Indian village would be found along the Little Big Horn, and there certainly hadn't been any reason for him to discard that belief. The Indian scouts' sighting, along with that of Charlie Reynolds', should have been ample reason to believe the location, whether Custer had actually seen it or not. We can add to that Custer's acceptance of scouts' reports before, and Red Star's account certainly doesn't sound like it was made up.

Red Star at the Crow's Nest:

> Custer asked by signs of Red Star if the distance was short, [to the Crow's Nest] and Red Star made signs that it was. When they got to the foot of the hill, Red Star signed that this was the place. They climbed the hill, and came to the scouts. Charley Reynolds came up and he and Custer went ahead leaving the others behind. Charley Reynolds pointed where Custer was to look, and they looked for some time and then Gerard joined them. Gerard called back to the scouts: "Custer thinks it is no Sioux camp." Custer thought that Charley Reynolds had merely seen the white buttes of the ridge that concealed the lone tepee. Charley Reynolds then pointed again, explaining Custer's mistake, then after another look Custer nodded that he had seen the signs of a camp. Next Charley Reynolds pulled out his field glasses and Custer looked through them at the Dakota camp and nodded his head again.[25]

One should note that Red Star stated that the distance was short, and we know that as Trumpeter Martin and Sgt. Kanipe said, Custer was usually galloping, which is why several of his men later on were not able to make it up the bluffs before their horses went down. In other words, Custer would have made it from Halt 1 to the Crow's Nest in thirty minutes or less.

Red Star said that he delivered Varnum's message as the sun was rising. This could mean Red Star arrived before 4:13 or a short time afterwards. Although Michael Reynolds' time of Custer's arriving at the Crow's Nest by 4 a.m. appears to be too early, it might not be that far off. What are the times being used by Gray, Liddic, and others for these events? Liddic has generally accepted Gray's time of events so I will refer to Gray's time-motion analysis. Gray has Custer receiving the message from Varnum at 7:30 a.m.[26] I disagree. I would place the sighting of the village by 3:05 a.m., and by 3:30 a.m. Varnum would have accepted the sighting and sent Red Star with his message to Custer. According to Gray the Crow's Nest was 4 3/4 miles from Halt 1.[27] Using a conservative estimate of 5 a.m. as the time Reno and Benteen had the regiment moving from Halt 1, and that they traveled two miles when they were met by Custer, I would say it was around 6 a.m. that Custer informed them of the sighting of the Indian village. Custer most likely told them that at first he couldn't see the village, and Benteen acted as if he hadn't seen the village at all or even believed there was one.[28]

Benteen was given the lead as they left Halt 2, but Custer soon took over, and they traveled another mile and halted again (Halt 3).[29] With the time taken at

Halt 2 and the distance then traveled to Halt 3, it could have been getting close to 8 a.m. Custer and Adjutant Cooke went to the side and after about fifteen minutes Custer made the division of the command. In his report following the battle, Reno said that by 8 a.m. they had crossed the divide and were in the valley of one of the branches of the Little Big Horn.[30] This was what is now called Reno Creek. (I will use Reno Creek rather than Sundance, Ash, or other names that have been used.)

Remember, the officers had adjusted their time, so these early reports reflect the actual time they were using. Let's compare the times used by Gray, Liddic, and the coterie for the above mentioned events with the early reports.

We have already established that according to Gray, Custer didn't receive Varnum's message until 7:30 a.m., and after informing his officers he left for the Crow's Nest by 8 a.m.[31] You now have at least four and a half hours since the Indian village was spotted. Custer then takes an hour to go the 4 3/4 miles to the Crow's Nest.[32] Custer must have walked his horse. How does this time compare to Reno's earlier report? Reno has Custer crossing the divide and reaching Reno Creek by 8 a.m.,[33] while the experts have Custer just taking off from Halt 1. And we are to believe there wasn't a timing cover-up?

What one sees by Gray's time-motion analysis is his recognition of the large gap between the sighting of the village (3 to 4 a.m.) and the Reno Court time for the division of the command (12:10 p.m.),[34] and consequently the need to extend time in order to cover the gap. You have roughly a four hour period (4 a.m. to 8 a.m.) before Custer begins his jaunt to the Crow's Nest, and it then takes him a hour to reach the Crow's Nest.[35] Come on, this is the news he has been waiting for—keep in mind that this is the attack-minded Custer. You have reports that Custer was at the Crow's Nest by 4 a.m. and 6 a.m., and according to the first stated times one would have expected Custer to have arrived. By the time of the Reno Court it must have been obvious to Reno's counsel that the times had to be changed or Reno would be facing a court-martial, so the times were changed. This was not that hard to accomplish, since the army and the officers did not want Reno to face a court-martial. The only important time change necessary was when the division of the command took place. The officers only needed to be unsure of the time. Because of the officers' testimony, particularly that of Lt. Wallace who was keeping the official time, this was accomplished. Later, officers and historians filled in the timing gaps. Gray has done masterful work in doing this, and Liddic's acceptance is typical of other writers.

Reno's official report had to be covered-up. Liddic brings this out but fails to follow through with it. Why wasn't Reno hammered with questions? What does it take to realize the lack of follow-up questions represents a cover-up in process? The official recording time of Benteen's arrival on the ridge was around 2:30 p.m.,[36] along with the common knowledge that it was at least 5 p.m.,[37] before they went to check on the gunfire coming from the Custer battlefield: these times could not be justifiably explained. Both Benteen and the packs had orders to support Custer, and Reno was aware of the orders. The concern for the wounded, the need for ammo, and extending the time the packs arrived was not enough to fill the 2 1/2 hour gap, so the time had to be changed.

Liddic nor others have explained the difference between the early time given for events to those times used at the Reno Court. Time is a major cover-up that effects one's whole conception of Custer, and the battle. After the battle it was recognized that an immediate attempt to check on the gunfire coming from the Custer battlefield might have saved many of the men. There was also the realization that all of the 7th may have been killed, but that possibility wouldn't have excused their failure to make the attempt. Without a time change that failure would have resulted in a court-martial for Major Reno. Why the various army factions needed to prevent the court of inquiry from leading to a court-martial is understandable; what is not is how historians have gone along with this cover-up.

The two essential cover-ups were the supposed lack of orders Custer gave and the time change. Claiming that the orders were insufficient was necessary to protect Reno's flight from the valley, and the time change was needed in order to justify the delay before going to check on Custer. Reno's flight from the valley was covered-up by saying that Reno only received orders to move against the village and he would be supported by the whole outfit. Reno, by the time of the Reno Court, only believed this support was coming from behind. When in the timber Reno didn't see this support, so he fled the valley in order to save his men.

Right after the battle Reno and Benteen realized it was necessary to deny the orders received and therefore any knowledge that an offense was underway. They knew they couldn't say Custer gave orders to Reno that he was to attack the village from the south while Custer would be enveloping the Indians and moving against them from the north, and that Benteen's orders stated that when he reached the valley he would aid Reno and would be on his left.

By the time of the Reno Court, Reno's counsel would have known they had to change the time in order to cover the gap from when Benteen arrived on the hill and when they went to check on the gunfire coming from the Custer battlefield, and to maintain that the only order that Reno had was to attack the village and he would be supported by the whole outfit.[38] Benteen also needed to have failed to receive any offensive orders, indicating that Custer had no idea of just where the Indian village was or that there even was such a village.[39] This excused his actions and also benefited Reno.

Gray has the arrival time of the regiment at Halt 1 as 3:15 a.m., in contrast to Reno's initial recording of 2 a.m. and Benteen's at about 2:30 a.m. Both Reno and Benteen had the regiment leaving by 5 a.m., and we know Custer left before that time. Red Star said he arrived with his message from Varnum to Custer as the sun was rising, and yet Gray doesn't have Custer receiving the message until 7:30, and Liddic refers to the time as before 8 o'clock. I can't imagine anyone saying that they arrived somewhere when the sun was coming up and it was actually three hours after it had risen. Certainly not anyone accustomed to the outdoors as these scouts were. As for Custer, this was the information he was waiting to hear, and though he still may have expected to wait until the next morning to attack the village, this wouldn't have stopped him from being in a hurry to check out the sighting for himself. Remember, this is Custer, whose faults have been described as being too reckless not too cautious.

SOURCES

Overfield II, *The Little Big Horn, 1876, The Official Communications, Documents, and Reports, With Rosters of the Officers and Troops of the Campaign..* Here-in-after cited Overfield II.

Nichols, (ed) *Reno Court of Inquiry, Proceedings of a Court of Inquiry, in the Case of Marcus A. Reno.* Here-in-after cited Reno Court.

Graham, *The Custer Myth.* Here-in-after cited Graham.

Gray, *Custer's Last Campaign.* Here-in-after cited Gray.

Liddic, *Vanishing Victory, Custer's Final March.* Here-in-after cited Liddic.

Carroll, (ed.) *The Benteen, Goldin Letters,* Here-in-after cited Caroll.

Hammer, (ed.) *Custer in 76.* Here-in-after cited Camp.

1.   Overfield II, 42.

2.   Ibid., 45.

3. Liddic, 10.

4. Overfield II, 43.

5. Carroll, *The Benteen, Goldin Letters,* 180.

6. Graham, 136.

7. Willert, *Little Big Horn Diary*, 260; Stewart, *Custer's Luck,* 225.

8. Carroll, 180.

9. Ibid., 180.

10. Gray, 228.

11. Brady, Indian Fights and Fighters, 371.

12. Ibid., 371.

13. Graham, 194.

14. Carroll, 18.

15. Carroll, (ed.) *Custer's Chief of Scouts,* 61.

16. Gray, 225.

17. Carroll, *Custer's Chief of Scouts,* 62.

18. Gray, 228.

19. Carroll, 180.

20. Michael Reynolds speech; Letter to Richard Upton.

21. Graham, 15.

22. Carroll, 180.

23. Graham, 33.

24. Reno Court, 402.

25. Graham, 33.

26. Gray, 228.

27. Ibid., 228.

28. Reno Court, 402.

29. Carroll, 181.

30. Overfield II, 43.

31. Gray, 228.

32. Ibid., 228.

33. Overfield II, 93.

34. Reno Court, 20, 21.

35. Gray, 228.

36. Overfield II, 43.

37. Graham, 230.

38. Reno Court, 561.

39. Ibid., 402; Graham, 129.

2

TIMING DIFFERENCES

The Reno Court was a cover-up that has profoundly affected the view of the Battle of the Little Big Horn. The officers went along with Reno's Defense even though they had little use for Reno's actions. As Captain Benteen wrote to Judge Goldin: "… but as to queries before the Court of Inquiry, there I would answer now as I did then, and shield Reno quite as much as I then did, and this simply from the fact that there were a lot of harpies after him."[1] The officers only needed to know they should not reveal their knowledge or understanding of orders, nor get involved with definite answers to timing questions. They were not going to be asked many questions on either subject. I am also sure that their beliefs were similar to Captain Benteen's, that Reno's flight from the river "had been a rout—a panic—,"[2] and more than likely that he had been drunk, as Reno himself was later to have said.[3] The Court could not have avoided asking questions on the drinking and cowardice, but even without pressure the officers would have been inclined to protect Reno. Officers would have been free to answer questions on anything other than orders, conduct, and time, no matter how contradictory, since they were generally irrelevant and verbiage questions.

Reno's counsel's summation made clear the military position on answers that contradicted the officers that were made by non-officers whether enlisted soldiers or scouts or civilians. The following portrayal illustrates the problem facing the Recorder in formulating a brief.

Counsel Gilbert:

> … A military court is always, as far as I am informed, composed of officers higher or at least equal in grade, to the one who is interested in its proceedings. The reason for the rule is, I think, plain. It is found not merely in the greater impartiality which higher rank confers, not merely in the greater knowledge and ampler experience which attends it, but also in the fact that the independence of every officer requires that those who live in the suburbs of the Army, to whom he must give preemptory orders to which the only

answer is unquestioning obedience, shall not be his judge in matters which concern his life or his honor.

Apply the reason which governs the selection of military courts to the kind of testimony by which you, as members of this Court, would be governed, and you will see that some of the testimony requires a rule of rigid construction.

Let it once be understood that an orderly, a private soldier of limited intelligence, who follows at the heels of his commanding officer is evidence to establish an important order as much as the officer who rides by his side; that an Indian interpreter on his first expedition can give reliable testimony upon military matters; or after being dismissed for stealing, can sit in judgment on the courage of his superior; or that a mule packer struck in the face by an officer for being where it was thought he had no duty to be, can originate a charge of drunkenness against that officer, and unsupported by any other witness, save that of another mule packer, can insist on this story in a Court of Inquiry.

Let it once be understood that name and character and fame lie in the keeping of these followers of an army, and the sense of subordination is gone, and the desire to conciliate becomes stronger than the desire to command. The character of an officer will then depend on the favor of the camp followers, and they will profit by that knowledge.

The charges against Major Reno rest largely on the testimony of two mule packers, a doctor, an Indian scout, a sergeant and an Indian interpreter.... [4]

The authorities seem to have accepted this pitiful attempt to belittle and discredit witnesses that were not officers. These witnesses, at the Court, were not under the direct control of the military. What is most interesting is that the enlisted men whom the Court could not avoid calling, almost destroyed the Court's case. Answers by Sgt. Culbertson, Reno's orderly Davern, and Custer's orderly Martin innocently exposed cover-ups. Neither the Court, the Defense, or the Recorder asked penetrating or probing questions into the exposed openings that led to cover-ups of orders and time. Reno and Benteen were the major recipients of the orders that were under question. Since Benteen wasn't on trial he could cover his own orders, but Reno's orders needed officer verification. Lt. Wallace, the itinerast who was not assigned to any company, was then placed by Reno's side. He then testified to Reno's version of his orders and the other officers accepted their rendition, as they did Benteen's. Officers were under military control.

As Girard was told by an unnamed officer:

> Well, Gerard, they have got the whip over us; they have somethings in the pidgeon holes that could be used to make me feel rather uncomfortable and I thought there was no use trying to stand up against the whole gang by myself.[5]

Jay Smith in a 1992 article in the *Research/Review,* said he couldn't understand the following statement by General Phil Sheridan because it went again Cavalry tactics, particularly against Indians. Successful maneuvers involved an envelopment—a basic cavalry tactic.

Sheridan said:

> If Custer had waited until his regiment was closed up and crossed it at the point Major Reno did, and had made his attack in the level valley, posting some of his men in the woods, all of the Indians there could not have defeated him.[6]

Smith went on to say that Sheridan's results are clear, "he silenced his other commanders such as Ronald S. Mackenzie, Nelson A. Miles, and Eugene A. Carr. None of these officers wrote about Custer's tactics.

Smith also pointed out how Sheridan could hold this power over officers, and he used Robert Utley's explanation on the length of time required to move up the ranks and how one word from Sheridan meant that they could forget about a promotion.[7]

Time was a different story from the orders because there were too many accounts of the actual or general time of the day when actions took place, so it was better for the interrogators not to ask specific questions. In the Girard "watch" incident it was necessary to put pressure on him by the Court, or by the Recorder on behalf of the critic's script. If the time between Reno's retreat, Benteen's and the packs arrival, and their move to aid Custer could not be accounted for it would be a serious military offense resulting in not only a court-martial but a conviction. The failure to ask discerning questions as to time, and to disregard its importance can be seen in Reno's counsel's summation in which he said:

> The question of time and distance with such differing evidence has been given is, not to my mind, of great importance except as it determines the relation of one command to another, and this relation and position can, as

the Court has no doubt already observed, be fixed independently of watches. Where Custer's column was with reference to that of Reno can be definitely placed without regard to the time of day. There will be, I think, but little difficulty upon that point.[8]

So the three and four hour differences in the time of events doesn't really matter. One might note there is no talk of different time zones, which has been used as a blanket excuse, or "old" time vs. "new" time. If any objective analysis is used, can one still believe the Reno Court wasn't a cover-up?

Keeping the above in mind let us examine some of the machinations that had to have taken place. The testimony at the Reno Court is used and footnoted time and again to support a writer's view, but there is no attempt by writers to put themselves in the place of Reno's counsel, Lyman D. Gilbert, and that of the "interrogator" Recorder, Lt. Jason Lee. What were the problems they faced, and what would their briefs need to consist of? Underlying this is the recognition, as I have already said, that the army and the officers did not want Reno found guilty. This was not an impartial trial. The army didn't want Reno court-martialed, and they didn't want Lee to ask certain questions or probe into answers too deeply.

Reno's counsel must have known that the major criticism of Reno in the bar rooms would have been that he was a coward, that he panicked, and that he was drunk. Reno's Defense would have found these charges the easiest to get the officers to not necessarily deny but to mitigate

Jay Smith adequately expresses this view in the following statement:

> What a strange turn of events; the testimony showed that Reno was stupid and inept, and was probably drunk. Yet, his name was cleared because he was not a coward, and by extension Captain Frederick W. Benteen was cleared too. Logically then, the fault for the defeat lay with the Field Commander of the Regiment, Lieutenant Colonel George A. Custer.[9]

The counsel, as he brought out in his summation, would also know that if these officers could agree on essential issues, any contrary evidence by enlisted men, scouts, or civilians would not be effective. As Colonel Wesley Merritt, one of the court judges said after the trial, "Well the officers wouldn't tell us anything and we could do nothing more than damn Reno with faint praise."[10] And as Benteen is quoted as saying, "We (officers) must defend the regiment." The officers were not about to accuse Reno as many believed Reno's panic flight is what saved them, even if many of their comrades died in that flight. Many others were at least close to panicking on the retreat from Weir Point. The concern for the living would have offset any desire to defend Custer's actions on the two critical issues—orders and time.

Orders were the major premise that needed to be covered-up. The site of the village being in the Little Big Horn valley had been suspected even before the sighting from the Crow's Nest. An objective analysis of what Custer must have thought would acknowledge that he was operating on that assumption. There shouldn't have been any contrary evidence to have changed his mind on the village's general location, and he should have made plans to attack the village by the time he divided his command. He also had no reason to change his mind that he would be facing, if he could bring them to battle, one thousand to fifteen hundred warriors. Even if you were afraid the Indians would scatter you would have made plans to attack the Indians in their village along the Little Big Horn. This is why an essential question centers around whether Custer at the Crow's Nest saw or accepted the scouts' sighting of the village. There should be no doubt as to the answer.

If one studies Custer's orders as reported by the two orderlies, Davern and Martin, it doesn't take a genius to see that Custer wanted Reno to attack the village from the south, and he would be supported on his left by Benteen. Custer would attempt to flank the Indians, separating the warriors from the noncombatants. Custer planned on sandwiching the warriors in between his troops and those of Reno's and Benteen's. He may also have planned to use one or two of his companies to cordon off the noncombatants (see addendum map). These orders would indicate that an offense was underway. Reno's Defense needed to deny that Custer had any plans known to either Reno or Benteen, except that Reno was to cross the Little Big Horn and would be supported. That it was an all out offense should have been common knowledge, but Reno's and Benteen's statements that they had no understanding of any plans by Custer or where or what the other was doing was accepted by the Court and has continued to be by the Little Big Horn coterie. The only officers that needed to be convinced by Reno's Defense to change times or orders would have been Lt. Wallace, Lt. Hare and possibly Lt. Varnum. The other officers merely had to pretend ignorance. The two orderlies had to be asked, and they actually said too much, but the interrogator didn't attempt to ferret out or even follow-up on their remarks. Reno's counsel in his summation made sure to downplay Davern's testimony (see addendum). If the Reno Court was not a cover-up, one needs to explain why. Trumpeter Martin, Custer's orderly, who undoubtedly had knowledge of not only the orders Custer gave Reno but when and if attack orders were sent to Benteen, was not questioned on any other orders but the written message he carried.

Even these orders were not examined in any detail. When Custer's orderly is not asked about other messages or orders Custer sent, and is in fact prevented from mentioning them,[11]—it should make you realize that the Reno Court was a cover-up of the key issues. If it does not, you can continue to believe the scenarios protecting the actions of Reno and Benteen while condemning Custer's. The court concentrated on asking Martin questions on topography and distances in order to mix him up so they could then dismiss him. Martin's testimony on the location of the packs had to be ignored.

Where does all this leave Recorder Lt. Jason Lee, the prosecutor? He knows that officers, on the key questions of orders and timing, are not going against Reno's and Benteen's testimony. I don't believe Lee was an inept interrogator, but one that was prevented by the army from asking penetrating questions on the key issues that could have led to a court martial of Reno and indictments of Benteen, and possibly others.

Lee needed to present a case against Reno even though he knew that it would not lead to any court-martial charge. Reno's Defense had attempted, or I should say was successful in creating the idea that Reno and Benteen had no knowledge of any offensive plans of Custer or what was expected of either of them, and that Reno believed Custer was to support him from the rear. Reno, of course, had no idea that Custer planned on flanking the Indians. Reno appeared not to know that a major fear of the army was that Indians when knowing troops were moving against them would scatter rather than engage them—or that a basic cavalry tactic was envelopment. Reno's Defense heard that some soldiers thought Custer's adjutant, First Lieutenant Cooke, after delivering his message to Reno, would have gone with him to the ford. This enabled the Defense to use this in support of Reno's claim that he expected Custer to support him from the rear. Reno said he sent McIlhargey with a message to Custer that the Indians were in force in his front.[12] At that time there were no Indians moving against him. Reno then moved to attack the village, but fearing an ambush he formed a skirmish line. The Indians were becoming stronger so he moved his troops into the timber. When in the timber he couldn't see the support he was promised, and being afraid that he couldn't hold out, he fled to the cliffs in order to save his troops.

If this were an impartial trial Lee would have questioned all of the officers with more astute and discerning questions as to orders and time. After Lt. Hare's statement that he heard afterward that enlisted men had seen Custer on the ridge,[13] Lee should have bombarded Reno and the officers with him in the valley with questions as to the sightings. Instead the Defense used Varnum's late sighting to bring out that Custer had plenty of time to support Reno even by flanking the

Indians. That he still hadn't attacked the village excused Reno for fleeing to the bluffs. Lee, if this was an impartial trial, would have made sure Lt. Gibson was a witness, for Gibson would have known the orders Benteen received, and where and when he received them. Lee definitely should have asked Martin questions on orders other than the written one Custer gave him. The time gap should have been examined. Lee, knowing he could not ask those questions, came up with his (or Whitaker's) schematic ploy, one that has twisted and prevented an accurate assessment of Custer and the battle. Girard was to say the Rees told him the Indians were not fleeing as Custer had thought, so, after warning Reno, he went to inform Custer. The warning of Reno, that Reno denied, was so Reno should expect Custer to be coming to aid him even if not from behind. The use by the Defense of Cooke going to the ford enabled Lee to have Girard meet Cooke behind a knoll and inform him that the Indians were not running and to give this information to Custer. Girard was then able to make it back and join Reno. This information prompted Custer to take his five companies in an attempt to flank the Indians instead of following Reno. Reno's fleeing to the ridge enabled the Indians to leave Reno and meet Custer, in force, at the ford. Reno's fleeing the valley then caused Custer's defeat. Lee could not have expected this ploy to be successful against the testimony of Reno, Benteen, Wallace, and other officers. What it has done is put forth the belief that Reno's movement down the valley preceded Custer's flanking move, thereby supporting Reno's and Benteen's accusations that Custer had no prior plans to flank the Indians until he heard from Cooke. This is preposterous, but has been effective and has been accepted.

There undoubtedly were machinations employed by Reno's Defense as represented by his counsel Mr. Lyman Gilbert, and the Recorder or Investigator (Prosecutor), Lt. Jason Lee, and collusion with the Court itself. I do want to reiterate and take this a little further, as the picture presented by the Reno Court has been so instrumental in shaping writers' scenarios.

The Court established certain basic assumptions that have been accepted and were derived from the schematic ploys used by the Court, the Defense, and the Recorder. The army and their desire not to have the battle and its participants subject to further investigations underlie both Major Reno's Defense and 1st Lt. Jason Lee's interrogation.

The Defense only needed to keep the officers in line, and it would be impossible for the Prosecution (I will use this term) to offset their testimony. The Defense's primary position was that Major Reno and Captain Benteen had no idea of Custer's plans, and weren't even sure that he believed there were Indians or their village that lay ahead. Reno's orders only said he would be supported by the whole troop, and he believed this meant that Custer and his five companies would follow him into battle. Benteen's only orders were to "pitch into" any Indians he saw on his reconnaissance and look for a valley. What valley he didn't even know.[14]

These and the following specious tenets were then accepted or brought forth by both sides. Jason Lee's case against Reno was sound, as was his presentation, but he failed to probe beneath the central but superficial positions taken by the Defense. This had to have been due to the army's desire to acquit Reno, and not Lee's ineptness.

Reno's counsels main position was that Reno expected Custer to follow him into battle. This was an inherent falsehood as Custer was not going to follow Reno into battle under practically any condition imaginable. Officers compliance only supports confirmation of their collusion. This meant the full extent of Reno's orders had to be covered-up. Reno's adjutant, Hodgson was killed so the Defense placed Lt. Wallace by Reno's side (which he wasn't). Wallace then could testify to Reno's version of his orders. Adjutant Cooke had given Reno the orders from Custer, and since some enlisted men reported Cooke going to the river with Reno, this was then used as proof that Reno was right in expecting Custer to follow him. Officers, even though not there gave the needed support. However, Cooke only went to where Reno crossed over Reno Creek on his way to the ford. The Prosecutor represented the military as well as the critics of Reno, the main critics being the scout Girard and Mr. Whitaker. Whitaker was not allowed to be a witness or question witnesses, but undoubtedly played a part behind the scenes. After the battle he had been primarily responsible in blaming Reno for the defeat suffered by Custer, which forced Reno to call a court of inquiry.

The Prosecution knowing it would do no good to deny that Cooke went to the ford realized they could use his going to their advantage. They said the Rees informed Girard that some 1500 Indians were moving against Reno. Girard supposedly told Reno of this and that he was going to inform Custer. Cooke's going to the ford enabled Girard to meet Cooke behind a knoll close to the ford with the information to take to Custer. Girard was then able to return and go down the valley with Reno. The information Cooke took to Custer, that the Indians were not running but coming to meet Reno caused Custer, who was still waiting around Reno Creek, to decide to flank those Indians instead of following Reno.

Custer, even if he hadn't initially seen the village, by this time would have been aware of it. Custer, after sending Reno his attack orders, would not have sat around Reno Creek for thirty to forty-five minutes. He would have gone to the bluffs to personally observe the village and the Indian situation.

Whether Reno used the ploy that the Indians were moving to confront him first or whether this was the sponsored scheme of the Recorder, Girard, or Whitaker doesn't really matter. Reno said he sent Pvt. McIlhargey with a message to Custer that the Indians were strong in front of him. Since he didn't receive a reply he then sent Pvt. Mitchell. The Indians were not strong in front of him in fact there were only a few horse herders at the time they started down the valley. The Rees didn't report any Indians, and Reno's message by way of McIlhargey and Mitchell had nothing to do with Indians in front of him. Reno's concern had to be where his support was, and whether he should wait for it or not. The support he was wondering about was not Custer but Benteen. Reno knew Custer was planning on flanking the Indians, and there is too much concrete evidence, along with common military sense to believe otherwise.

The Prosecution's script had Reno going down the valley ahead of Custer on the ridge. Girard's message is what caused Custer to flank the Indians, which means we have Custer sitting around Reno Creek, after giving his orders to Reno, for thirty to forty-five minutes. Times and locations vary but Lt. Hare's report should have been fairly accurate. He said it took about twenty or thirty minutes to reach the ford. You then had three companies in column of twos crossing a girth high river, while their horses drank, Reno sent a messenger, they then passed through fifty yards of timber, reformed, waited for a reply, then sent another messenger, and still were able to move down the valley by the time Girard returned from giving Cooke a message behind a knoll that was within fifty yards of the river. So when Custer arrived on the ridge Reno was establishing his skirmish line. This is the picture that the Prosecution portrayed. They then used the relative position between Reno and Custer to back the following script. Reno, because of Girard's warning, should have known Custer would be supporting him even if not from behind. His leaving the timber when he did released the Indians to rush back to the village, meet and overwhelm Custer before he could launch his attack at Ford B which would have provided Reno with the support he had been promised. If you can correlate this action with a timing math and have it come together you are a mathematical genius.

Taking this timing another step, and realizing that by now there is no way Custer would not know the Indian village lay behind the bluffs to his northwest, but you still have Custer along Reno Creek waiting to follow Reno. If you do then your study of Custer is different than mine. Custer would have been on his way to the ridge right after sending Reno his attack orders. And you have testimony by the Crows to support that supposition.

Reno's Defense could not bring out the numerous sightings and reports of Custer on the ridge as they were moving down the valley. There is no way the officers would not have been aware of them. This would indicate they had to have been told not to mention those sightings, and the questioners not to ask. However, those sightings were not a problem as they had been made by enlisted men who were not at the Court. If this had been an impartial court, Lt. Hare's remarks should have brought out additional questions—that it didn't is a sign of Court and officer complicity.

The Prosecution also didn't want the sightings brought out since it would have meant that Custer had plenty of time to have attacked at Ford B. Since there were no signs of an attack they wanted any sightings of Custer to be further back on the ridge. This would then support their brief that Girard's warning via Cooke caused Custer to move to the ridge, and by the time he arrived Reno had already set up his skirmish line. Reno then flees the timber before Custer can reach Ford B to attack the village. Girard in order to support this specious account testifies that while Reno is fighting in the valley he sees Custer on the ridge in the area of where Reno later entrenched. Girard, in answer to a question as to how far Custer would have gotten by the time Reno fled to the bluffs, pointed out a spot further down and still some distance from Ford B. The Recorder's script then had Reno knowing Custer would be supporting him, and since he was in no immediate danger that he should have held in the timber. By fleeing he allowed the Indians to return in time to overwhelm Custer.

Varnum's sighting of "E" Troop near Weir Point, as Reno was setting up his skirmish line, enabled Reno's counsel to say that Custer had plenty of time to have attacked at Ford B. Since there were no signs of an attack, Reno was justified in going to the ridge. The paradoxes between the sighting of Custer back by Reno's later entrenchment at the time Reno was setting up his skirmish line, compared to Varnum's sighting beyond Weir Point of "E" Troop at the same time, doesn't seem to have created any questioning or need for an explanation. Reno's counsel does use Varnum's sighting to show that Custer must have or would have been met by an overwhelming force of Indians even before Reno retreated, and therefore his flight to the bluffs had no effect on Custer's defeat. This definitely has Reno still fighting in the valley at a time Custer could have reached Ford B.

To further illustrate the farcical, and disturbing nature of this cover-up Court, is Reno's counsel's summation, in which he attempts to nullify Martin's statement that Custer at Weir Point (the only place this observation could have been made) saw a "napping" or "sleeping" village. Reno's counsel:

> If the mind can believe testimony and draw any inference from it, it is over-whelmingly clear that Custer had reached the ford "B" where he could have crossed to the Indian village before the Indians, whom Reno was diverting by his attack in the timber, could have reached that point, and from the known character of Custer for valor and for bravery it was equally plain that, notwithstanding the thousand Indians whom Reno detained at the upper end of the village, there were Indians at the ford "B" in such overwhelming numbers as to make it a matter of madness for Custer and his command to engage them there. That explains the fact of the sleeping village which Martin says that Custer saw.[15]

◆   ◆   ◆

The statement of General Custer made to his officers before Benteen diverged from the column, showed that after fullest care he disbelieved in the presence of the Indians. The announcement made by Girard just before Reno left the tepee, a short distance from the river, disclosed the belief the Indians were running away. The sleeping Indian village seen by Martin, and, as he testifies also, by General Custer, when the command of the latter was so close to the place of its heroic but final struggle, further attests the ignorance of the number and plans of the Indians, and of the preparations they were making for resistance.[16]

I consider the above statements ridiculous for several reasons. Maybe the statements aren't farcical but the acceptance of them is. The fact that you have contradicting testimony that cover a given period, and which are accepted by all sides without questioning, certainly is. Custer was seen at the time Reno was establishing his skirmish line back where Reno later entrenched, and at the time Reno was retreating Custer was just past Weir Point. You then have Varnum at the time Reno was establishing his skirmish line seeing "E" troop on the ridge across from the skirmish line close to point 2 on Maguire's map,[17] which would place Custer beyond Weir Point. Varnum's sighting is used by Reno's counsel to indicate Custer had plenty of time to have reached Ford B and attack the Indians while Reno was still fighting in the valley. Yet if that is true, and since you have Reno moving across Ford A and down the valley ahead of Custer's move to the ridge, you then have Custer both behind and ahead of Reno. However this dichotomy hasn't raised questions then or since.

Then to nullify the sleeping village testimony, which in itself would indicate Custer was ahead of Reno, you have the Indians aware of Custer and by overwhelming numbers they were waiting for Custer. And, of course, Custer would not have been able to see them when he looked at that sleeping village. Hundreds of warriors had to have been hidden along the banks, but even Bouyer didn't see them.

There might be some excuse for historians at that time to be taken in by the cover-ups, but for those today to still be is—I was going to say laughable but a better word would be pathetic. Indian testimony brings out clearly that Reno's firing awoke the village. Liddic uses Foolish Elks statement that at the time Custer arrived at the ford most of the warriors were still preparing to go and fight Reno, which would mean Reno was still fighting in the valley. I have not seen any testimony by Indians that they were waiting in large numbers for Custer to move to Ford B.

Where were the 1500 to 2500 warriors that were seen by Girard's Rees, and were inferred by Reno to have been in the valley. Trooper testimony does not support it nor does Indian. Any such number of warriors would not have allowed army troops to move toward their village without attempting to prevent it. They would not have used the village for an ambush attempt, but instead would have used either an all out attack or harassing attacks in order to protect the village. That there were none should be enough evidence for any historian to not only question but reject testimony of such sighting by Girard and Reno. It is surprising that with all the erroneous statements that Benteen made which are recognized and accepted, and then to believe Benteen's statement, as presented by Reno's counsel, that Custer back at the division of the command "disbelieved in the presence of Indians" is absurd and yet was accepted and still is by so many.

Reno's troopers' testimony of seeing Custer and his battalions on the ridge while they were going down the valley should be examined. These sightings were known by officers, as Lt. Hare's slip-up brought out. Why weren't the officer's put to third degree questioning? These were fundamental questions to have been asked during any legitimate attempt to determine what happened at the Battle of the Little Big Horn. They were interrogative questions which reflected on Reno's actions so they couldn't have been shunted off as were other questions. The lack of such an investigation should prove that there was no effort to go beyond spurious questions and excessive cover-up verbiage. The Reno Court of Inquiry was a cover-up to protect Reno, Benteen, other officers, along with the 7th Cavalry's and the army's image.

SOURCES

1. Graham, 194.

2. Ibid., 195.

3. Ibid., 340.

4. Reno Court, 596.

5. Camp, 238.

6. Smith, "What Did Not Happen," *Research/Review*, June, 1992, 9.

7. Ibid., 9, 10.

8. Reno Court, 598.

9. Smith, *Research/Review*, June, 1992, 7.

10. Stewart, "The Reno Court of Inquiry," *The Montana Magazine*, Vol. II, #3, July 1952,43; Graham, 337.

11. Reno Court, 390.

12. Ibid., 561.

13. Ibid., 307.

14. Graham, 180, Reno Court, 402.

15. Ibid., 561.

16. Ibid., 611.

17. Ibid., Maquire Map.

3

THE TIME GAP

In my chapter breakdown I will be in essence analyzing how Liddic has dealt with the two major cover-up issues—Custer's orders and the time gap. Many of the references to the times and orders will be repetitious, but I believe necessary in order to bring out the weakness of the coterie's position. Their positions may vary with Liddic's to an extent, but primarily on other or minor details.

Liddic brings out that Custer on the night of the 24th said that "beyond a doubt that the village was in the valley of the Little Big Horn."[1] We should then remember that in Custer's mind the valley of the Little Big Horn was where he would find the Indians, and that view would only have been enhanced, not diminished. Custer was even warned by Girard that he could expect to find the fighting strength of the Indians wouldn't be less than 2500.[2] According to Liddic, on the morning of the 25th the Rees carrying Varnum's message arrived sometime before 8 o'clock,[3] which would keep him on track with Gray's 7:20 a.m.[4] Red Star should have been sent by Varnum by 4 a.m., and reached the camp site by 4:30 a.m. Red Star, although wanting to have breakfast, was sent to Custer with his report. Custer, after informing his officers, then took off for the Crow's Nest. Being anxious to see for himself, Custer would have left before 5 a.m., and could have reached the Crow's Nest by 5 a.m. This is later than what Michael Reynolds reported, and somewhat earlier than White Man Runs Him. Gray has Custer leaving at 8 a.m.[5] and taking a hour to go to the Crow's Nest. Already the authorities have closed the timing gap 3 hours.

Following the battle and with the criticism of his actions intensifying, Reno would already be rationalizing. He would want to extend the time he fought in the valley. This is revealed in the following General Rosser letter to Major Reno:

> You do not state, but I have the impression from some of the accounts sent in from the field, that you began your skirmish with the Indians about half past twelve to one o'clock. That you re-crossed the river and occupied the bluff about two o'clock. Now, to the reporter of the New York Herald you

state that you made a reconnaissance in the direction of Custer's trail about 5 o'clock. The Indians appear to have withdrawn from your front as soon as you re-crossed the river. Why, then, could you not have gone in pursuit of Custer earlier?[6]

These earlier times correlate with other accounts from both Indians and whites, and the times used by the officers at the Reno Court do not, but their time has been accepted by the historians even though they don't correlate. We might recall that Sgt. Kanipe had Reno arriving at the Little Big Horn by twelve o'clock,[7] and Trumpeter Martin said that from the ridge Custer saw the village around noon.[8] This shows the need for Reno's Defense to extend the time, and you can combine that with an understanding that Reno's official report would have, most likely, already reflected his attempt to make it appear he fought longer in the valley than he did. The question General Rosser raised is the quintessential question, and the one Reno's counsel had to come up with an answer to. If Reno was on the ridge by 2 o'clock, why didn't he go to check on Custer for three hours? If the time Reno used in his official report was the one used at the Reno Court, the 2 1/2 hour difference between Benteen's arrival and the move to check on Custer would constitute a court-martial offense.

Let's look again at some of the time changes. According to Gray, at 3:15 a.m. Custer's troops on their night march to reach the divide by morning came to a halt along Davis Creek.[9] This halt is referred to as Halt 1. Liddic brings out that the command was not ready to move from Halt 1 until 8:45 a.m.[10] Reno in his official report of July 5th, 1876, said that on the night of the 24th the command came to a halt at 2 a.m.[11] when Custer was told by his scouts that he could not cross the divide before daylight. They "rested for three hours at the expiration of which time the march was resumed."[12] That would make it 5 a.m. not 8:45 a.m. Benteen had the regiment coming to a halt around daylight. He said they rested for about an hour and a half and then they moved out.[13] This would place the time close to Reno's 5 o'clock. It seems that the need to change the time at the Reno Court in order to erase the time gap is obvious, and that the Reno Court was a cover-up by not only Reno and his counsel, but Benteen, other officers, and the army. The Reno Court represents a blatant attempt to conceal the truth.

Custer arrived at the Crow's Nest. Liddic has Custer nodding to Charlie Reynolds that he does see the signs of a camp. This would be smoke from the village since the bluffs blocked the view of the actual village.

Liddic then says, "we will never know if Custer thought there was a village ahead."[14] We may never know but we certainly can deduce that he did. Let us remember that on the 24th, Custer said that he was sure they would find the Indians on the Little Big Horn. Then on the morning of the 25th Custer went to the Crow's Nest and, according to Red Star and accepted by Liddic, nodded his head that he saw the signs of the camp (village).[15] These signs were the horses grazing and the smoke rising from the village. The bluffs cut off the actual sighting of the village. However, Liddic is saying Custer did not know that this smoke came from a village north of Reno Creek's entrance into the Little Big Horn. There were maps of the region that the officers should have seen, and we know Custer would have seen them. The *Army and Navy Journal* of 1871 said that "any person in charge … should by previous inquiries, have learned as far as possible all about the road or country he is to pass over from day to day." Let's give Custer a little credit as a commander. Remember that the Crow scouts knew every "nook and corner of the area."[16] Do you think that if Custer had any doubts of the village location that he wouldn't have asked the Crows? You might even remember that the Crows said Hairy Moccasin had gone ahead and reported back the location and the size of the Indian encampment, and that they were not running.[17]

Liddic uses Godfrey's statement to Walter Camp that Custer thought there was a village ahead.[18] He said Custer expected to find Indians strung out along the river, but was unsure whether they would be found upstream or downstream from where he might strike the river.[19] This statement is then twisted. Did Custer know there was a village where he saw smoke coming from? Yes he definitely did. Did Custer wonder if there were any other camps, whether upstream or downstream? Undoubtedly, but his main concern would have been if there were any to the south of the known camp. This was the main reason that he sent Benteen to the "valley." Custer would not have forgotten the Washita.

Why is it hard to understand that acting as if Custer didn't recognize the obvious was necessary for Reno's Defense to protect Reno, and by doing so Benteen? It was imperative that they had no knowledge of any plans Custer would have made. In order for them to say this, Custer could not have been aware of the village until he came to the Little Big Horn. The term "reconnaissance in force" fits into this scenario and has been adopted by the historians over the years. This then justifies Reno's and Benteen's actions or I should say lack of action. Reno and Benteen had to plea a lack of knowledge of any plans that Custer might have had. To me, what is amazing is how for a hundred and thirty years this cover-up has been successful.

Custer, according to Liddic (and Gray and others), spent roughly an hour and a quarter at the Crow"s Nest.[20] This I cannot imagine. This time doesn't connect with Reno's statements as expressed in his official report,[21] nor with Benteen's account found in his *Narratives.*[22] This is another example of officers covering up for Reno in order to prevent court-martial charges that would have implicated more than just Reno.

Liddic then says it was about a quarter after ten when Custer rode down from the observation point and rejoined his command at about ten thirty.[23] This does not coincide with Reno's earlier report or Benteen's. Benteen, after moving out from Halt 1 about 5 o'clock, said they went about a mile or so and halted[24] (Halt 2). This is where Custer met them and reported the scouts' sighting. Benteen said Custer didn't believe the sightings. We know (or should know) Custer did accept the scouts report. Why would Benteen say Custer didn't see or believe the scouts? Because if Benteen said Custer saw or accepted the scouts sightings, it would mean that Custer made plans to attack the village. What about the timing? Could Reno's and Benteen's report of the regiment moving out by 5 a.m. have taken them over 5 hours to go the several miles they reported, or could this again be an example of a time change to cover the time gap?

There is a statement used by Godfrey that I really like. It has been quoted by so many, but has failed to be applied. It is the one where Godfrey informed Walter Camp that Custer was "possessed" with the idea the Indians would not stand and give battle but would run at the first sight of the cavalry.[25] Then Liddic uses a second of my preferred statements: "… judging from past performance, attack and victory was inseparable."[26] I have used this one already,. These statements are essential to apply and remember in analyzing the battle.

Then an interesting remark is made by Liddic, that the officers (this is at the first halt) listened intently to Custer's decision to attack.[27] Wouldn't Custer be planning to attack the Indians, and wouldn't those Indians be living in villages? Doesn't a decision to attack mean there is something to attack and you would make plans for that attack?

SOURCES

1. Liddic, 23.

2. Reno Court, 85; Liddic, 23.

3. 3, Ibid., 25.

4. Gray, 228.

5. Liddic, 28.

6.   Graham, 230.

7.   Camp, 92.

8.   Reno Court, 394.

9.   Gray, 228.

10. Liddic, 27.

11. Overfield II, 43.

12. Carroll, 180.

13. Ibid.,180

14. Liddic, 26.

15. Ibid., 26.

16. Ibid., 14.

17. Curtis, *The Papers of Edward S. Curtis Relating to Custer's Last Battle,* 41.

18. Liddic, 26.

19. Ibid., 26.

20. Ibid., 26; Gray 228.

21. Overfield II, 43.

22. Carroll, 180.

23. Liddic, 28.

24. Carroll, 180.

25. Liddic, 28.

26. Ibid., 28.

27. Ibid., 30.

4

CUSTER'S ATTACK PLAN

The first column of Liddic's new chapter is entitled "Separation of Forces" which illustrates the thinking that has permeated the views of Custer and the Little Big Horn battle.

Liddic starts out by saying Custer had reached the conclusion that he must immediately attack the village.[1] Two things should be noted in this statement: (1) Custer is planning to attack, and (2) the village. To me this says that Custer is aware of where the village is, and he is planning on how he can attack the village. If so, what would he recognize and consider in his plan? First, what did Godfrey say Custer was "possessed with?" Wasn't it that the Indians would not stand and give battle but would scatter? Secondly, attack and victory were inseparable. In order to prevent the first what would Custer plan on doing? Would it be to follow Reno or encircle the Indian village? To accomplish the second would he have waited along Reno Creek until he received messages from Girard and McIlhargey, or would he have already gone to the ridge in order to reconnoiter the village and decide how to implement his offensive plan.

Liddic now says that Custer is planning to attack a village of unknown size without fixing the precise location. Let's remember that Custer has said he is expecting 1000 to 1500 warriors, and that he has been warned he may face as many as 2000 to 3000. It is true that he doesn't know its exact size or extension, but would that really bother Custer or affect his plans? Liddic says Custer doesn't know the precise location—doesn't he? He nodded that he saw what the scouts were pointing out, which would have been smoke from the village. Custer must have known it was located behind the bluffs north of the confluence of Reno Creek with the Little Big Horn River. If Custer didn't know he would have asked his Crows, who, if you remember, knew every nook and corner of the region.

Liddic believes that whatever plans Custer formulated at the Crow's Nest would have to be modified or totally disregarded.[2] Why? Liddic doesn't give any reason, nor have I read of any writers giving any. Custer does know where the village is, and he is afraid they are aware of his troops and will scatter before he can bring them to battle. He is not concerned, at this time, with camps or Indians to the north as his command that is moving down Reno Creek can deal with them, but he has to be concerned if there are Indians waiting to attack from the bluffs or from camps lying in the valley upstream. He doesn't want to launch an attack on the known camp and then have Indians from camps to the south attack the companies he will be sending to attack the known village. He sends Benteen to the left to make sure there are no Indians waiting to ambush his troops and that there are no other camps. Custer, as Liddic points out, fears the Indians will scatter. Would Custer plan to follow Reno? Reno should have realized Custer would have planned on flanking the Indians. As long as Custer recognizes there is a village and knows the general location, then the exact size or precise location is immaterial.

The authorities do not question why Custer sends two additional messages to Benteen after giving him orders to go to the left at the division of the command. Custer when giving his initial orders had to have told Benteen more than go to the left, so why isn't Benteen's statement of what the other two orders consisted of questioned? The first courier, Trumpeter Voss, supposedly just told him to go beyond the first bluff, and the second messenger to go to the valley.[3] Would it take an initial order and then two messengers to get Benteen to go beyond the first line of bluffs, and if no Indians were found to go on to the valley? And to carry such simple messages, why would you send the second message by a staff officer? Why wouldn't you send Martin or some other courier?

According to the generally accepted view, Custer, as he continued down Reno Creek, not knowing the terrain or the exact location of the village, was not able to make any workable plan. Consequently Custer's move down Reno Creek was a "reconnaissance in force."[4]

Custer didn't communicate any plan to his officers (although I can't imagine them not knowing what he planned) because he wasn't sure of what Benteen might find on his excursion to the left. Custer, knowing as he did where the village was, would have made a simple plan, such as any commander would have made. If Benteen did not run into any Indians he would continue on to the valley. Benteen (contrary to what he claimed), even if he hadn't been told, would know it was the Little Big Horn valley. Anyone should be able to see through his pretense that he was valley hunting "ad infinitum."[5] We might remember he was the one that said he believed the scouts.[6] Custer, having given Reno three companies, would expect him to cross the Little Big Horn and move against the village. Custer was moving slower than he would have liked so that the rest of the command did not out distance Benteen. Benteen, when he reached the valley, would move in support of Reno. Because Custer was afraid the Indians would scatter, he would attempt to flank and encircle the Indian village. Up to this point Liddic brought out the necessary ingredients, but to then say no workable plan could be made is, to me, absurd. When Custer was ready to put his plan into action he did send orders to both Reno and Benteen as expressed by Custer's and Reno's orderlies. The lack of plans, this "reconnaissance in force," was created because the authorities didn't see the real reason why it was necessary for Reno and Benteen to say they didn't know of any plan in order to prevent themselves from being blamed for Custer's defeat. Because writers accepted this charade, Custer's knowledge and ability was made to suffer.

Benteen, as he was being sent to the left, supposedly questioned Custer's dividing the command and told Custer that they should keep the command together.[7] This sounds like another attempt by Benteen to portray himself as the superior military leader, and assert that if only he had been in charge things would have turned out differently. Benteen then protected himself from any involvement in the manipulation of time by claiming that according to Wallace's watch it was ten minutes after twelve when he was sent to the left.[8] Neither Reno's or Benteen's initial references to time would sustain any after twelve o'clock division of the command.

Liddic seemingly recognizes Custer's legitimate reasons for sending Benteen to the left, and then reverses his astute observations by saying Custer could have reaped the forenamed benefits by delaying Benteen's departure until he had better intelligence of what lay ahead.[9] Liddic then describes several benefits. What he doesn't say is that Custer had to assume (and his statements and actions indicate he is under this assumption) that the Indians were aware of his troops. He undoubtedly would have wanted to hurry and attack the known village, but he didn't know when the Indians may have become aware of his troops and prepared an ambush. He needed to send—not just some scouts—but enough men that could create a defense or an attack while notifying Custer. For Liddic to bring out the different positions is commendable, but since this one is an essential factor in determining the main premise surrounding Custer's actions and their connection with coverups, he should have made sure the dots are connected.

Liddic clarifies the above point that I am attempting to make, which is to tie in minor premises with the major premise. Liddic uses a letter that Private John Donouhue sent to the *Bismark Daily Tribune*:

> Major Reno you will charge down the valley and keep everything before you: Captain Benteen will take the extremeleft. I will take the extreme right myself with five companies. General Custer here described the point that

Major Reno should strike the camp supported by Captain Benteen and his three companies. "I will strike them on the opposite point and we will crush them between us."[10]

This coming from an enlisted man points out the common knowledge of Custer's plans, that have been so successfully covered up by the officers in order to protect Reno and Benteen and the overall 7th Cavalry's image.

Here again Liddic fails to connect the dots. Why? Is it because Donoughue was just a private, and an officer, Captain Benteen, said he didn't think Custer needed a plan since he didn't know where the Indians were.[11]

I will try to analyze both accounts. I'll take Benteen's first. Benteen we know tried to bring out that Custer had not seen what the scouts had at the Crow's Nest, and didn't even believe there was a village.[12] Liddic accepted that Custer did see or assented to what the scouts said they saw. I have tried in my writing to indicate as objectively as possible why Benteen (and Reno) had to say Custer did not see the village. If he hadn't seen the village then he wouldn't have made any plans, so they could say they had no knowledge that an offense was underway, or that he planned on flanking the Indians. After the battle, when their actions were increasingly criticized, the need to rationalize those actions became apparent. It was absolutely necessary to cover-up their orders and their time consuming delay in going to check on Custer.

Donoughue, according to Liddic, was wrong because "Custer had no tactical plan, and such reasoning is deeply flawed."[13] Liddic, and other writers, can't seem to acknowledge that from the time of the sightings from the Crow's Nest, Custer knew the general location of the Indian village, and that it lay behind the bluffs along the west side of the Little Big Horn river. He knew from maps and the Crow's reports that Reno Creek would meet the Little Big Horn to the south of the Indian village. He sent Benteen to the left for the reasons that I have given. Since the terrain would be more difficult and Benteen might run into Indians and need help, the other troops had to move at a comparatively slow pace. Custer's fear was not that he would be defeated but that the Indians knowing of his troops would scatter. As I've said many times, it wouldn't take a military genius to realize the need to not only attack the Indian village from the south but also from the north in an attempt to prevent the scattering. At the division of his command he had already planned on how to attack the village. He knew he had to make sure there were no Indians or camps to the left or south of the known camp. He gave Benteen three companies in order to make sure there weren't. He then gave Reno three companies—again, no military genius was needed to know that when the time came they would attack the village from the south. Custer, knowing the packs would trail, gave them an enlarged company for protection. He gave himself 5 companies.

Let's go over this fairly slowly: What is Custer afraid the Indians know? He is operating on the assumption that they have discovered his troops. What does he fear besides an ambush or that there are camps to the south of the known camp? Is it that there isn't a village? No, he has seen and accepted the scouts report on the village. Is it the camps precise location? No, Custer's only fear is that the Indians might scatter. To prevent that possibility would a commander plan to follow his other companies in an attack on the village? No, I don't think that would stop the Indians from scattering. Is flanking an opponent an army maneuver? Yes, it has been used. Has Custer ever used it? Yes, he has. Might he think of using it even at the time he divided his troops? Yes, as long as he knew the general location of the village. Would it have to be a precise location? No, that wouldn't be necessary. Would he plan on any companies supporting the three he knew he would be sending to attack the village from the south? Yes, if the three companies he sent to the left didn't find any Indians when they reached the Little Big Horn valley, they should move to support the other three. They would reach the Little Big Horn valley further upstream and to the southwest of the crossing made by the other three companies. They would then be expected to move on the left of the other three in the attack on the village. Could this be considered a "tactical" military plan? Yes it could.

A central question concerning Private Donoughue's report is if there was any verification of his letter. And the answer is yes there was. Reno's orderly Davern said the same thing at the Reno Court. According to Davern, Reno was to attack the Indian village and Benteen would be on his left.[14] A follow up question that should have been asked is: Was anything said as to what Custer and his five companies were going to do? The fact that such a question was not asked, and the interrogation on this central issue was cut short, should in itself be evidence of a cover-up. Doesn't the fact that there weren't any questions asked of Martin on the orders Custer gave, except on the orders he carried to Benteen, signify a cover-up? Shouldn't there have been some curiosity as to whether any orders were sent to Benteen at the time Custer sent orders to Reno? Martin some years later gave Colonel Graham an account of the orders similar to what Donoughue and Davern reported.[15] What more should writers need in order to realize that the view presented by the officers at the Reno Court was a cover-up?

Why is it so hard to understand that when Custer divided his regiment he would already have made plans to attack the village? He had assumed since he left the Yellowstone that the Indians would be found along the Little Big Horn, and he hadn't ran into any contrary evidence. The sighting from the Crow's Nest should have cemented his conception. The way he divided the regiment in itself would indicate his plan. If there were no Indians to the south he would have six companies attacking from the south and five from the north, with an enlarged company protecting the packs. This plan is "tactical" and it is sound, and it is the plan that Donoughue, Davern, and Martin—those not in the cover-up for Reno, Benteen, and the regiment—would have expressed. This plan would have remained intact until Custer learned that Benteen had not moved to the valley, and instead had returned to the main trail. And, considering the situation at the time Custer learned that he was back on the main trail, there is no way Custer would have wanted him to cross the Little Big Horn to support Reno.

Liddic doesn't connect Low Dog's sleeping[16] and that it was about noon to the early reports as expressed by Reno, Benteen, and others. He states that Indians would often say whatever the interrogator wanted them to say (and he could have added that they were usually paid for it). Liddic notes that Custer's slow "deliberate pace" was so he didn't outdistance Benteen.[17]

Liddic also states that Varnum reported to Custer his sighting of the main village, along with its size and location. This information he gave Custer, "about an hour or more before Reno was ordered forward."[18] Liddic mentions that Hairy Moccasin, one of the Crow scouts, said he went to "a butte on the head [sic] of Reno Creek" and he saw the village. He reported the information to the commander and that the village wasn't breaking up."[19] This happened earlier than Liddic is reporting. However, within six miles of the Little Big Horn, Custer knew not only where the Indian village was but its size. However, he still made no plans to attack the village. He was still on his "reconnaissance in force." We know that he had no plans because the authorities have said Custer was planning on supporting Reno by following him. According to them, Custer was in Reno Creek valley watering his horses and preparing to follow Reno when Cooke came with a message from Girard that the Indians were not running, and the warriors were moving to meet Reno. This news compelled Custer to suddenly decide to flank the Indians, but he didn't believe it necessary to inform Reno, Benteen, or the packs. This is where those opposed to, and critical of Custer should really condemn him—if for nothing else his stupidity.

Getting back to Liddic's account. Shortly after 2 o'clock Custer had Reno cross over to the north side of the Creek. The lone tepee was less than a mile ahead.[20] We now have at least six hours that have gone by since Custer knew the village had been located. A person could have walked twelve miles, but the attacked-minded Custer's 7th Cavalry had only moved ten, and they still had four to go to reach the river.

I believe Liddic is correct that Lt. Gibson located the valley and didn't see any Indians or camps and reported this to Benteen. Benteen should have been in Valley 3, and had to make the decision whether to continue following his orders to go to the valley or return to the main trail. He said he didn't follow orders, but excused himself by saying his return to the main trail saved Reno.[21] Liddic realizes that Benteen should have sent a message informing Custer that upstream was clear of Indians, and that he was returning to the main trail. However, since he hadn't, Custer would have assumed Benteen was still moving to the valley. Custer's plan, and the orders he sent to Reno and Benteen, would have been the same: On reaching the valley Benteen should move in support of Reno's attack on the village, while Custer would attempt to encircle the Indians. Custer would have sent orders to Benteen, carried by the Sgt. Major. Benteen's denial was a necessary cover-up.

Liddic states how Benteen's testimony, "shifted about constantly with half-truths, evasions, and falsehoods: by the time the Inquiry ended he had spread enough whitewash to cover Chicago. There can be little doubt Custer's senior captain dramatically changed his story three years later when called to the witness stand at the Reno Court."[22]

With this accurate assessment of Benteen, it seems odd to me that Liddic didn't carry it a step further and connect the Reno Court with the need to cover-up testimony in order to prevent court-martial charges being levied against Reno and an indictment of Benteen.

Lt. Hare remembered that Custer picked up the pace as he neared the Lone Tepee and nearly overtook his scouts. Liddic reports that Hare thought Custer seemed very impatient. What Liddic doesn't bring out is that the messenger sent to Hare was the Sgt. Major.[23] Benteen said that the second messenger he received after moving to the left was the Sgt. Major. There are several questions this should raise: (1) Could the Sgt. Major have taken a message to Benteen and still made it back in time to be sent to Lt. Hare? (2) Why wouldn't Custer have sent a regular orderly to Benteen, since the order was only to go to the valley? (3) If Custer thought those orders were that important, why wouldn't he have sent orders to Benteen when he was about to launch his attack? (4) Would there be any reason Benteen wanted to hide the time he received Custer's second courier? (5) Carrying it another step, would Benteen want to hide orders that Custer was launching his attack on the Indian village? And, if so, why? The answers to these questions shouldn't be hard to find.

Liddic said it was toward 2:45 p.m. when some of the mules made a mad dash for the morass. Lt. Wallace recorded the last official time at 2 o'clock near the site of the Lone Tepee, about three and a half miles in a straight line from an excellent crossing of the Little Big Horn. Liddic goes on to say that, "never the less one can't escape the relationship between time and distance no matter how much distortion is attempted."[24]

If some of the pack mules made a break for the morass and became stuck around 2:45 p.m.,[25] why is nothing mentioned that it was about one o'clock when Benteen said he watered his horses and they were just ahead of the packs?[26] However, according to the coterie, it was about 2 hours later when the mules rushed for the morass. They, of course, ignore earlier accounts, like those of General Rosser that Reno arrived on the ridge about 2 p.m.[27] These they brush off because Lt. Wallace recorded that Custer was at the Lone Tepee at 2 o'clock.[28] The question that I would like answered is, Why aren't the officers' time differences explained—if there is a rational explanation—between those they gave right after the battle compared with the times used at the Reno Court. If I gave an essay question to my class and they failed to explain in a logical way answers to the dichotomy found between answers given by officers before the trial and after the trial, those students grades would definitely suffer.

Liddic ends the chapter by reporting on the dust that was seen ahead and the belief that the Indians were running away. However, according to his version, this wasn't enough to cause Custer to feel the need to try and flank the Indians.

SOURCES

1. Liddic, 31.

2. Ibid., 31.

3. Reno Court, 403.

4. Liddic, 31.

5. Reno Court, 421, 431; Liddic, 34.

6. Graham, 179.

7. Liddic, 33.

8. Ibid., 33.

9. Ibid., 33.

10. Ibid., 34

11. Ibid., 34.

12. Reno Court, 402.

13. Liddic, 34.

14. Reno Court, 332.

15. Graham, 289.

16. Liddic, 36.

17. Ibid., 36.

18. Ibid., 36.

19. Ibid., 37.

20. Ibid., 37.

21. Graham, 194; Reno Court, 430.

22. Liddic, 38.

23. Camp, 65.

24. Liddic, 40.

25. Ibid., 40.

26. Graham, 180.

27. Ibid., 230.

28. Liddic, 40.

5

CUSTER'S ORDERS TO RENO AND BENTEEN

Liddic writes that as Custer passed the Lone Tepee he reacted to only what his senses told him and what his eyes saw, not the information he had been presented. He had now seen some Indians in flight, so he sent Reno and his three companies after them. Liddic has Custer first attempting to send the scouts in pursuit, but they refuse.[1] It is my understanding that they refused because they thought they were to lead the attack on the village, whereas Custer only wanted them to go after the Indian horses. One way or another, I question Liddic's interpretation of Custer's response to the dust and fleeing Indians. Custer would not have expected Reno's troops to catch the Indians. What Custer realized is what he had been afraid of, and that was the Indians scattering. This had been his fear all along, but now it appeared he was right. What Custer now knew was that he could not wait much longer to launch his attack on the village. He called Reno to the front at this time but not to chase after the fleeing Indians. Custer had been hoping to hear from Benteen that there were no Indians or camps upstream from the recognized camp location, which was the focal point of the plans he made back at the division of the command. His interest in the Indians seen fleeing was that they would warn the village, and he now knew he could not wait for Benteen's report before he launched his attack. However, he would have wanted to send orders to Benteen which is when I believe he did.

Writers should look beyond what the officer's said in their cover-up attempts, and instead listen to what the enlisted men said. This is particularly true when it is Reno's and Custer's orderlies. Why wasn't Martin asked what Custer's orders to Reno were until forty years afterwards? Why didn't some of the historians take Martin to the battlefield and have him show them the specific locations that are still disputed? What might be the reason that they didn't, besides lack of vision?

Reno at the Reno Court said he only expected his support to come from the rear. Liddic points out that ten days after the battle in his report Reno said, "It was evident to me that Custer meant to support me by moving further down the stream and attacking the **village** [my emphasis] in the flank."[2] Liddic then describes Davern's report of the orders Cooke gave to Reno.

The following is another prime example of not connecting the dots. Liddic does admirable work in bringing out the dots, and then not only fails to connect them, but actually erases the ones that he already brought out. He then reverts back to the accepted scenarios.

Let me try to explain. From page 46 in Liddic's book, I will start with his dot connecting and then get to his erasures, leaving the gap that has bothered me for years in the coteries' scenarios.

> Reno's orderly, Private Edward Davern 'F' Company, agreed with the Major's story and related how Cooke gave the order. Cooke said: "Girard comes back and reports the Indian village three miles ahead and moving. The General directs you to take your three companies and drive everything before you." Davern also added Cooke further said that"Colonel Benteen will be on your left and will have the same instructions." But Reno in a letter published in the New York *Herald* less than six weeks said there was "No mention of any plan, no thought of junction, only the usual orders to the advance guard to attack at a charge." The Major further wrote that the Adjutant's exact words were: "Custer says to move at a rapid gait as you think prudent, and to charge afterward, and you will be supported by the whole outfit." Custer's orderly John Martin remembered that Custer told Cooke to direct Reno to go down and cross the river and attack the Indian village. Martin further said Custer would support him with the whole regiment. According to Martin the plan was for Custer to go down to the other end and drive them, and he would have Benteen hurry up and attack them in the center. Martin, as an orderly would have been in an excellent position to be privy to any conversation between the lieutenant colonel and his adjutant.[3]

Liddic then gets into extraneous material that makes his book interesting and essential for an overall understanding of what happened, but sidetracks him from the real issues. After several paragraphs he does again get back to a connecting dot:

> At the Court of Inquiry, Reno swore under oath he had never received any direct orders from Custer, and the only order he received was to 'advance'

from the Adjutant beyond the Lone Tepee. However, we know Cooke assigned Reno his battalion at the divide, his battalion was brought to the head of the column by Custer as they approached the Lone Tepee, and, of course, the order to advance. It would seem Benteen was not the only one at the Court of Inquiry who dipped into the whitewash bucket.[4]

If you dip once, might you dip again? Liddic, after bringing out these cogent dots proceeds to erase them:

> I believe Girard, Herendeen, and Porter were correct in what Reno was directed to accomplish. Custer's orders to Reno were to bring the fleeing Indians to battle, and he didn'timagine he was sending him to attack a village. The reports Custer heard indicated the presence of a village, but there was still no specific knowledge of its size or exact location, except it was about three miles ahead, with plenty of inhabitants, and they were probably dismantling the village. The immediate circumstances confronting Custer would indicate he never expected his major to do any serious fighting.… Thus Custer's orders to "attack the village" was an afterthought by those who so heard, and consequently in a very human trait, they telescoped the village they were soon to confront with what they had been ordered to achieve a half hour earlier.

> … To reiterate, if Reno was correct and was ordered to attack a village, it must have been based on inference by Custer or Cooke, as neither had seen a village.[5]

A major fault of Liddic is his inconsistency. Does he believe Reno was sent to catch some fleeing Indians or to attack the Indian village. One would think from the above that Reno was only sent to bring the fleeing Indians to battle. This coincides with Liddic's and the authorities acceptance of Reno's and Benteen's statements that Custer had no plans and his move down Reno Creek was a "reconnaissance in force." However, Liddic also reports:

> At the Crow's Nest, Custer nodded his head indicating he had seen signs of a camp.… Custer studied the area once more and told Reynolds he was right, the signs were visible.[6]

Interestingly, Reno and Benteen testified at the Reno Court of Inquiry, Custer said he had not seen the village himself and although the scouts said there was a village he didn't believe it. However, their suspicious self-serving testimony is off-set by the recollections of Lieutenants Gibson, DeRudio,

Godfrey and Edgerly who clearly remembered Custer said the scouts reported a village and pony herds in the valley. In addition, the Arikara and Crow scouts positively declared Custer saw the signs of a village from the Crow's Nest. If Custer didn't believe there was a village along the banks of the Little Big Horn why would he commit 600 men to attack an illusion.[7]

He [Custer] had reached a conclusion that he must immediately attack the village ... [This was at the time he divided his regiment.] He must have known he was throwing the dice in attacking a village of unknown size without fixing its precise location.[8]

Reno at the Reno Court said, Cooke came to me and said, "General Custer directs you to take as rapid a gait as you think prudent and charge the village ..."[9]

This is important because one's view of Custer and in the overall sense the battle, rest on which of the two views you take. However, this is only true if you recognize the underlying meaning and incorporate it into your scenario. Liddic presents both views, but again fails to either recognize the inconsistency or its effect. Even though he brings out as shown above, numerous statements that indicate the village was Custer's objective, he has Custer's actions reflecting the lack of knowledge of the village location. He is then accepting Reno's and Benteen's testimony that they failed to know, or to have received, any attack plans. And since they didn't receive any they can then say Custer didn't have any, and his only plan was to follow Reno. Benteen is left out completely until hearing from Martin. However, if Custer did know the location of the village, at the time he divided his regiment, he would have already made provisional plans to attack the village, and these plans would include Reno, Benteen, the packs, and his five companies.

The failure to see the significance of Custer agreeing to the scouts sighting of the village from the Crow's Nest allows you to accept the schematic ploys Reno and Benteen used to excuse themselves from the debacle that took place.

Liddic includes two of the essential and basic dots: Davern's remembrance of the orders Cooke gave to Reno, and Martin's version of the orders Custer told Cooke to give Reno. Two orderlies who would not have been in on the cover-ups. The orders are the quintessential element (or should be) of any analysis of Custer, Reno, Benteen, and the other major participants in the battle. Any objective study should be cognizant of the cover-ups surrounding the battle, and the Reno Court of Inquiry. I have tried to bring these cover-ups out in my previous books and articles, and already have in this manuscript. Will it have any effect on those Custer buffs that have similar scenarios etched on their minds as those presented by Liddic? No, I don't think so, not when it hasn't so far. What their scenarios signify or portray is that Custer had no plans, and therefore Reno and Benteen had no knowledge that he was planning an attack. This belief, of course, is derived from what Reno and Benteen said, and as officer's their statements and testimony is militarily superior to two enlisted orderlies. Reno and Benteen said they had no knowledge of, and, in fact, didn't believe Custer had any plans. They said he couldn't have had any plans since he hadn't seen, and didn't even believe there was an Indian village. This led to the infamous march to the river being labeled as a "reconnaissance in force." This view has been accepted by most writers." Liddic does believe Custer thought there was a village, but since he couldn't have known the "precise" location of the village he wouldn't have made any plans to attack it. Liddic also considered Custer's movement to the river a "reconnaissance in force."

According to Liddic's scenario, Custer, when he sees the dust raised by the fleeing Indians, reacts "only to what his senses and what his eyes saw, and not the information he had been presented."[10] He then attempts to send the scouts after the fleeing Indians, and when they refuse to go he orders Reno to bring them to battle. Although I think Liddic's timing is off as to when Reno received his orders from Cooke, the main question is how did he expect Reno to catch those Indians? It was common knowledge that it was practically impossible to catch fleeing Indians. This would certainly be true with Indians having the head start that these did. In questioning whether Reno was sent to catch these fleeing Indians, I can't recall reading of any urgency in Reno's "pursuit." I don't think there should be any question that the "village" was the target Custer sent Reno to attack.

In dividing his command, Custer gives Benteen three companies, Reno three, the packs one, and he keeps five. What does Custer fear from the Indians? He fears the Indians will scatter before he can bring them to battle. Custer does know the following: (1) The general location of the Indian village. (2) The path of Reno Creek, and its confluence with the Little Big Horn . (This he would know from maps, and from Bouyer and the Crows.) (3) Fearing the Indians would scatter, one has to consider Custer completely void of any rational thought if he planned on having his whole regiment cross the Little Big Horn and move from the south on the Indian village. Would he want some of his troops to attack from the south? Yes, he would. At the division, who, in his mind, would he assign to that attack? Wouldn't common sense tell us that it would have been Reno's three troops. Why was Custer moving comparatively slow until the Lone Tepee?

Wasn't it so they wouldn't outdistance Benteen? Where did he want Benteen to go to make sure there weren't any Indian villages? To the valley. When he reached the valley, and hopefully he wouldn't have found any villages, what might Custer have wanted Benteen to do? Might it have been to move north down the valley in support of Reno? Custer's and the armies basic fear was that the Indians would scatter once they knew about the troops. What might Custer have planned for his five companies? Could it be that he might have planned on flanking the Indian village? Ideally, he would have six companies attacking the village from the south, and five from the north.

Other questions: What did Reno's orderly say were the orders Cooke gave to Reno? What did Custer's orderly say were the orders Custer gave Cooke to give to Reno? Was Benteen to receive any orders? If Benteen was sent orders, who most likely carried them, and when? Why wasn't Reno's orderly asked additional questions concerning Custer and what he might have been expected to do? Why did they cut off Davern's questioning, and why did Reno's counsel attempt to brush off and dismiss Davern's remarks? And probably the most important question concerning the Reno Court, is why wasn't Custer's orderly asked any questions as to the orders Custer gave to Reno, and whether he gave any to Benteen?

Then to the erasure of the essential dots by Liddic. Liddic brings out the two basic dots: What Reno's orderly Davern said were the orders Cooke gave to Reno, and what Martin said the orders were that Custer gave to Cooke (even though he wasn't asked of this until forty years later). Did these orders and the lack of this inquiry or follow up on them at the Court present any unanswered questions to Liddic? No, we can dismiss what the orderlies said and implied because Reno said they weren't the orders he received, and Benteen also said he had no knowledge of any orders or plans that Custer had. So the officers' accounts nullify those of the privates, even if the officers' denials were necessary to prevent them from being court-martialed and blamed for the wiping-out of Custer's five companies.

Liddic brought out two of what I consider the necessary dots: The two orders that the orderlies remembered. They both had Benteen being sent orders from Custer. However, they were not asked, nor have the coterie been concerned as to when the orders were sent or who carried them. Shouldn't these have been requisite follow-up questions? These orders indicated that Benteen was to aid Reno and Custer would be flanking the Indians. If Benteen didn't run into any Indians or their camps this would have been Custer's plan from the division of his command. The only "reconnaissance in force" by Custer was his holding back because of his concern for Benteen's reconnaissance.

The essential position one needs to take is an acceptance of Custer at the Crow's Nest seeing or agreeing with the scouts on the location of the village. This shouldn't be that difficult, because the only ones who said he didn't were Reno and Benteen. And we should understand why this was necessary in order to prevent themselves from facing court martial charges and being blamed for the defeat of Custer. Liddic accepted the sighting, but used Custer not knowing the precise location of the village to say that he would not have had any plans to attack. If Custer knew the general location of the enemy, even if not the exact position, he would make plans to attack. The only reason to change those plans is if he found out some part of them wasn't taking place as contemplated. Custer knew that Benteen could have confronted enough Indians that he would have needed help, or, as he later found out, that Benteen had not followed orders and deviated from his plan by returning to the main trail. By then Custer knew he didn't want him to cross the Little Big Horn in support of Reno, but instead wanted him to support his five companies. I'm also certain that the packs had initial orders to hold as they neared the Little Big Horn until they received further orders.

Liddic reports Reno's and Benteen's "whitewashes" or cover-ups, but then accepts their version of the orders they received in contrast to the orderlies version. The orderlies had no reason to lie or distort the orders, but Reno and Benteen did.

Liddic then writes:

> It wouldn't have been unusual for Custer to wonder about Benteen's whereabouts. Why hadn't he rejoined the main trail, or why hadn't he reported what he discovered? If Stabbed's account is accurate, he must have been dispatched as a messenger to find out the answers. If Custer dispatched this messenger, his request would have had to have been in writing as Stabbed spoke no English, and no interpreter accompanied him. One battle student suggested that the messenger was the Sergeant Major, and that Stabbed escorted him. What would have the message contained? Probably, as noted, Custer would have asked why he had not heard from the senior captain? What were the conditions on the back trail? Were there any camps in the lower valley? In addition, could Custer have given Benteen further orders, such as, he was to join the attack or to come in on the left of the eight advancing companies? The possibilities of Stabbed going to Benteen and returning would create enough interesting scenarios to keep battle historians busy for the next hundred years.[11]

At least Liddic mentions the older Ree, Stabbed. It is very doubtful Custer would have sent Stabbed alone with a written order. Stabbed should have been sent with a soldier in order to help locate Benteen, but they would not have been sent to find out information on the Indians. It isn't that Custer wasn't concerned, but he would have expected Benteen to notify him if there were Indians, and the fact that Custer had not heard gunfire would have allowed Custer to assume that Benteen was still moving to the valley of the Little Big Horn.

Liddic raises the question of what the message contained, and he suggests orders, but then leaves the question up in the air. One needs to understand that this is the period during which Benteen and Reno had to cover-up the orders they received. There is no way, in my mind, that Custer would have sent the Sgt. Major to Benteen at the early time and with the message that Benteen claimed he carried. As he neared the Lone Tepee, Custer was concerned with the Indian situation as illustrated by his sending the Sgt. Major to Lt. Hare, a short distance ahead, for a scouting report.[12] We know Custer was picking up the pace as he neared the Lone Tepee, and censured the Rees for not going ahead in pursuit. Custer undoubtedly knew that he would have to launch his attack on the village as he neared the Little Big Horn. Since he believed Benteen had not encountered any large number of Indians, he expected to be able to initiate his attack plan. Custer had not informed Benteen or Reno of the plan because of the provisional characteristics associated with it. However, once he knew he was going to launch his attack on the village, he would have sent a staff officer, his Sgt. Major, with orders for Benteen when he reached the valley. He wouldn't have sent the Sgt. Major alone, but would have wanted him to be accompanied by an Indian scout. As they first moved into the bluffs and from a high knoll, they would not have been able to see anything of Benteen, but Ridge C would have appeared to be a good lookout point to find Benteen. Possibly they first saw Lt. Gibson with his six men. One way or another they located Benteen. He was already moving to the main trail. The Sgt. Major would then have written a message notifying Custer, and sent it with Stabbed. We know Stabbed met the slower Rees following Custer's trail,[13] and when they got on the ridge Stabbed went further down to where I assume he met Custer's rear guard, or the last of Custer's five companies to leave the ridge. One should mention that Soldier, one of the slower Rees that Stabbed had caught up with, said that as they came onto the ridge he could see Bob Tail Bull far out on the left.[14] This would mean that Reno was still on his way down the valley, and since Soldier did not say he saw Custer's men still moving to or on the ridge, they must have left the ridge on their way to Medicine Tail

Coulee and Ford B. As I said before, Stabbed could have met the rear guard or even the last of the five companies to leave.

I think it is ridiculous to believe that the Sgt. Major was sent with the trifling message Benteen said he delivered, and at the time Benteen reported receiving it.[15] Again we should recall the orders the orderlies said Custer gave, and that they were given to Benteen. The initial orders were based on the assumption that Benteen would go to the valley. He would reach the river above Reno's entrance and in moving down in support of Reno would be on hs left. And at all times keep in mind that Reno and Benteen were attempting to hide actions that could be blamed for the demise of Custer's five companies and instigate a court-martial. If this is too hard to believe or digest, read and study today's cover-ups by officials.

Liddic then reveals another cover-up, but fails to follow it up:

> It was about 2:15 in the afternoon [I will skip all the references that it was actually before or near noon] when Reno's battalion moved forward; ... The major was about three and one half miles from the Little Big Horn River. [this distance is questionable as Varnum referred to it as about two miles from the river. and most reports say a mile and a half.] Varnum had rejoined Custer and saw Reno's battalion moving off at a trot. He asked his commander where they were going, and Custer replied," to begin the attack. [I thought, according to Liddic, that Reno was sent after some fleeing Indians. To begin the attack sounds more like it is aimed at a certain location. If chasing fleeing Indians shouldn't Reno have been moving faster than a trot.] He asked Custer for further orders and was told that he could go with the advance if he wished. As he rode past his lieutenant colonel for what would be the last time, Hare and the scouts around him joined Varnum. While the small party passed the main column, Varnum noticed his friend and roommate George Wallace riding at the head of the troops and called out, "Come on Nick, with the fighting men. I don't stay back with the coffee coolers."

> Custer just smiled and waived his hat, and Wallace also joined the advance.... Varnum's recollections strongly imply that Wallace perjured himself at the Reno Court of Inquiry when he stated he always rode "near Major Reno" and gave testimony as if he had.[16]

This should ring a bell. What sort of a bell? A very loud one. I wonder what it takes for people to realize that the Reno Court was an enormous cover-up to protect Reno, Benteen, other officers, the 7th Cavalry, and the army. Why would

Wallace have lied? In order to protect Reno, Benteen, the 7th Cavalry, and the army.

Reno's adjutant Lt. Hodgson had been killed, so they needed some officer to corroborate what Reno said his orders were. Who was unattached and could be placed by Reno's side? Who else but Wallace? Would Wallace have done it if it only protected Reno? Possibly, but they needed to protect all of the above. Does this make Wallace a bad person? No, you or I, or at least I, would have done the same thing.

Liddic follows the accepted line that it only took ten minutes for Reno's three companies to cross Ford A. I love the way time can be extended or shortened when necessary to protect a scenario. I cannot see three companies approaching a timber—lined ford, changing to column of twos, some scattering as stated by Wallace, the horses drinking, and still have it take only ten minutes. In this case writers are accepting the time element needed to have Reno's troops moving down the valley ahead of Custer's on the ridge.

Liddic:

> While Reno was moving to the advance, Custer followed at a much slower pace. He was still giving Benteen time to catch up with the rest of the regi-ment while Reno carried out his assignment.... To insure his orders to Reno were being carried out, Custer asked Cooke to follow after Reno.... Myles Keogh also joined the Adjutant. These two key figures from the right wing weren't just "pirating on their own hook." They were sent by Custer with a specific mission to accomplish. It is conceivable, at this point Custer intended to follow Reno, probably in a reinforcing position. It is doubtful the Lieutenant Colonel would have ever sent these two important officers to follow up on the advance if he expected to change his plans to a supporting position and move in a different direction. This is another indication that Custer closely followed Reno almost to the ford itself and did not turn to the right several miles or more from the Ford 'A,' as some battle students claim.[17]

Liddic said Custer was going slow to enable Benteen to catch up to the rest of the regiment. (This was as they were nearing the Lone Tepee) As I have been pointing out, Custer would have been torn between two realizations: (1) He had to be sure of the Indian situation to his left and whether there were any other Indian camps upstream from the known village. (And it was a known village.) (2) He knew he should be launching his attack on the village. We know he picked up the pace as he passed the Lone Tepee.

Always keep in mind the army's and Custer's basic fear, and that was that the Indians would scatter once they knew troops were in the area. This should make it quite clear that Custer would have had no plans to follow Reno, and he wouldn't have given any orders to Cooke to go with Reno to the river, and certainly not Keogh. We should try and keep the dots in line. One of the prime dots is to understand that if Reno (and this applies to Benteen) knew that Custer planned on flanking the Indians, especially if this was brought out in their orders, they would have been subject to a court-martial. The most important link in Reno's defense case was Private Wilber's statement that Cooke sat on the bank on his horse. Wilber said: "We were galloping fast, and just as we got to the river Cooke called out: 'For God's sake men, don't run those horses like that; you will need them in a few minutes.'[18] Wilber said he didn't see Keogh. Besides the fact that in no way was Custer planning on following Reno, and recognizing the need for the Defense to find such support for Reno's version of his orders, I don't accept Wilber's account because Sgt. Culbertson had a similar story. However, it took place at the tributary crossing rather than at the river. Culbertson said, "as we were crossing the tributary to the Little Big Horn, while on the way to the crossing ford, I heard Adjutant Cook tell the men to close up, there was hot work ahead for them."[19] Then Dr. Porter, who was by Reno's side, said that after Reno received his orders, "The Adjutant rode back and Reno went on to the crossing, … [20] Private Morris said Cooke never went to the ford and he was in a position to know. I think it is fair to assume that Wilber got the two crossings mixed up. The officers that said Cooke went to the ford were not with Reno. These reports would have been part of the Courts' cover-up. The essence of the Defense's case was that Reno expected Custer to follow him, and he did not know Custer was flanking the Indians. Reno certainly would have realized by the time of his court of inquiry that if he professed to knowing Custer was flanking the Indians it meant he should not have left the valley, and in doing so he would be facing court-martial proceedings.

Benteen made enough statements that he had orders to go to the "valley," and since Custer had not heard from him, he would have assumed Benteen would be nearing the valley (the Little Big Horn Valley). Don't brush off, as Reno's counsel did, Davern's remembrance of Custer's order to Reno, and that Benteen would have orders to be on Reno's left. If one needs verification of that they need only look at what Martin said Custer's orders were. Custer didn't need any message from Girard to have planned on flanking the Indians.

Liddic uses Godfrey's statement that Cooke and Keogh were both at the ford crossing for a short time. Godfrey was not there so this is hearsay, or he was simply trying to support Reno or refrain from upsetting Reno's case. Liddic then is in error since he has Culbertson saying Cooke was at the river,[21] when that is not what Culbertson said, and the footnotes used are also not correct.

The authorities go along with Girard's prosecution ploy that the Ree's told him that fifteen hundred Indians were coming up the river to meet the soldiers.[22] This ploy fit in with Reno's that he sent McIlhargey to tell Custer the Indians were strong in front of him.[23] If any Ree told Girard of the Indians coming to meet them, I haven't read of it, nor have I read of any Sioux or Cheyenne account that there were. The evidence supports that there weren't any for, besides testimony, if there were it is amazing how fast they disappeared as Reno moved down the valley. This was the time you would have thought the Indians would be attempting to stop or at least harass his troops. Girard was attempting to accuse Reno. Reno, after the battle, couldn't say he sent McIlhargey to find out if he should wait for Benteen, so he used Girard's and the Recorder's ploy that the Indians were in force in front of him. These remarks by Girard and Reno are accepted by the coterie, preventing any real analysis of their effect.

So Cooke receives the messages from Girard and McIlhargey. Girard returns to Reno's command, but McIlhargey continues on. Why does McIlhargey continue on if his message is to only notify Custer of the Indians that Reno is now confronted with? Couldn't he, like Girard, have allowed Cooke to deliver the message, and he could then have returned to Reno?

Liddic does mention that McIlhargey could have ridden a longer way to deliver his message, thus precluding any safe return to Reno. Liddic, in supporting the early meeting with Cooke, believes he may have stayed with his own company ('I'), or he may have felt there was a greater chance of action and "glory" riding with Custer.[24]

Liddic has Custer receiving both messages while still on Reno Creek; if so, wouldn't McIlhargey have found out that because of the messages, Custer now planned on flanking the Indians? Since Reno, according to Liddic, had no idea of Custer's plans,[25] shouldn't Custer have sent McIlhargey back to inform Reno that he now planned on flanking the Indians?

There is nothing wrong with the reasoning that if up until then Custer had not planned on flanking the village, receiving these messages would have caused him to do so. Custer would have realized that with the Indians attacking Reno, the village could be vulnerable to a flank attack and "a strike at the end of the encampment to put a stop to any further flight."[26]

This is sound reasoning if that was the situation at the time. However, I don't think it was for a number of reasons: (1) You are assuming that from the time

Custer was at the Crow's Nest, he either didn't accept the scout's sighting or because he couldn't see the precise location of the village, he wouldn't have made any plans to attack. This, to me, is absurd. Even if he hadn't seen what the scouts pointed out, Custer would have assumed the scouts were right, and then made plans to attack the village. Custer would have recognized that there were variables that could change those plans, but he would have still made them. (2) As he neared the Little Big Horn, scout's reports, such as Hairy Moccasin's and Lt. Varnum's, would have made him aware of the village its size and location. (3) In accepting the view that Custer planned on following Reno until he received these messages, you are saying that Custer didn't believe the Indians were aware of his troops so he had no fear the Indians would scatter. However, we know that he decided to attack that day because he feared the Indians were aware of his troops. (4) Custer had no plans for Benteen, he was only sent to the left to find out if there were any Indians and their camps. Custer also gave him orders to go to the valley, but had no other plans for him, even at the time he began his attack, so Benteen was kept in complete ignorance until receiving Martin's message. This defies logic. (5) Custer must have had some inclination that there was an Indian village on the other side of the bluffs from all the signs, reports, etc. He sent the Crows to the ridge, but according to the accepted testimony he personally must not have had any desire to go and check out the situation for himself. Is this reasonable? According to any history of Custer he would have been out in front leading the attack or searching for the enemy. Once he gave Reno his attack orders and gave his five commanders permission to allow their horses to drink, Custer would have been off to the ridge to check on the situation in the valley for himself.

Getting back to the messages. If Custer had received those messages, he would have sent McIlhargey back to Reno to let him know that he had changed his mind from following him to flanking the Indians. This signified several things: (1) That Custer had already gone to the ridge. (2) Custer would not have sent Cooke to the ford with Reno. Cooke most likely accompanied Custer to the ridge. (3) There were no Indians in front of Reno's troops at that time. Girard's message was concocted as a plot at the Reno Court in order to charge Reno with fleeing from the valley when he should have known Custer would be moving to help him. His fleeing the valley allowed the Indians to leave, meet Custer, and defeat him. Reno should then have been court-martialed, since his actions were instrumental in Custer's defeat.

Liddic has Benteen arriving back on the main trail about three o'clock. He quotes Private Morris and Godfrey on the slowness of Benteen's pace. He brings out that Custer was less than six miles away in the vicinity of Sharpshooter Ridge, and Reno was down in the valley about five miles ahead, heavily engaged. He has Lt. Mathey driving mules past a half dozen others mired in the morass at a little after 3:30 p.m. They go on to the Lone Tepee where McDougall with "Kanipe in tow" meet them and the command is now together. [27]

What has always been difficult for me to understand when reading past and present accounts of the battle is how writers can ignore the difference in time between officer's earlier and later testimony. I will not list the accounts of participants, officers, enlisted men, scouts, and the hostiles that state the battle began about noon or earlier while Reno Court estimates are around three o'clock.

Benteen said he was at the morass about 1 p.m. of a "hot summer day."[28] Liddic correlates his time with Gray and others, listing it as about three o'clock At the morass Benteen should have been within 6 miles of Reno Hill. Using Benteen's estimate that he was at the morass about 1 p.m., (and not using the more likely time of 12:45 p.m. or earlier) and that he left by 1:20, he should have had no trouble, even if walking his horses, reaching Reno Hill by 2:20 or 2:30. A person can walk a mile in 20 minutes, and run 6 miles in an hour. In his report following the battle, Reno has Benteen arriving on Reno Hill by 2:30 p.m.[29]

According to Liddic, Custer made his third critical decision as he turned to the right. The question Liddic asks is what caused Custer to change from what had seemed to be a reinforcing role to one of supporting.[30] Liddic gives several reasons, including Girard's report that the Indians were coming to meet Reno. Liddic's reasoning lacks tangibility but expresses the accepted belief.

Liddic now states that we must take into account Custer's aggressive nature and that to him, attack and victory were the same.[31] I don't know where this aggressive nature was up until now—and I might add afterwards. I'll go back over Liddic's hypothesis again—briefly. Custer had known since the Crow's Nest (actually believed even before) that there was a village behind the bluffs west of the Little Big Horn. He feared the Indians may have seen his troops and would scatter, but he still planned on reinforcing Reno. He had no plans for Benteen except to have him look for Indians and go valley hunting. However, we now remember Custer is an attack-minded leader, so he is not going to wait and follow Reno, he is going to attack by flanking the Indians. He still doesn't plan on including Benteen. If Custer is such an attack-minded leader then he would never have planned on following Reno, and he would have included Benteen. Either Custer is inept or this line of reasoning is.

Liddic:

> By going to his right Custer has been roundly criticized for not informing Reno of his change in plans. Custer knew Reno wanted to be reinforced; he had sent Reno to stop the flight of a body of Indians, and now he received two reports they were coming out to meet Reno "in strong force." If Custer's intent was to reinforce rather than support (and we have no way of knowing what additional instructions were given to Major Reno.) Then his failure to apprise Reno of "this sudden and variant change at best constitutes a lack of good faith." However, Custer might have thought he would execute his attack well before any messenger would get through to his vice commander. Also,without a doubt, Custer still believed the village was breaking up and the "strong force" Reno reported was only the rear guard.[32]

There are major premises that I keep coming back to, and undoubtedly will continue to do so since I have brought them out in my other books and articles, yet many experts have ignored them. Maybe repetition will help.

(1) There was no change in Custer's plan. He planned on flanking the Indian village since the division of his command. (2) He didn't send Reno after some fleeing Indians because there was no way they would have caught them. Reno's actions or statements do not support such a premise. (3) Liddic, in saying "There is no way of knowing what additional instructions were given to Major Reno,"[33] might give Custer credit for a little insight plus military knowledge and assume that Davern and Martin may have been right in the orders they said Custer gave Reno and implied were sent to Benteen. This should be connected to an understanding of the pressure Reno and Benteen were under, and the necessity for them to rationalize their actions by covering-up their orders. (4) In the same paragraph Liddic states that Custer sent Reno after the fleeing Indians, and also that Custer still believed the "village" was breaking up. If Custer believed this, he should have recognized a long time back the necessity of flanking the Indian encampment and the need to send some companies from the south (i.e., Reno and Benteen) to attack that village.

When Custer reached the ridge a lot of the Indian village would not have been in view. The relative position between Reno's troops as they moved down the valley and Custer's troops on the ridge is an essential dot that needs to be connected. I have Custer leaving the ridge while Reno is still part way down the valley. I base this on testimony, timing, and common sense.

Two interesting comments should be factored in: (1) A July 15, 1876 letter by Dr. Holmes L. Paulding (Dr. Paulding was with Colonel Gibbon's command) to his mother. (2) A letter dated Aug. 8th, 1896 from the Office of the Chief Signal Officer, Captain Thompson to then Attorney at-Law Theodore W. Goldin:

Dr. Paulding wrote:

> "While Custer was fighting, Reno with his three Companies went up the river & crossed in the timber & then charged from the valley toward the upper end of the village one (1) or two (2) miles away. As they galloped over the plain they heard several volleys from where Custer was, and soon after engaged themselves."[34]

Although Dr. Paulding may have misinterpreted comments from 7th Cavalry officers, it would appear to have been a common recollection.

Captain Thompson asks Goldin if:

> .... I have just heard that Reno's men while fighting on the bluff, or perhaps it was while his line was extended across the plain before he took to the timber, at any rate, the point is that sometime during Reno's stay in the valley, and before he made his wretched scramble to the bluffs, some of his men are said to have seen Custer fighting across the river, perhaps two miles or so away.... should have gone all these years unmentioned, yet that is just what the Indians say took place—that Custer's first fighting was done in full presence of Reno's command ... [35]

The essence of the two comments is that Custer planned on enveloping the Indian encampment, that he moved ahead of Reno, and that he had engaged the enemy while Reno was still in the valley.

One needs to analyze all of the following elements in determining Custer and Reno's relative position: Reno's Ford A crossing; Sharpshooter Ridge; Weir Point; Cedar Coulee; Western and Middle Coulee; where Martin received his message to take to Custer, Martin's sighting of Reno fighting in the Valley; Reno's enlisted men's sighting of Custer along with the Rees; the slower Rees when arriving on the ridge noticing Bobtail Bull far out on the left of Reno's men going down the valley; and Lt. Hare's inadvertent remark that he had heard later that enlisted men had seen Custer on the ridge. However, the most important factor is Martin's account of seeing a peaceful village, kids playing, etc., along with Curley's reference to similar remarks by Bouyer, and the three Crow's statements given to Edward Curtis and General Woodruff. These peaceful sightings would not have taken place from Sharpshooter's Ridge, or after Reno had gone into action. The measurements given by General Woodruff, and his and Curtis' remarks, have Custer going to Weir Point and seeing a peaceful village. As I have said before I question if all of Custer's troops had left the ridge, but Custer was on his way to Medicine Tail Coulee, and personally may have reached it, as Reno was establishing his skirmish line.

Underlying one's analysis should be the understanding that so many views have been shaped by Reno Court testimony, and one must recognize the case Reno's Defense was making as well as the case Jason Lee was attempting to create. Jason Lee deserves credit in realizing that he couldn't combat officer testimony with the witnesses he could call, and the army restrictions he was operating under. He then accepted the Defenses' strategy which put Reno ahead of Custer. This ploy also included these elements: Custer did not have any prior plan to attack the Indian village; his trek to the Little Big Horn was a "reconnaissance in force"; he only planned to follow Reno; there were no plans for Benteen; and Custer didn't plan on flanking the Indians until he heard Girard's and McIlhargey's messages. The Recorder accepted the Defense's position that Cooke had gone to the ford with Reno in order for Girard to tell Reno the Rees had informed him that the Lacotah were coming down the valley and he was going to tell Custer. Girard was then able to meet Cooke and still go with Reno down the valley. Reno should then have known Custer was coming to his aid even if it was not from behind. Reno should then have stayed in the valley, and that by fleeing he enabled the Indians to leave and concentrate on Custer. The fleeing caused Custer's defeat. The picture they created portrays an abject Custer who lacked the insight to plan an attack, and when he finally did decide to attack he still didn't notify his subordinates of his plans. The Reno Court cover-ups led to the belief that Reno's troops moved down the valley ahead of Custer on the ridge. Custer's flanking move was too late, and justified Reno's flight to the bluffs. The acceptance of this has distorted timing, the overall view of the battle, and particularly Custer's ability as a commander.

SOURCES

1. Liddic, 45.

2. Overfield II, 49; Liddic, 46.

3. Ibid., 46.

4. Ibid., 46.

5. Ibid., 47.

6.   Ibid., 26.

7.   Ibid., 29.

8.   Liddic, 31.

9.   Reno Court, 561.

10. Liddic, 45.

11. Ibid., 48.

12. Camp, 65.

13. Graham, 38.

14. Ibid., 38.

15. Reno Court, 403.

16. Liddic, 48.

17. Ibid., 49.

18. Camp, 148.

19. Reno Court, 380.

20. Ibid., 199.

21. Liddic, 49.

22. Ibid., 49, 50.

23. Ibid., 50.

24. Ibid., 50.

25. Ibid., 46.

26. Ibid., 50.

27. Ibid., 52.

28. Graham, 180.

29. Overfield II, 43.

30. Liddic., 53.

31. Ibid., 53.

32. Ibid., 53.

33. Ibid., 53.

34. Dr. Holmes L. Paulding, *Montana The Magazine of Western History,* Autumn 1982, p. 43.

35. Graham, 211.

6

RENO IN THE VALLEY

Liddic brings out accusations of Reno's drinking. He also mentions the Ree scouts along with Lt. Hare going down the valley after the Indian ponies. What is instructive is that they had advanced about a mile when they saw a herd of ponies.[1] One can't help wonder where the 1500 Indians the Rees warned Girard about were, or the strong force Reno complained about. Liddic uses Private Tom O'Neil's statement to Walter Camp in which he remembered passing the Rees on the way to the crossing ford. The Rees picked up "handfuls of grass and dropping it and pointing to the Sioux, who could be seen down and across the river, indication that the Sioux were as thick as grass."[2] According to Liddic this is probably when Reno sent his striker McIlhargey to speed up his reinforcement.

I have always understood that a historian should essentially question everything. I am sure from all the signs that the scouts had been seeing for some time, and since some of the scouts had been to the bluffs with Varnum, that they were aware of the Indian village, its location and realized the large number of warriors there were. They then threw up the grass and pointed in the direction of the village, indicating that the Sioux were as thick as grass. I question if there was any knoll near the crossing ford where they could have even seen the beginning of the Sioux village, and as Liddic states there weren't any Sioux warriors and only a few herders that might have been seen. The first time there were reports of seeing Indians was as they neared the village. Varnum and the scouts could see some Indians riding back and forth. We should also remember that the Rees were about to lead Reno down the valley, and I question if the Rees would have done that if they had seen as many Sioux in the valley as the grass episode implies. We should also remember that the hostile Indians did not report any number of warriors in the valley, and most of the Indians were not aware of Reno's troops until the first shots were fired. We can add to that the peaceful look of the village as reported from the ridge by the Crows and Trumpeter Martin. I think it is fair to say there was no large force of Indians in the valley at that time.

I agree Reno sent McIlhargey to Custer because he wondered where and if he should wait for his support, but there is no question in my mind that he knew that the support from behind was to be Benteen. We won't, at this time, go again into Custer's knowledge of the village and it's location, or the orders he gave as stated by Davern, Martin, and recognized by enlisted men such as Private Donoughue. McIlhargey should have caught Custer's men as they were still watering or starting for the ridge. Custer would already have been on the ridge. The other officers were in no position to have told McIlhargey whether Reno should wait or not. McIlhargey would have had to continue on, and by the time he would have caught and reported to Custer, Reno would already have started down the valley. I won't get into timing here, only to say that the time used for Reno, after getting his orders to go to Ford A, cross, go through the timber, reform, send messengers and expect a reply, is too short a period. It did have to be made short in order to have Reno preceding Custer, incorporate the time change, and lengthen Reno's actual fighting time in the valley.

Liddic:

> If one can believe Reno's testimony about "nothing to guide my movement," there is little doubt there was a complete misunderstanding between Custer and Reno regarding his mission. It would appear they attended different meetings together. Clearly Custer was operating under one set of perceptions and had directed his subordinates according to his intended tactical plan(s). The fear the village was escaping, I believe, drove these perceptions and developments. Did this correspond to Reno's perception, and what in reality awaited ahead of him? Allowing that Reno was correct in his recollections and the rest wrong, Reno was ordered to advance at a pace he was to select, look for and to charge the village/Indians. The Major hadn't any personal knowledge and had only been given reports of Indians ahead, one of which he dismissed. Before asking for "support," a more prudent course would have been to carry out the orders given until the true situation in the valley was disclosed.... Custer's tactical perceptions tragically clashed with the reality of what transpired before Reno's eyes. But weren't these Indians his objective, as well as the campaign's? Custer dispatched his second in command to look for a village of recalcitrant Indians, and since the Major hadn't lost any of those Indians, he didn't need to find any ... unless his commanding officer was with him.[3]

Liddic says if one can believe Reno's testimony there was a complete misunderstanding between Custer and Reno regarding his mission. What he is actually saying is that Custer didn't give clear orders so that his subordinates were not aware of his plans. If Custer was alive what do you think he might have said about the orders he gave? Don't you think they might resemble what Davern and Martin said, more so than what was reported by Reno and Benteen? If we connect what was said with the major premise, which is who was mainly responsible for the disaster that took place, was it Custer or was it Reno and Benteen? If as Reno and Benteen claimed they had no knowledge of Custer's plans, and we believe Custer's response and actions depended on a "reconnaissance in force," then we must blame Custer. However, if Davern and Martin were correct and their remembrance of the orders were those given to Reno and Benteen, then the blame should be placed on Reno and Benteen.

Liddic says Custer's fear that the village was escaping is what drove his perceptions and developments. I've tried to point this out throughout my writings of the campaign, and this would have been true after the sightings of the village from the Crow's Nest. Liddic reverses himself as he acknowledges Custer's recognition and concern with the village and not just some fleeing Indians. In doing so, he implies Custer not only knows its general location, but is primarily interested in its scattering and not its precise location. Underlying such an explanation should be the recognition of the need for Reno and Benteen to cover-up this knowledge, and that Custer's central interest has been the village. This should be discerned from their statements covering-up Custer's orders. Custer's knowledge and concern with the village would have been expressed in planning how to attack the village. Custer would have recognized the necessity of this following the Crow's Nest, and it led to not only his division of the command but the way it was divided.

Liddic says, "Custer's tactical perceptions tragically clashed with the reality of what transpired before Reno's eyes."[4] There is no question Reno expected support, and it should have been from both Benteen and Custer. Since neither could be seen, this placed Reno in a quandary that he was not capable of dealing with, and which caused him to flee to the bluffs. However, the reasons why "Custer's tactical perceptions tragically clashed with the reality of what transpired," was not due primarily to the fault of Reno or Custer's plans. What went wrong was: (1) Benteen failed to move to the valley and be in a position to support Reno on his left. Six companies hitting a peaceful village would have created a great deal of havoc. (2) Custer failed to attack the Indian encampment with his five companies from the north, at a time the camp would have been in a near state of panic. Six companies attacking the village from the south and five companies from the north should have enabled the 7th to win a victory. The effect of the attack would have been aided by the arrival of the packs and their enlarged company. This, as I have brought out many times, leads to the main question concerning the battle: Why didn't Custer attack the village from across Ford B? Contrary to the authorities Custer moved to the ford at the time Reno was still fighting in the valley, and this was when the village would have been in a turmoil. Why wasn't there an attack? Writers have spent a lot of time on other questions and very little on this key connection to the major premise.

Liddic spends some time concerned with Reno's companies and the number of men and whether the counts were correct. He believes Wallace's calculations "were sadly inadequate." [5] It's fine to bring out the distortions, but this concern should be applied to more critical matters.

Reno's three companies start down the valley and "it was before 3:15 p.m."[6] The time corresponds with Gray's and other writers. You have different accounts of the gaits, but Liddic quotes Private Morris that they moved down the valley faster than he had ever ridden before.[7] This is in contrast to Private Taylor's remembrance, who said, "they were at a fast walk, then as they could see the pony herds near the foothills on their left, they were given the command to "trot." Then as firing broke out they were given the command to charge".[8] The key thing is not so much the gait as the lack of Indians until they near the village. This should be related to the stories that Custer changed his plan of following Reno to one of flanking the Indians. It should also be noted how the village was shut off by the trees. The important point being that it is unlikely that much or any of the village would have been seen from Ford A or Sharpshooters' Ridge—certainly not enough to have prevented Custer from going to Weir Point to see the exact size, state, and extent of the village. This would be especially true if I thought Custer hadn't made any plans to attack the village because he didn't know the "precise" location of the village.

Liddic brings out the following views as to whether Reno should have charged the village or was correct in setting up his skirmish line:

> Lieutenant Edgerly told a fellow officer that if Reno had charged through the village, Custer and Benteen would have been with him shortly with an expensive victory as a result. Mrs. Spotted Horn Bull, who was in the village that afternoon, agreed with Edgerly.... Captain Charles King, 5th Cavalry,wrote that a bold and dashing charge was required.... Lieutenant Edward Mclemand, 7th Infantry, heard from 7th Cavalry officers that it was Reno's lack of aggressive and controlling leadership that had allowed the troops to slip from offensive to defensive. Captain Thomas French, Company M, had no idea why Reno halted as it wasn't the kind of fighting he

was used to; "When you saw your enemy you went right at them." He thought the only chance Reno had was to "charge headlong through them all."

… However, the battalion hadn't made any real contact with the Indians at the time of the halt. Varnum told the Court of Inquiry, prior to the halt, "There was no absolute contact between the command and the Indians." Only a few scattered shots had been fired by either side, and the nearest Indians were at least 500 yards away…. Most of the battalion officers defended the Major's decision to abandon the charge. Lieutenant Hare was of the belief Reno couldn't have lasted another five minutes if he had not halted, and not a man would have gotten through the village. Hare thought Reno's order to halt was "the only thing that saved us."

DeRudio was in complete agreement with Hare…. DeRudio was quick to add that he thought the position the troops took after the halt threatened the village….

Just as Reno couldn't have known about the "ravine," he also could not have known how many Indians were in his front at the time he halted. He stated he saw between 500 to 600 Indians to his front. Wallace estimated the total was over 200, and they were all in or near the ravine which was about five hundred yards from where they halted. He added later that their numbers increased only after the command to dismount was given. Varnum didn't venture a guess as to the number, but he said the valley was "full of Indians" and they were riding in every direction. However, as the troops advanced towards them they "retired before us." Sergeant Ryan wrote there were few Indians until they reached the area of heavy timber and dismounted. Sergeant Culbertson also said there were few Indians near the troops. He estimated there were no more than 250 altogether to their front. Girard recalled there were really no Indians to speak of until Reno dismounted, and even after the line was formed the Indians remained about 1,000 yards from the troops. Girard who had experience judging Indian numbers, said there were less than 100 warriors in front of the skirmish line. Hare agreed with Girard and testified that up to the time the command halted there were probably only fifty or more Indians riding up and down to their front. But he added as soon as the command had stopped, hundreds of Indians moved down to the left and rear.

Herendeen, who was in position on the extreme left and about "100 yards in front of Reno's line, was in excellent place to observe the whole panorama down the valley, but he didn't see any Indians in the immediate front of the command. In fact Herendeen remembered even after Reno established his line, "There were no Indians near enough to shoot at; and they were few in number. The Indians were all further downstream and they didn't move toward the battalion until the troops halted. Herendeen said the entire number of Indians that Reno fought in the valley "could not have exceeded 200 warriors." ... Dr. Henry Porter supported the scouts, and said that the nearest Indians, only 75 or 100 of them were fully 800 or 900 yards away and "there might have been 50" who confronted the troops. He added there were a good many more down the river, but he could not see how many.

Just as the question over who gave Reno his orders to advance after the Lone Tepee, the numbers of Indians confronting Reno broke down between the company commanders and the civilians and junior officers. The Captains agreed with the Major and saw many Indians, while the civilians and junior officers saw very few. [9]

Reno's halt reflects Reno's character in contrast to other more daring cavalry leaders. Whether or not his halting saved his command or whether it might have prevented a victory is pure conjecture. I think it is more important to recognize, as Liddic does, that there were not many Indians confronting Reno when he brought his troops to a halt. However, the more important question to consider is why Girard said the Rees told him the Indians were not running and were coming up the valley, and why Reno said he sent McIlhargey because the Indians were strong in his front. These are definite distortions of a situation that has affected the view of the battle. Both reports have been used to substantiate the claim that Custer was planning on following Reno, that he was still along Reno Creek, and these reports are what caused him to decide to flank the Indians. These views underscore Reno's and Benteen's claim that they had no idea of any plans that Custer had—in fact they didn't think he had any—and that he failed to believe his scouts on the location of the village. This led to the belief that his trip to the Little Big Horn was only a "reconnaissance in force." It has also led to the view, as Liddic appears to have accepted, that Reno was only sent to chase and bring to battle some fleeing Indians. Then possibly the most damaging view created, because of its effect on the formulation of battle scenarios, is that Reno preceded Custer, and that Reno was setting up his skirmish line when Custer was just arriving and starting down the ridge. This works to Reno's advantage to have

Custer trailing, not only for the reasons mentioned, but because this means that Custer would not have been in a position to support Reno when Reno would have been looking for support, thereby justifying Reno's "charge" to the bluffs. This meant that at the Court the Defense had to prevent the sighting of Custer on the ridge as Reno was moving down the valley. So then something had to be done about Varnum's sighting of 'E' Troop, which according to Lt. Maquire's map location is beyond Weir Point. Since the skirmish line is just being set up, you have (as Varnum states at the Reno Court[8]) plenty of time for Custer to attack the village. However, as 'E' troop was supposedly in the center of Custer's column, that would place Custer ahead of Reno, which would mean that Custer hadn't planned on following Reno and that he had not been waiting along Reno Creek. This could mean that Custer actually knew where the village was and had made plans to attack it. Reno's Defense then had to worry that Davern's and Martin's actual knowledge of the orders Custer gave was not brought out. They particularly didn't want it known that orders were sent to Benteen, and who the courier was. Reno's counsel's only hope was that there were so many conflicting reports that investigators wouldn't do any real analyzing. Reno's defense knew that if they could control officer's account of orders, and limit questioning of Davern and Martin, the court would not go against the major officer's testimony. As Liddic noted, there was a difference between company commanders' descriptions of the number of Indians Reno faced with those of civilians and junior officers. This is why this period is so important, and it is here one can find the answer to the major premise as to who was primarily at fault for the destruction of Custer's five companies, even though it will not be a definitive answer. This is because there is still the need to determine why there was not an attack on the village by Custer's five companies, and why they moved to the north. It is unlikely that anyone can find a conclusive and acceptable answer to these last questions.

Liddic brings out the difference between Reno's official report following the battle with his Court of Inquiry testimony:

> How much did the lack of Custer's support influence Reno's decisions in the valley fight? Reno recorded his thoughts on this matter when he first penned his official report ten days after the battle. "It was evident to me that Custer intended to support me by moving further down the stream and attacking the village in the flank." Hare said that Reno knew Custer had not followed him up and everybody "supposed that he would attack the village somewhere else and that was the only way he had of going to the village. Private Newell remembered that he saw Custer's battalion on the bluffs as they charged down the valley. In addition Varnum said he saw Custer's troops "going on

the bluffs" about the time the skirmish line was formed. He knew they were giving support by "going to attack the lower end of the village, either from the bluffs or into the village." …

Not withstanding what he officially submitted to his superiors, Reno testified three years later at his Court of Inquiry that he had "official information" that he would be supported by the "whole outfit." When asked if he believed Custer would have supported him in some "other way except by following in your rear," Reno replied, "There was no other way to support me." Making sure the Court understood what Reno meant, the Recorder asked if a flank attack would be considered as support? The reply was "Not under the circumstance." With Reno's battle report in his hand, the Recorder asked if Reno did not state that very thing in his report? Without changing his expression Reno answered, "I may have said that." Recorder Lee was not to be put off by this answer by the Major. Lee was searching for the reason behind the decisions Reno made and his apparent failure to understand what were Custer's objectives, laid before the Court. The Recorder then asked if Reno went into the fight with any confidence in his commanding officer. Ordered to answer after trying to avoid the question, Reno replied, "I had no confidence in his ability as a soldier."[10]

Liddic points out the difference between Reno's official report with his Court of Inquiry testimony, and does his usual admirable work in presenting the contrasting views. His failure is to connect with or recognize that the Reno Court was a cover-up and why. Certain questions had to be asked at the Court but there was no real grilling or probing as there should have been.

Hare's "everybody" supposed that he (Custer) would attack the village "somewhere."[11] One might note again the use of village. Although not stated as such the all inclusive everybody and somewhere would most likely represent the general view of officers without direct orders from the time of the division. The key components to keep in mind, are: (a) that Custer did accept the general location of the village, and (b) Custer's fear that the Indians were aware of his troops and would scatter before he could bring them to battle. I cannot see any objective analysis that wouldn't agree that Custer recognized the first, and that his big fear would be the second. A competent commander wouldn't go twelve miles without having a plan of attack, and Custer was a competent commander. Custer would have formed a provisional attack plan at the division, which would encompass the following: Six companies attacking the village from the south and five from the north. Either this would have been his plan or Custer was unbelievable obtuse.

Liddic does a credible job of pointing out distortions made by Reno and Benteen, and yet accepts their most essential cover-up that Custer failed to see or accept the scouts' sighting of the village from the Crow's Nest. This cover-up is essential because it enables Reno and Benteen to claim Custer had no plans, they knew of no plans, and he gave no orders except those they expressed. It isn't enough to point out distortions or "whitewashes" at the court without attempting to determine the reason for the rationalizing or the outright lies. Liddic along with the coterie appear to have accepted these cover-ups.

According to this established scenario Custer was still watering in Reno Creek, and Reno had crossed the Little Big Horn. Reno wondered where his support was and so sent his striker McIlhargey with the message to Custer that the Indians were strong to his front. Girard had also given such a message to Custer's Adjutant Cooke. The messages, according to the accepted script, caused Custer to decide to flank the Indians although he didn't notify Reno or Benteen. Without analyzing the time, or wondering why Custer (and this was Custer—remember the attack and victory synonym) was still down by Reno Creek, the scenario has Reno going down the valley and setting up his skirmish line while Custer was just reaching the ridge. The reported sightings have Custer being seen close to what became known as Reno Hill. This was both good and bad for Reno. Good, in showing that Custer had no plan of attack, except to follow Reno, until he received Girard's and McIlhargey's reports. It was bad in that Custer couldn't have reached Ford B in time to provide the support that Reno would have been looking for, so Reno should have remained in the timber for a longer period. It enabled Recorder Lee to then say that Reno's fleeing to the bluffs when he did, allowed the Indians to leave, confront Custer, and by their now overwhelming force defeat Custer. To combat this schematic plot, Reno's counsel used Varnum's sighting of 'E' troop on the ridge north of Weir Point to show that Custer could have attacked the village and provided Reno's support while Reno was still on his skirmish line or in the timber. Since this didn't happen, Reno was justified in fleeing to the ridge in order to save his troops.

What is amazing to me is how the sightings of Custer on the ridge by enlisted men and the Rees are passed over. Lt. Hare made a blunder at the Reno Court in stating that Custer had been sighted on the ridge by enlisted men. He attempted to smooth it over by saying he only heard of it later. This should have opened a flood gate of questions, but did it? Were there probing questions by Reno's counsel? Were there any by the Recorder? You know the answer.

Liddic reports how Private Newell said he remembered seeing Custer's **battalion** (my emphasis) on the bluffs as they charged down the valley.[12] The Rees statement that they saw Custer above where the Hodgson marker was later placed could also have been brought out.[13] Liddic could have mentioned Thomas O'Neill who said, "when about half way down to where skirmish line was formed he saw Custer and **his whole command** (my emphasis) on the bluffs across the river,[14] Corporal Stanislas Roy said, "After passing ford we formed in line and while forming I heard some of the men say "There goes Custer." He could be seen on hills to our right and across river."[15] ... And, we might recall what Henry Petring said, while in the bottom going toward the skirmish line, "I saw Custer over across the river on the bluffs, waving his hat. Some of the men said, 'There goes Custer, he is up to something, for he is waving his hat.'"[16] I realize these are not officers, but shouldn't it be clear why the Defense had Custer sitting around Reno Creek until he heard from Girard and McIlhargey. Is there anyway Custer could have preceded Reno down the valley if he hadn't planned on attacking the village and flanking the Indians? If the enlisted men saw Custer isn't it reasonable to believe that the officers were also aware of him. Doesn't the lack of questioning on this issue represent a cover-up by the Court? If Custer had been on Reno Creek when he got the report from McIlhargey wouldn't he have sent McIlhargey back with a message to Reno, particularly if Custer hadn't given any orders to the effect that he was flanking the Indians, but he now knew he would?

Liddic describes Recorder Lee's questioning of Reno, and points out how Reno's official report following the battle contrasts with his testimony at the Court. Liddic gives Recorder Lee credit that he wouldn't be put-off by Reno's answers.[17] Lee then asks Reno his opinion of Custer. To me this is a put-off because Lee does not continue to ask Reno questions such as why Custer wouldn't have planned on flanking the Indians since he was concerned with the Indians scattering, or, if there were sightings of Custer from the valley, etc. Dropping such questions and going into personal opinions was a put-off.

Liddic continues:

> In view of what these officers thought about the "support" Reno could expect, Custer was providing it for him but from a different direction. Numerous officers and men had seen Custer on the bluffs and with very little mental agility understood what he was trying to accomplish. Reno's sudden blindness on the valley floor is as inexplicable, as would be his later deafness on the bluffs. Probably the Major and certainly many of his soldiers were aware of the direction this "support" had taken, and ten days later Reno so admitted in his report. I doubt if Custer's failure to follow behind Reno had much to do with the latter's decision to halt at the point he gave the order; shortly, however, this perceived lack of "support" would loom large in

Reno's decisions. I submit it was only afterwards, with the need to provide a cover story for his failure to press the attack, Reno began his construction of excuses;....[18]

Again Liddic does his usual excellent work in bringing out the general situation but again fails to connect it to the overall picture. Instead he analyzes Reno's problems and rationalizations for what he did in the valley, and the reasons for his move to the bluffs. What I am accusing Liddic of is exemplified in his statement that, "Reno's sudden blindness on the valley floor is as unexplainable, as would be his later deafness on the bluffs."[19] Both are explainable. If Reno and the officers admitted at the Court that they saw Custer on the ridge, no matter where, then Reno would have had no excuse for leaving the timber, particularly when considering the few casualties that he suffered, and the few Indians he was facing at that time. Why, as Liddic brought out, did the commanders see more Indians in the valley than the others? There can only be one acceptable reason, and it is that the commanders were in on the cover-up and were attempting to justify Reno's flight to the ridge. At the Court, Reno and these officers couldn't say that they saw Custer on the ridge for it would have meant that they knew he was attempting to flank the Indians, and Reno should have remained in the valley no matter if his troops were wiped out. All of this points to only one thing: The Reno Court was a cover-up, and the army did not want Reno to be convicted and have to face a court-martial. It should prove that Custer had plans to flank the Indians, that he was ahead of Reno, and that he did have time to attack the Indians at Ford B. The sighting of his battalion on the ridge should also substantiate the fact that Custer went to Weir Point and he didn't go down Cedar Coulee.

Liddic brings out the different views as to how far Reno advanced, his skirmish line, etc. He goes on to say:

> The ponies rounded up by the scouts were escorted to the east by their captors. Although they had captured a number of horses in the valley, most of these were lost by the time they had reached the bluffs because of the Indians' pursuit. From the scout's description, they reached the top of the bluffs about a half mile below Reno Hill. Custer had just passed this point about five minutes previously. This would have been before 3:30 p.m. Strike Two recalled that some of Custer's stragglers had fired upon them thinking they were the enemy. Soldier also confirmed there were stragglers from Custer's command, but the soldiers didn't shoot at them. These troopers were too busy attending to their faltering mounts.[20]

I disagree with Liddic on his use of timing, since 3:30 p.m. is at least two hours later than when this was taking place. Liddic brings up all the distortions but fails to make the important time connection. However, at this point my concern is with the position of the scouts, the troops, and their actions. We need to recognize that Custer"s troops were ahead of Reno's going down the valley. The sighting of Custer on the ridge by Reno's troops as they were reforming and part way down the valley should establish this. In other words Custer had not passed there 5 minutes before, but twenty to thirty minutes. Curley on his way back from firing on the village Indians from near Bouyer's Bluff, met or saw these Indians. The scouts would have been at the front of Reno's move down the valley. Strike Two, Little Sioux, and several others saw and went after several Dacotah women. They crossed to the east side of the river and then saw on the flat some Indian horses. They then went after them. According to their account the Indian village was just stirring, and they heard firing on the left and right. This would indicate both Reno's and Custer's troops were now engaged.

The scouts then drove the horses up the ridge, and were joined by Stabbed and others. We should recall that Stabbed had joined Soldier and the slower Rees that were trailing Custer. When they got on the ridge they saw Bobtail Bull "far out on the end of the line and many Dacotahs riding behind the ridge on the left."[21] This means the Ree scouts were still in the valley and Reno had not set up his skirmish line.

When you combine the Ree accounts they bring out a consistent story. Both Little Sioux and Strike Two mention the soldiers that fired on them. Strike Two said, "While we were driving horses up hill from river, some soldiers passed by and fired on us by mistake, and one of the captured horses was killed."[22] They were joined by other Rees when they reached the ridge. Stabbed, who had gone to those soldiers with what I assumed was a message, informed the soldiers that the Indians driving the horses were scouts. When the scouts reached the ridge with the horses they were joined by Soldier, Stabbed, and others. They drove the "horses back and got them in a good position."[23] What Strike Two then mentions I find very interesting because it fits into my conception of events. Strike Two said that here a soldier "with stripes on his arm came along (probably Kanipe) and asked, 'How goes it.'"[24] This would not have been Kanipe since he had already left, but I believe it was the Sgt. Major on his way back from taking Custer's attack message to Benteen.

The soldiers that fired on the scouts as they were driving the horses up the ridge, as Liddic points out, were not stragglers, but were most likely a rear guard or the last of Custer's five companies to leave the ridge.

Liddic spends some time in analyzing Kanipe's ride to where he sees the Ree scouts, the packs, and Benteen. Outside of disagreeing on the time element, Liddic does masterful work in laying out the dispute over whether Kanipe actually delivered a message from Custer to Lt. Mathey or Capt. McDougall or both. I would agree that Kanipe most likely delivered a message to both officers. McDougall's testimony to Kanipe certainly indicate that Kanipe delivered Custer's message to McDougall.[25] I don't think there is any question that at the time of the Court there was a cover-up. The two officers had not followed orders from their commanding officer to hurry and bring the packs not to Reno but to Custer. I am not sure of military protocol, but I would think orders from one's commanding officer would hold precedence over those of other ranking officers.

Liddic emphasizes different aspects of the fighting in the valley, and the move from the skirmish line into the timber. He then examines the different views as to whether Reno could have and should have set up a defense in the timber.

Liddic:

> The troops now were in a new line along an old dry cut bank of the Little Big Horn facing to the west and southwest about 300 yards from their former skirmish line.

> The protection afforded by the cut bank was much better than the exposed line on the valley floor. With a little work, it could have been made into a defensive position which would have been held indefinitely. Reno, as a professional military man, should have known there was no precedent for organized troops numbering more than a hundred and armed with breach loading weapons, being overwhelmed by any combination of Indians.... Captain Benteen thought the position that Reno assumed in the timber was a "No. 1 defensible position," and it could have been held with 120 men for 5 or 6 hours. DeRudio was more emphatic and said that the timber was "impregnable and nothing but fear could have prompted his (Reno's) retreat.[26]

> ... Later at the inquiry, Reno was asked if he didn't think with the number of Indians he claimed to have seen "that Custer might not be in the same predicament as he?" Astonishingly, Reno replied it had not, and men "could hold off quite a number of Indians if properly disposed." It is little wonder the Recorder could only stare at the Major after this incredible admission.[27]

.... I believe we can add the captain's name [Moylan] to the growing list of those who blanched over their testimony at Reno's inquiry.[28]

I keep wondering why Liddic and other authorities can't admit that the Reno Court was a cover-up. I believe Captain Carter expressed it better than anybody, and that his observations were correct. Carter was aware of what the officers said after the battle in contrast to what they said at the Reno Court. The following are some of his comments in his letters to Colonel Graham. Colonel Graham's rebuttals, which can be found in his book, *The Custer Myth,* are typical of the experts.

Captain Carter:

> ... I do most emphatically discredit their statements, [officers] and in view of what I myself have heard and read from equally credible witnesses, I am sure they did not tell the *whole truth;* and I also believe that it was predetermined among themselves after their previous discussions about Reno's conduct in the Post Trader's store at Fort Abraham Lincoln, when it had become known that the regiment was being assailed by the press and people on all sides. Reno was being ostracized to the extent that he felt forced to demand a Court of Inquiry, and the enigma of cowardice was likely to be attached to their regimental colors, and guidons, and handed down to future generations as part of the history of the United States Army.... Since that testimony at the Reno Court ... the regiment has been known as the "Fighting Seventh."

> It never has appeared that those officers who testified at that Court were ever cross-examined by anybody as to anything they were trying to hold back. The testimony clearly shows that they were doing this very thing.... not one of them *volunteered* to tell the *whole truth,* as conditions and facts have since developed—so long as no one asked them to do so.

> ... to bring it out by a drastic course of cross questioning, and as you yourself know and as I know has generally been the policy at any Court of Inquiry or General Court Martial. Even Godfrey expected to be recalled to give additional testimony, but found that the Court had closed and adjourned. Of course in its finding no Court Martial was found necessary or for the best interest of the service, therefore the *whole truth* has long been buried in oblivion. Why does Hare pay no attention to your letters? Why is Edgerly so mealy-mouthed, even to me, his own classmate.

> I simply discredit, I repeat, the testimony of these officers—after knowing of their daily conversations in the Post Trader's store at Fort Lincoln, the ostra-

cizing of Reno for nearly 3 years, or until he felt compelled to ask for a Court of Inquiry, and then their going as a body before that Court and testifying just exactly to the reverse of what their talk had been. Even Benteen testifying in Reno's favor.

I feel that if they had been properly cross-examined, his (Benteen's) act in throwing down the Chicago paper in the train when he was traveling with Godfrey to Chicago, and in which paper was a bitter article accusing the entire 7th Cavalry outfit of cowardice, would have been brought out; ... [29]

As I said, I go along with Captain Carter's observations as to the officer's testimony at the Reno Court. It is interesting when the officers in their testimony make an inadvertent statement, and then realize it does not fit into the picture that they are drawing, and, as Carter claims, it left the door open, but there were no follow-up questions. I also think it is enlightening in reading Captain Carter's account of the conversations at Fort Lincoln, and his criticism of the testimony at the Court—how they are aimed at Major Reno, and primarily his actions in the valley. I think it illustrates a natural failure by the officers in that they refrain from bringing out the cover-up of "orders" because of the particular effect it would have had on Benteen's actions, as well as other officers besides Reno. "Timing" didn't become an issue at Fort Lincoln.

Several other comments by Captain Carter concerning the testimony at the Court deserve noting:

.... and my absolute belief that the testimony of those officers you have quoted to me who went before that Court is not only worthless but, in view of what has come to light since the battle of the Little Big Horn, should be utterly discredited, he volunteered [a retired Brigadier General whose name Carter does not reveal] to tell me that in conversation with one of those officers he was told by him that *they had all agreed to tell but one story.* This general officer declined to give me the name of the officer, saying, "he is dead," and "it would serve no good purpose, especially as Mrs. Custer is yet living." ... The fact is that I have always believed those officers went to Chicago pledged to give that testimony in order to uphold the good name and honor of their regiment. In this they have thus far succeeded and pinned the proud name "The Fighting Seventh" to their regimental color and guidons but I believe a stiff cross-examination might have brought out the *"whole truth."* [30]

One of Colonel Graham's statements to Captain Carter is also noteworthy:

> You ask where I get the idea that Custer was attacked before Reno left the timber. I got it from the testimony of Trumpeter Martin, the stories told by the Indians and what seems to me the inevitable logic of the situation. Unless Custer stood still for three quarters of an hour, he must have reached the point where the Sioux met him before Reno retreated.[31]

I think that the Crow scouts recognized this time gap while going with Edward Curtis and attempted to exploit it to their advantage. They then had Custer watching Reno in the valley, and created their account of the proceedings. I have dealt with this in previous articles and my last book.

Liddic, in bringing out the action surrounding Reno's retreat from the timbers, refers to Lt. Hare's account:

> … Hare disagreed with one action and confirmed another when he said Reno made his decision to leave the timber precipitously, but to the uninformed there always "is certainly more or less disorder about cavalry column moving at a fast gait." Hare then clarified this assertion and said as he rode out onto the prairie he could see "the three companies were individual together—well closed up, they formed three angles of a triangle; A company on one side, G Company on another, and M company on the other and they were going at a fast gallop." It is a wonder a brass band wasn't playing. Hare didn't just varnish his testimony at Chicago, he whitewashed it; any resemblance between this part of the lieutenant's testimony at the Court of Inquiry and the truth is purely coincidental.[32]

Another example of a whitewash, but still no connecting dots with the essential premises. As Captain Carter and Judge Goldin pointed out, that after the battle Lt. Hare would never talk about the battle. Besides the statements Liddic uses, I think one should recognize that Hare was in a position where he knew how the cover-ups were protecting Reno and condemning Custer. When Custer, as they approached the Lone Tepee, sent the Sgt. Major to Hare for information, I believe the information Custer wanted had not only to do with the Indian village but whether or not the scouts had seen any signs of Benteen. Custer at this time knew he was about to launch his attack and that it couldn't be held off much longer. Hare would most likely have told him that the scouts had not seen any Indians or camps to the south of the known camp. This meant that Benteen should have had clear sailing (except for the terrain) to the Little Big Horn valley. Custer could then precede with his attack plans. He would have wanted to send orders to Benteen prior to his actual launching of the attack, and by more than just a regular courier. The Sgt. Major qualified. However, Custer would not have wanted him to go alone, so he would have had Hare assign a scout to go with him. That scout would have been Stabbed. Lt. Hare was aware of these things, but if he brought them out, even after the battle let alone at the time of the Court, he would have really opened up a can of worms that encompassed not only Major Reno but Captain Benteen, and this would have thrown a monkey wrench into all of the cover-ups. I would say this played on Lt. Hare's conscience the rest of his life. He knew he was protecting the 7th's image, but helping to convict Custer as a commander.

Liddic seems to have accepted that Kanipe met Benteen a little before 4 p.m.; he has Reno still fighting in the timber "a little before 4 p.m.;"[33] These times sound about right except they are two hours later than they would have occurred. Herendeen, who was left behind when Reno "charged" from the timber, heard volley fighting from the Custer battlefield at about 4:15 p.m.[34] I disagree as to where Kanipe received his orders to take to the packs, but it would have been at least the five cross-country miles that Liddic refers to. Considering the pace Benteen was supposedly traveling at, he wouldn't have reached Reno Hill before, let's say (using accepted time), 4:45. There were all the intervening happenings before they began their move to check on the gunfire. This move has been pretty much accepted as taking place around 5 p.m. However, according to accepted views, after Benteen arrived the Indians left, Reno was concerned with Hodgson's body, and Hare was sent to bring up some of the ammo packs. The ammo was supposedly passed out; the wounded were taken care of; Captain Weir took off and Lt. Edgerly with Weir's company followed; Benteen and the rest of the companies then joined the procession. This timing doesn't add up. Then Herendeen says he heard volley firing coming from the Custer battlefield about 4:15 p.m. Reno was still in the timber about 4 p.m. Reno then leaves and makes his mad dash for the bluffs. The Indians close in, and for the next twenty minutes or so there must have been quite a bit of firing going on. Herendeen and several others were hiding in the timber and should have been preoccupied, so I doubt that they would have heard the firing coming from the Custer battlefield. I do think if you throw the other times back at least two hours, Herendeen's 4:15 could be about correct. Most of the Indians during this time would have left, and the firing around Herendeen's location had pretty well ceased. Herendeen and his group then went to the ridge about a "quarter after five." If you can squeeze in all of the prior times stated and still have Major Reno's command moving to check on Custer by around 5 o'clock, you have taken a different mathematics course than I have.

One might also attempt to throw in Benteen's account of how far back the packs were, and since Liddic is using Gray's timing, realize that the ammo packs didn't arrive on the hill until 5:19.[35]

Liddic does mention that Reno's retreat from the timber showed no signs of a tactical maneuver.

SOURCES

1. Liddic, 59.

2. Ibid., 60.

3. Ibid., 60, 61.

4. Ibid., 61.

5. Ibid., 61.

6. Ibid., 62.

7. Ibid., 62.

8. Taylor, *With Custer on the Little Big Horn*, 36.

9. Liddic, 63, 64.

10. Ibid., 65.

11. Ibid., 65.

12. Ibid,. 65.

13. Graham, 39.

14. Camp, 106.

15. Ibid., 112.

16. Ibid., 133.

17. Liddic, 65.

18. Ibid., 65, 66.

19. Ibid., 66.

20. Ibid., 69.

21. Graham, 38.

22. Liddic., 69.

23. Ibid., 69.

24. Ibid., 69.

25. Ibid., 72.

26. Ibid., 73, 74.

27. Ibid., 74.

28. Ibid., 76.

29. Graham, 309–316.

30. Ibid., 316.

31. Ibid., 312.

32. Liddic., 78.

33. Ibid., 76.

34. Ibid., 79.

35. Gray, 273.

7

CUSTER'S TRIP TO MEDICINE TAIL COULEE

Liddic:

Sergeant Kanipe turned his horse towards the end of the column, and began his ride across country to find the pack train and deliver Custer's orders. Just before dispatching the courier, Custer had ridden to the edge of the bluffs, near Reno Hill, close enough to look down on the Little Big Horn River and they were in "plain view of the Indian camps.[1]

I don't believe Custer could have seen enough of the Indian village from near Reno Hill to say they were in "plain view of the Indian camps." Custer would have gone to the ridge and was able to see the southern end of the village. As Edward Curtis and General Woodruff brought out, Custer would have seen only a few tepees,[2] and that is why he continued on to Weir Point. One might recall Benteen's assertion that it was when he arrived on the highest point (Weir Point) that he had his first glimpse of the Indian village.[3] And, in determining where Sgt. Kanipe was dispatched from, I would say it was from near Weir Point. Kanipe was undoubtedly the messenger Martin started to mention at the Reno Court before he was cut off.[4] Camp said, "Knipe is very positive and emphatic in expressing his recollection that Custer and all his men proceeded north along the bluffs so far west that they had full view of Reno's men and the Indian village all the time instead of some distance back and out of sight as stated and mapped by Godfrey."[5] Here we have a primary source, one of only six that were with Custer on the ridge that survived, saying they moved north along the bluffs, which indicates a movement further north than Reno Hill. As I brought out in my last book, Custer came to the ridge after giving Reno his attack orders. He then signaled his men, and in going to meet them would have crossed what was later the location of the pack mules and horses during the Reno Hill engagement. After meeting with his company commanders, Custer returned to where he had left the Crows and checked on events in the valley before proceeding to Weir Point. The troops followed Custer to Weir Point, and as Kanipe indicated, moved north close to the ridge and in sight of the valley. Reno would have been moving down the valley at that time, but had not begun firing. This is substantiated by the sighting of a peaceful village that was said by both Martin and Curley's report of Bouyer's statement. This also places Custer ahead of Reno's move down the valley. Kanipe went on to say that "Custer was trotting and galloping along with companies in columns of twos, all 5 companies abreast, the men cheering and eager for a fight and that after the highest point (my emphasis) on the bluffs was reached, the men through their eagerness, broke into something like disorder, as previously noted."[6] I won't bring up all the references to the highest point and that it signifies Weir Point. It is true Sharpshooters' Ridge is as high, but since they weren't using an altimeter I think it is safe to say that any such reference is referring to Weir Point.

It is difficult for me to read these accounts and believe that Kanipe received his message to take to Benteen near Reno Hill. And, though Liddic concedes that Custer could not see all of the village from the vantage point by Reno Hill, he then has him going to Sharpshooters' Hill. I am saying much the same thing, except that Custer took off for the bluffs after giving Reno his attack orders and his own company commanders orders to water their horses. He wasn't sitting back along Reno Creek waiting for messages from Girard and McIlhargey before moving to the ridge. He then went over to meet his men, whom I assumed came onto the ridge just south of Sharpshooters' Ridge. Custer may even have gone up Sharpshooters' Hill, but I can't believe that he and Martin were able to see a peaceful village with children and dogs playing. I think Goldin's account that Custer went back to the rim where he was seen by the Rees and some of the men of Reno's command would then have taken place.[7] As Curtis and Woodruff pointed out, Custer went to Weir Point where the observations of a "napping" village took place.[8]

Liddic believes that beside from observing the village, on Sharpshooter's Ridge, Custer would have noticed Benteen back on the main trail. I doubt this because (contrary to the accepted beliefs) Benteen should have been nearing the main trail or was just entering it. Custer had not seen Benteen's battalion moving to support Reno, so when giving Kanipe his message near Weir Point, Custer would have told him that if he saw Benteen to give him that message, not that he had seen Benteen or the message would have been sent to Benteen, as Martin's was with additional orders for the packs.

Liddic states:

> … and that Custer from this observation point had the three other elements of his command in visual sight before he proceeded further to the north and into battle. This is an important point, for if Custer knew where all three of his battalions were before 3:30 p.m., the charges that he had scattered his command beyond recall is false.[9]

I am always amazed at how Custer students, and many I am sure are Custer buffs, seemingly fail to realize their scenarios go beyond portraying a commander that made some mistakes, to one that is a lousy commander. It doesn't take a lot of insight to know that Custer saw or credited his scouts with seeing the Indian village from the Crow's Nest. Custer had already taken his scouts' word that his troops had been observed and decided he must attack that day.

Let's use my questions and what the coteries are actually saying:

Q. If Custer has decided to attack that day because of the scouts' report, which implies knowing there was an Indian village, shouldn't Custer then make plans to attack that village?

A. No, because even though he accepted the scouts' report that the Indians had sighted his troops, he didn't see or believe that his scouts had located the village.

Q. Even if he did question his scouts' sighting, wouldn't a good commander make temporary plans to attack in case the scouts were right?

A. No, because even if the scouts were right about the location, Custer doesn't know the actual size of the village.

Q. Didn't Reno's and Custer's orderlies say that Custer sent orders to Benteen in which he planned on Benteen supporting Reno on his left while Custer was planning to encircle the village?

A. Yes, but we (the authorities) don't believe them.

Q. Why don't you believe the orderlies?

A. Because Reno and Benteen said they didn't know of any such plans, and Reno didn't believe Custer was a competent commander.

Whether these authorities recognize it or not, what they are saying makes Custer out to be not only a bad commander but a stupid one as well.

Custer traveled fairly slow down Reno Creek until he reached the Lone Tepee because he knew Benteen was crossing more difficult terrain, and Custer wanted him to be able to keep abreast of the main command. Custer had sent Benteen to the valley, and would have known that when Benteen reached the valley he would be to the south and west of Reno's crossing.

Continuing my questions:

Q. Wouldn't Custer have sent Benteen orders for when Benteen reached the valley?

A. No, we have to remember that Reno and Benteen said they had no idea of any plans or where each other even were.

I hate to say it but let's be realistic. One reason that Custer's offensive plan didn't work is that Benteen and Reno deviated from the plan. All the dots are there but one—and that is the answer as to why Custer didn't attack at Ford B.

Liddic, after presenting a number of varying estimates on the size and number of Indians in the village, goes on to say:

Some students think Custer made a third observation and obtained his clearest view of the valley from Weir point. Among the more noted students who thought so were Kuhlman, Dustin, Stewart, and Gray. However, if one places any credence in what Trumpeter Martin recalled and the area's geography, Custer didn't go to Weir Point. Martin described Custer's lookout as "a big hill that overlooked the valley." He further clarified this location as "the highest hill, the very highest point around there." Today, if one is approaching from the south, as Custer did, Weir Point does not appear as the highest hill in the area. The features of Sharpshooters' Ridge was much more pretentious when viewed from this perspective. In addition, Martin was specifically asked at the Reno Court if Weir Point and the lookout were one and the same. He replied they were not. Martin was sure this was the point, not Weir Peaks, from which they looked over the valley because on his way to Benteen, he saw Reno's command in action from the same ridge from which General Custer saw the valley.... the Crows followed the bluff's edge until they reached Weir Point; their accounts do not mention Custer being with them or on Weir Point by himself, or with his staff.

Martin said that after Custer made his observation, he rode back down to where the troops were, and he and the Adjutant discussed the situation. Martin said Custer remarked, "The Indians were asleep in their teepees," ... Many battle experts have taken Martin to task for claiming Custer was under the impression or said that the Indians were "asleep;" when a full regiment of cavalry had already begun their attack ... It's possible the village was in the condition Martin so reported and would lead one to assume it was surprised or figuratively "asleep." He told Camp that when Custer was at the observation point, they saw children and dogs playing among the teepees and a few loose ponies. Martin further related the officers discussed where the warriors could be.... But, it was supported by the Crow scout Curley, who said after Custer turned toward the river, the four scouts and Mitch Bouyer looked down upon the village and also noted there were very few Indians around, and Bouyer remarked the Indians were not in the village.[10]

I disagree with Liddic and the consensus of views as expressed above. I would start and finish with this question: How stupid do you believe Custer was? Whether you recognize it or not, that is what you are making him out to be. (There are many words that could be used but I'll stick with stupid.) I can't help but wonder how he ever got to be a general.

Liddic starts out by saying that Martin was coming from the south to the ridge, and that the highest hill one sees from there is Sharpshooters' Hill. I question that, but will not take issue on that point; however, moving to the ridge from Reno Creek is a minor part of Martin's remembrance. He passed along the ridge several times, fought on the ridge, and though Sharpshooters' Hill might be as high as Weir Point, it doesn't stand out as such. When "the highest point" is referred to, it isn't Sharpshooter's Hill, it is Weir Point. Liddic will make this same assertion.

One thing to remember is that so many of the statements made by Martin came during the Reno Court and reflect their efforts to confuse him, and so provide an excuse to dismiss him. The questioning of Martin is the most pathetic aspect of the Reno Court of Inquiry. The Court knew that Martin held the key that could have unlocked the door to all kinds of revelations that they didn't want to come out.

Liddic then says that Martin, in Graham's abstract of the Reno Court proceedings, said that the lookout and Weir Point were not the same thing. I have not been able to find in the Reno Court proceedings such a question being asked. Martin, when going to Benteen, saw Reno's command in action from the same ridge that Custer saw the valley. Liddic's belief is that Custer went to Medicine Tail Coulee by way of Godfrey's Gorge or Cedar Coulee, and if correct, I then question if Martin, when going with his message to Benteen, would have gone up either Sharpshooter's Ridge or over to the western crest where he would have been in a position to have seen Reno's troops in action. Martin would have taken the easier path along the ravines east or west of Sharpshooter's Ridge.

Liddic should have made a strong disclaimer to those who discounted Martin's account because a "full regiment of cavalry had already begun their attack." The dots need to be connected. It should be recognized that an essential premise, no matter where the lookout was, is the fact that Martin, on his way to Benteen, saw Reno in action in the valley. This means that Custer had plenty of time to reach Ford B in order to attack the village, during a period when the village was primarily concerned with Reno. Custer should have realized this particularly if he had gone to Weir Point and not down either Cedar Coulee or Godfrey's Gorge. It is hard for me to see how the sightings of Custer and his battalion on the ridge by Reno's troops as they were moving down to their skirmish line can be dismissed. Liddic, and the authorities, should also recall Kanipe's statement, "that Custer and all his men proceeded north along the bluffs so far west that they had a full view of Reno's men and the Indian village all the time instead of some distance back and out of view …" Kanipe also said that after the highest point on the bluff was reached … "[11] Then there is the question asked of Martin **that can be found in the Reno Court proceedings**: Q. That place from which you saw the village and children, dogs, and ponies, was at the highest point down the river below where Major Reno made his stand. A. Yes sir. The highest hill, the very highest point around there.[12]

Captain Carter questioned if Varnum, from the skirmish line, would have been able to distinguish the gray horses on the ridge. I realize at that time there would have been more smoke and dust being stirred up; however, I believe it is doubtful if Martin, without glasses, would have been able to make out dogs and children from Sharpshooter's Ridge close to two miles away. It may have even been difficult from Weir Point, but in looking down there wouldn't have been the distance or the ridge impediments there were from Sharpshooters' Ridge. Liddic and the advocates of the sightings from Sharpshooters' Ridge admit that Weir Point would have definitely blocked off the main village. If Custer couldn't make plans to attack the village at the division of the command because he didn't know the precise extent or location of the village, he should have definitely wanted to go to Weir Point at this time to determine the extent of the village, the action going on, and how best to attack the village.

The Crows at the time, and the sources that Liddic uses, don't mention Custer being at Weir Point, but since the Crows go to or near Weir Point and their observation is the same as Martin's, it certainly implies that Custer had been there. I think one needs to give the Court credit that they were smart enough to use different questions and methods to discredit Martin's testimony. The Court used Varnum's sighting of "E" troop on the ridge to show that Custer had plenty of time to support Reno, and by whatever ruse, Martin's placement on the map as to where he left Custer made it appear that Custer went to Medicine Tail Coulee not by the quickest coulee but instead by Cedar Coulee or Godfrey's Gorge. This would indicate why Custer didn't attack in time for Reno to have recognized that Custer was attempting to support him.

Liddic, in substantiating his belief that Custer didn't even go down Cedar Coulee to Medicine Tail Coulee but instead went down what is called Godfrey's Gorge, used the following to support his view:

> Many battle students believe Custer continued along Reno's Ridge until he came to a ravine that led in the direction of the river. This ravine, they claim, was Cedar Coulee, but was it? … Custer had seen all he needed to from his two lookouts.… Besides Custer couldn't see what was on the other side of Weir Point. That Custer didn't ride on the other side of Sharpshooters' Ridge toward Cedar Coulee, was confirmed by Edgerly, who told Camp that when he advanced to Weir Point, following after Weir, he saw no sign of Custer's trail … Martin said he gave the order "Attention," "Fours right," "Column right," "March," and the column passed down from the hill, and "Column left was then ordered. This was no doubt to move around an obstruction, … This is why Custer turned more to the east and into the broader Godfrey's Gorge.… Curley agreed with Martin's description of the route, and said, Custer passed into Medicine Tail Coulee from behind this ridge (Sharpshooters') and went down it going in a direction directly north, coming out about a mile from Ford B. Russell White Bear told Fred Dustin that the ravine Custer used "comes out two miles up Medicine Tail from the river. This move accurately describes the mouth of Godfrey's Gorge than Cedar Coulee.

> It was after 3:30 pm when the movement began.… Whereas Custer could only observe the advantage of one over another from some quick observation point rather than like us, being able to to travel over the alternatives and then make a judgment.… I conclude after a careful study of the sources and the areas geography, Custer's route to Medicine Tail Coulee was from Sharpshooters' Ridge, followed to the north by east, down into Godfrey's Gorge. It was here the troops struck Medicine Tail Coulee directly, or possibly crossed over the mouth of Cedar Coulee, into it.… There was no need to continue on to the north [from Sharpshooters' Ridge] as it would be out of

the way to reach the river, as well as taking up time. [this is hard to follow] Besides Custer couldn't see what was on the other side of Weir Point. He didn't want to expose his flanks to any possible harassment, and he could see the area, about what today is identified as Godfrey's Gorge, was clear.[13]

Liddic used Edgerly's account that when following after Weir he saw no sign of Custer's trail as evidence that Custer did not go to Weir Point. One should recognize that Edgerly's answer could be tied in with cover-up policies, and can certainly be debated. Using Liddic's reasoning you could say that because Captain Weir did go toward Weir Point, he was following signs that Custer's command would have made. And that Lt. Edward Maguire's map wouldn't have shown Custer going down what appears to be Western Coulee if Maguire hadn't been aware of something that indicated that was the route followed by Custer.

As interpreted by Liddic, Curley agreed with Martin's description of the route, and said, "Custer passed into Medicine Tail Coulee from behind the ridge (Sharpshooters') and went down it going directly north coming out about a mile from Ford B." I am glad Liddic used this source because my view of what Curley said is directly the opposite.

Camp referring to a Curley interview:

> From this point [Lone Tepee] he went with Custer's battalion as it came along, and when Custer diverged from Reno's trail, about 1 1/4 miles from the river, Bouyer and his four Crows went with Custer. Custer's route from this point was directly across the country, on the crest of a long ridge, running to the bluffs and coming out at a point about 500 ft. north of the Reno corral. From here Custer passed along the crest of the bluffs for fully 3/4 mile in full view of the river and of the valley over across it. Custer hurried his men, going at a gallop most of the time. Reno and his command were plainly seen by Custer's whole command while marching this 3/4 mile. On the first line of bluffs back from the river there are two high peaks marked "A" on the map, now called Reno peaks. For some distance south of these there is a high ridge running parallel with the river, but not so high as the peaks. Custer's command passed into the valley of a tributary of Reno Creek just behind this ridge and the peaks and went down it going in a direction directly north and coming out into the bed of Reno Creek [Medicine Tail Coulee] about a mile from its mouth at Ford B. From the moment Custer's command commenced to descent this tributary of Reno Creek, it passed out of view of Reno's battalion, but Bouyer and his four scouts kept to the left of

Custer, on the crest of the high ridge and peaks, and at all times could command a view of the river and the bottoms beyond.[14]

Curley, according to Camp, is saying that Custer's five companies came onto the ridge about 500 ft. north or Reno's corral. I believe this is somewhat twisted by Camp's interpreter. As I brought out in my last book, while his men were watering their horses Custer went to the bluffs somewhat below Benteen's companies location during the Reno entrenchment battle. He signaled to his men and then crossed over what later became Reno's mule and horse location to meet his men south and west of Sharpshooters' Ridge. He then went back to the ridge approximately 500 ft. north of Reno Hill. There he waved to Reno's men who were reforming after crossing Ford A. He and his men then moved the 3/4 of a mile to Weir Point. It is important to note that all six of the men who were the last to leave Custer, said that his command passed down the crest of the ridge in full view of the valley. They also referred to the two peaks, in other words Weir Point, not Sharpshooters' Ridge. These six were the four Crows, Sgt. Kanipe and Trumpeter Martin. Curley said it to Camp, and the three other Crows said it to Edward Curtis and General Woodruff and Martin said it in numerous statements, including his account of the commands Custer gave, and contrary to Liddic's belief, the orders to me had his command moving to the right around the Weir Peaks, and then a column left and they went down Western Coulee. We also have Kanipe referring to the men sighting Reno's command, and the reverse sighting of Custer's battalion by Reno's men as they moved down the valley. Curley mentions that the troops came out onto Medicine Tail Coulee about a mile from the river, this means Middle Coulee or Western Coulee. Since the Crows were quite specific with Curtis and Woodruff, and Woodruff's measurement said a half mile from the river, this means Western Coulee.[15] This corresponds to Lt. Maquire's map and the route he depicts Custer traveling to Medicine Tail Coulee.[16]

Liddic is right that many battle students believe Custer went down Cedar Coulee, in fact the battlefield maps have him doing so. However, Liddic prefers having him go down Godfrey's Gorge. In addition to the reasons we have already covered, he says that Custer did so because they led to the river. I must be entirely turned around, for to me they don't lead to the river but away from it.

Once again, a question and answer segment. "Custer had seen all he needed to from his two lookouts."[17]

Q. Could he have seen all of the village?

A. No, but why would he have wanted to see the "precise" location? The camp would just extend further down the river. The size or the number of warriors shouldn't really matter.

Q. Shouldn't Custer be concerned with the best route to flank the Indians?

A. No, not really. There must be a ravine leading to the village, and a ford he can cross, and you know what we said about the Crows and their knowledge of the region.

Q. Since Reno has or will be going into action, shouldn't Custer be concerned with finding the quickest route to attack the village and give Reno the support he promised?

A. No, Reno would be able to hold out. He has three companies and they should be able to set up a defense that can hold off any number of Indians for sometime, and Custer should be attacking by then.

Q. Wouldn't Custer believe the quickest route to attack the enemy would be to go to Weir Point and then continue north?

A. No, because Custer couldn't see beyond Weir Point. He would be exposing his flanks if there were some Indians, and he could see it was clear down Cedar Coulee and Godfrey's Gorge.

Q. Don't you think the orders Martin said Custer gave meant that his command had come to a halt to the south of Weir Point, the "column right" was in order to move around the peaks, and the "column left" was a move to the west, and they then went down to Medicine Tail Coulee?

A. No, as I said, he saw a clear move down Godfrey's Gorge to Medicine Tail Coulee, and the move to the left was just to get around some obstruction.

I needn't say it again, but I will. If this is what Custer thought and did, you have a—commander.

I disagree with Liddic's interpretation of Arikara and Crow testimony, from both a timing and a connecting standpoint, but I have detailed my analysis of their accounts in my articles and books. Little Sioux's account is noteworthy, although it jumps back and forth. Little Sioux was with Reno in the valley. Here is some of what he said taken from the Arikara Narrative:

> ... With Little Sioux were Red Star, Strikes Two and Boy Chief. As they stood there looking across the river they saw at the foot of the ridge (about where they were to cross later) three women and two children come across the flat running and hurrying along as best they could, ... Little Sioux fired twice at them and so did Red Star. Then all four of the scouts rode through the timber toward the river to kill them. But just at this point they saw across the river on the flat a large herd of about two hundred Dacotah horses ... [they went after the horses].... While they were driving the horses he first saw the tepees of the Dakotas, three-quarters of a mile away across the river. They had ridden farther ahead than the battle line of the soldiers, that is further downstream than the battle line of the soldiers, in order to head off and drive the horses back to where they could get them away from the Dakotas. [They drove the horses they still had up the bluffs, where Stabbed, Soldier, and other Rees joined them. The following is the important part of Little Sioux's narrative.] ... While he was driving off the horses on the flat he heard the battle going on very plainly on his right [Reno's] and his left also. Slightly behind him he heard sounds of another battle but not quite so plain. [The one on his left and behind him would have been from Custer's troops.][18]

This is important because it indicates Custer's fighting was taking place while Reno was still fighting in the valley. It is also worth noting that these are the Rees that Curley referred to meeting. Curley's interview with General Scott is one of the most meaningful since it ties together timing and action in a connecting way that I find lacking in other accounts.

Liddic attempts to relate the Crows' movement with Sharpshooters' Ridge and nothing beyond Weir Point. Custer's route to Medicine Tail Coulee, according to Liddic, would have been along Sharpshooters' Ridge and Godfrey's Gorge as indicated by the following:

> ... Meanwhile, Custer, as the battalion was being ordered, "Fours right," told Mitch Bouyer to inform his Crows they had accomplished what he had asked of them. They had escorted the soldiers "to the enemy and need not go into the fight." Bouyer and the Crows rode to a "bluff" (Weir Point) beyond the point where Custer had turned down" where they had an excellent view

of the whole valley. Bouyer told the four he was going with the soldiers and would fight with them.[19]

I don't follow how Liddic can take a cover-up by Goes Ahead and a disclaimer by Camp of White Man Runs Him's assertion that Custer sat on Weir Point, and say that it refers to Custer telling the Crows they were dismissed so they turned back. I realize this probably fits into Liddic's timing scenario since he has to have Reno engaged before Custer even reaches Medicine Tail Coulee, and it has to be two miles from the ford. However, he uses some statements that are misleading. Curley was given permission to turn back by Bouyer somewhere along the ridge below Weir Point. The three Crows said they were given permission in Medicine Tail Coulee. The bluff they then went to was Bouyer's Bluff, not Weir Point, and that was just above Ford B. According to Martin, the three Crows were with Bouyer and Custer when he received his message to take to Benteen.[20]

Liddic, as do other writers, seem bound to ignore passages from the same individuals that correlate both timewise and from an action standpoint. In other words, their scenario fails to connect the testimonial dots. They appear to have the village being sighted from Sharpshooters' Ridge, and Sgt. Kanipe receiving his message to take to the packs from near Reno Hill or Sharpshooters' Ridge. Custer's troops go on one side or another of Sharpshooters' Ridge and down Cedar Coulee or Godfrey's Gorge. They then have to have Martin receiving his message to take to Benteen from along Cedar Coulee or Godfrey's Gorge. Do they explain other remarks that would refute their claims? No, they are brushed-off or ignored. Let's look at a few.

Sgt. Kanipe:

> At this time Sergeant Knipe of Co. C saw Indians up on bluff some distance beyond where Reno later fortified. A little beyond this Tom Custer verbally gave Sergeant Knipe orders from General Custer to go back and order McDougall ... 21

> Knipe is very positive and emphatic in expressing his recollection that Custer and all his men proceeded north along the bluffs so far west that they had full view of Reno's men and the Indian village all the time instead of some distance back and out of sight as stated and mapped by Godfrey. Knipe says that Custer was trotting and galloping along with companies in column of twos, all five companies abreast, the men cheering and eager for a fight and then after the highest point on the bluffs was reached, the men through their eagerness. broke into something like disorder, as previously noted.[22]

We might also recall Martin's testimony at the Reno Court where he mentioned passing that high point on the ridge and going down a ravine to Medicine Tail Coulee, and that as they passed the high point or a little below it "he told his adjutant to send an order back to Captain Benteen."[23]

The last statement by Martin at the Reno Court was probably the order Sgt. Kanipe was to carry to the packs, in which he was to notify Benteen if he saw him. Martin caught the reference to Benteen and assumed it was to be taken to him. Gray pointed out how the questions quickly shifted to the order Martin carried.[24] If Custer had just passed this high point and was going down a ravine, and that is where Kanipe received his message, this would mean Weir Point. And if Kanipe saw Indians beyond where Reno fortified, and it was a little beyond this where he received his message to take to McDougall, it certainly would be close to Weir Point.

Were the Crows dismissed from Weir Point, and from there turned back south? One should keep in mind that the Crow's stories are distorted at times in order to rationalize their actions. This is true of any accounts, whether white or Indians, but there is a common grain that can be put together into fairly reliable testimony. I don't think there should be any question that the bluff referred to is Bouyer's Bluff not Weir Point. Each of the four Crows mention it and the firing at the Indians, and even a Lacotah and Cheyenne have mentioned three Crows firing from there.[25] One should remember the statement by Goes Ahead He said that Custer, at the time the six Crows joined the 7th Cavalry, told them that he understood they were good scouts, and "If we win the fight everything belonging to the enemy you can take home, for my boys have no use for these things.[26] This is why they would not have left until Custer's troops began their retreat from the ford, as can be seen in White Man Runs Him's account.

What can be noticed in practically any Indian testimony is the back and forth statements and often actual contradictions. Whether this is due to the interpreter or just what I wouldn't know, but one can find something to support your particular view in almost any interview. This is very true in analyzing the Crow accounts. As previously stated, they attempt to rationalize the criticism of their actions in leaving, and most likely they misinterpreted questions or their answers were. There is then the need to compare testimony and try to put together answers that correspond with other testimony.

This problem can be seen in the following Crow interviews.

Goes Ahead:

> ... When they had arrived at about the point where Lieutenant Hodgson's headstone was placed later, the three Crows scouts saw the soldiers under

Reno dismounting in front of the Dakota camp and thought that the enemy were "too many." Close to where Reno and Benteen later in the day were attacked by the Dakotas, on the ridge of hills above the river, the three Crow scouts were left behind and Custer's command went down the draw toward the lower ford on the run. Custer had told the Crow scouts to stay out of the fight and they went to the left along the ridge overlooking the river while he (Custer) took his command to the right.[27]

Camp interview with Goes Ahead:

... We saw Reno's battle and went back along bluffs and met Benteen's command. We three Crows did not see Custer after he turned down coulee to right. Did not see Custer fight. Did not see beginning or any part of it. Do not know whether Custer went to the river. We turned back to early to see where Custer went north of dry creek.[28]

From Goes Ahead's comments you would certainly think that the Crows never went beyond Weir Point and that they turned to the left while Custer went to the right. There are several things to consider or take note of: (1) The three Crows, during this period informed Curtis that they and Custer saw Reno's fight from Weir Point, and they do imply that Custer went toward the lower ford, which could not be said if he was going down Cedar Coulee or Godfrey's Gorge. This corresponds to both White Man Runs Him's and Hairy Moccasin's account to Camp. Camp in his letter to General Woodruff refuted the Crow's story as given to Curtis. He also mentions that Goes Ahead had said that "Custer had gone out of sight behind the bluff quite some time before Reno's fight began.[29] In other statements they have the soldiers seeing Reno's fighting, and they don't see Custer as he goes to Medicine Tail Coulee. There are so many contradictions in the Crows statements that it is certainly hard to piece together an accurate picture. I do think the following is a comparatively sound summation when coordinating their accounts.

The four Crows led Custer and his retinue to the ridge while Custer's troops were watering. The Crows went further down the ridge while Custer signaled to his men. He had the Crows remain on the ridge to watch developments in the valley. Custer then crossed over what later became Reno's entrenchment area to meet his men below Sharpshooters' Ridge. He then went back to the crest where he had left the Crows and Mitch Bouyer. This was above where the Hodgson marker was later placed, and Custer signaled to Reno's men who were now reforming after having crossed the ford. Custer went on to Weir Point with his men following. Custer, from Weir Point, saw a peaceful village. Reno had begun his move down the valley. Having seen the situation Custer knew he did not want the packs to cross the Little Big Horn, but to come to his support. He then had Tom Custer send Sgt. Kanipe with his message to the packs. Since he realized Benteen had not joined Reno or crossed into the valley, he mentioned to Tom to have the courier, if he saw Benteen, to inform him to also join him. He then moved his troops around Weir Point and took a Column left and went down Western Coulee to Medicine Tail Coulee.

The Crows then moved to Weir Point where they also saw a peaceful village. They then followed the ridge line toward Medicine Tail Coulee and moved parallel to Custer's troops. They saw Reno go into action, and Bouyer attempted to signal Custer. Bouyer knowing the battle had commenced told Curley he was too young and should return to the packs. Custer was now in Medicine Tail Coulee and Bouyer and the three Crows went down to meet him. Custer was informed that Benteen was back on the main trail. He then placed Captain Keogh and two companies in reserve, and they moved to Luce Ridge. Trumpeter Martin was sent back with his message to Benteen. Custer told Buoyer that he could dismiss the Crows because they had done their job. The Crows went on what is known as Bouyer's Bluff above the ford. They fired on the Indian village as Custer moved to the ford. Curley, who had remained on the ridge, also fired but from further back. The Indians at the ford were joined by those that were still preparing and those just leaving to fight Reno. Martin as he nears the high point hears the firing and looking back sees Custer's troops retreating. He has not yet seen Reno moving into the timber. The Crows fled back to where they met Benteen.

In the Crow interviews they mention their orders to hold before Weir Point, their sighting of Reno going into action, their dismissals, and Custer going to the ford. One can see their attempt to rationalize their actions by their account of Custer watching Reno from Weir Point and their attempt to get him to aid Reno. These interviews could be extremely difficult for a translator to put together in a coherent way. Within their statements one then finds contradictions. The following are some of the statements that I don't think one can dismiss because they coordinate with others from a time and event standpoint. They should then be accepted.

> Goes Ahead statement to Walter Camp: "Custer had gone out of sight behind the bluffs quite some time before Reno's fight began."[30]

> Curley: "These three Crows were with Bouyer and me as far as the bluff at the cut bank just south of Ford B and about 1500 ft. from that ford. While

we were here, Custer's command hove in sight, galloping right down the coulee toward the river."[31]

Custer's route according to Curley: "Custer left Dry Creek 900 ft. east of its mouth and struck the river 1,000 ft. downstream from its mouth."[32]

Hairy Moccasin: "We four scouts turned and charged north to where Custer was headed for. Three of us stopped to fire intothe village."[33]

White Man Runs Him: "The scouts took a position on the high bluffs where we could look down into the Sioux camp. As we followed along on the high ground, Custer had gone down Medicine Tail Creek and was moving toward the river.... Custer tried to cross the river at the mouth of Medicine Tail Creek, but was unable to do so. This was the last we saw Custer.[34]

White Man Runs Him: I know for sure that Custer went right to the river bank. I saw him go that far."[35]

Curley: "There were five of us altogether. We went further north on the high bluffs and came near the Indian camp just below the bluffs. Each of us fired two or three shots at the camp.

Custer had reached the river when we were at this point on the bluffs."[36]

White Man Runs Him: "Then Custer started moving toward the ridge. Mitch Bouyer noticed the scouts Custer had sent to look over the ridge had followed Reno, so he (Bouyer) called me, Curley, Goes Ahead, and Hairy Moccasin and said, 'Let us go over to the ridge and look at the lodges.' When we reached there we saw that the lodges were over in the valley quite a ways down the river, so we went on ahead, Custer following. This was about 9:15 a.m. (old time) "[37]

◆   ◆   ◆

What changed "old time" to "new time?" I have never found an explanation. And if "old time" was the time used when they set their watches, used during the battle, and right afterward, then that is the time that should have been used at the Reno Court. When did they change it to the "new time"? And, why wasn't everybody informed of an official change? Why were the officers the only ones effected? And how could the change be as much as three to six hours?

We then get to the question of Martin. I have spent many prior pages on Martin and why he saw the Indian camp from or near Weir Point, left within sight of the camp near Ford B, and that Custer went down Middle Coulee and not Cedar Coulee or Godfrey's Gorge. I have changed Middle Coulee to Western Coulee after reading Edward Curtis's and General Woodruff's measurements. Martin received his message to take to Benteen from 600 yds. or less from Ford B.

Liddic brings out the following as to where Martin received his message for Benteen:

> Exactly where Martin received the famous "last order" has been a subject of speculation among battle authors. Camp said that Martin told him that he left Custer about half way down the coulee. Dr. Stewart, Jim Willert, and Fred Dustin claim Martin left the command at the junction of Cedar Coulee and Medicine Tail. Dr. Gray infers that he was dispatched at the head of the coulee or gorge before the column entered it. Henry Wiebert believed it was at a point just as Custer entered Medicine Tail. Dr. Kuhlman opinion was that Martin was dispatched after riding 300 yards down the ravine. However, Martin should have known from what point he departed the column, and while the events were fresh in his mind, he told his story at the Reno Court of Inquiry. Martin testified that about the time the command had executed the "Column Left" a little below the ridge and almost to the head of the ravine, he was ordered to Benteen.... Martin recalled that he traveled south about 600 yards and arrived on the same ridge from which he had seen the village not ten minutes earlier. The trumpeter turned his head to the right and "looked down into the bottom, and saw Major Reno engaged.... The reason why Martin suddenly looked to his right was because he heard heavy firing in that direction. He originally thought it was from Custer's command but the battalion as yet hadn't even reached Medicine Tail. It was before 3:45 p.m. [It must be new time.][38]

In my prior books I wrote over a chapter on Martin, and brought out how Custer went to Weir Point; then to Medicine Tail Coulee where Martin received his message to take to Benteen; and that Custer didn't go down Cedar Coulee or Godfrey's Gorge. I've brought out the reasons why I don't agree with the above authorities. I will be glad to change my mind when I see any objective and logical evidence to the contrary. The above statements by Liddic and the others are definitely not a refutation. The Reno Court was an attempt to confuse Martin in order to dismiss him. As he himself said, he was not supposed to tell everything he knew.[39] Martin was the primary source that could have undermined the

Court's proceedings. This is why even after the Court he was never invited back to the battlefield by the officers. I can see why the officers didn't ask him since they already knew his statements would not coincide with the version they created for the Reno Courts, and has subsequently been maintained. However, historians should have questioned this, and invited Martin back to the battlefield. That they never did indicates their acceptance of officers' testimony, particularly Benteen's.

Contrary to Liddic, and the other experts, Custer had engaged the enemy and it was sometime before 3:45. Let's take a look at just some of the testimony that needed to be contradicted and not ignored.

Little Sioux:

> [At the time Little Sioux was driving Sioux ponies on the flat below Weir Point, and about the time Martin, on his way to Benteen, should have been sighting Reno on his skirmish line.] While he was driving off the horses on the flat he heard a battle going on very plainly at his right and on his left also. Slightly behind him he heard sounds of another battle but not so plain. [The very plain ones on his right would be from Reno's skirmish line. The ones on his left would most likely be from Nye Cartwright or Calhoun Hill, and those less plain from either Ford B or Custer's troops initial move north.][40]

Custer's route according to Curley:

> Custer left coulee of Dry Creek 900 ft. east of its mouth and struck the river 1,000 ft. downstream from its mouth. It is about 900 ft. further to the first high cut bank.[41] [It was during this time that Bouyer went from the bluffs above Ford B to meet Custer.]

You then have the following statement in a letter by Martin to Private Taylor. Martin:

> Mitch Bouyer was at the head of the column when Custer gave me the message. There were also three Crows as I remember.[42]

Martin to Camp:

> Custer first halted on Weir Hill and took a look at village.[43]

Martin to Camp:

> When I got up on the elevation I looked behind? Met Boston Custer half way between medium coulee and Weir Hill.... After this I heard a volley and

looked back and saw Custer retreating from the river. [Martin still hadn't seen Reno moving into the timber.][44]

Martin to Camp:

I showed (on June 27) Benteen where I left with note from Custer, and Benteen estimated the distance to be 600 yards to Ford B.[45]

Martin told Camp he was with Custer after he passed the high ground and left him just as the command started down a ravine to get off the bluff, some what to the right of highest ground and about 1000 ft. from it. [The high ground was the bluffs leading to Ford B, and 1000 ft. from it is inexact, but could be 600 yds. from Ford B or closer.][46]

Martin to Camp:

… I myself was with General Custer when he was much nearer the river than is the point where he was found dead and I saw him and his command right down on the flat within a few hundred yards of the river, retreating from it.[47]

Martin to Camp:

Custer first halted on Weir's Hill and took a look at village. Here he turned column to the right and went down coulee to Dry Creek (Walter Camp often used the term Dry Creek to describe Medicine Tail Coulee) and turned to the left and followed Dry Creek straight for the village. About half way down to Little Bighorn we came into full view of the village, and here he halted the command and Cooke wrote out the message to Benteen, and I started back with it on the trail. I did not follow Dry Creek all the way back to coulee running north and south but cut across the high ground.[48]

Halfway down to the river from Western Coulee would bring them within about 600 yards from the ford. Until then they would not have been able to see the village because of Bouyer's Bluff on the one side and the trees and cutbank on the other. Cutting across the high ground meant crossing the lower end of the bluffs which extend from Bouyer's Bluff back to Weir Point. Martin went into Western Coulee, and I believe, because of a somewhat better route, cut below a knoll into Middle Coulee and then back to the ridge.

Michael Reynolds, the son of the Crow Agent, who went with his father, and Edward Curtis and the three Crow scouts over Custer's route had this to say in a letter to Richard Upton:

> ... At this point, the command was halted and Custer with his brother Tom, a platoon of C Troop, Trumpeter Martini, and Adjutant Cooke rode down to within fifty yards of where Medicine Tail Creek entered the Little Big Horn River. Here, Mitch Boyer and the three Crow scouts, Goes Ahead, Hairy Moccasin, and White Man Runs Him met him. He looked directly across the river into the center of the Indian camp. He told Mitch Boyer to tell the Indian Scouts that they were dismissed and could go back to Reno. He ordered Cooke to write the famous message to Benteen and sent Trumpeter Martini off with it. [49]

If you believe Custer went down Cedar Coulee, Godfrey's Gorge, or Martin's Ridge then you should realize the following: (1) Custer was stupid. (2) Boston Custer shouldn't have wondered where Custer was. (3) Edward Curtis, General Woodruff, and the Crows were wrong. (4) Martin lied to Private Taylor. (5) Benteen didn't tell Martin he received his message 600 yards from Ford B. (6) Martin again lied when he said he was with Custer closer to the river than where Custer's body was found. (7) Martin didn't see Custer's troops retreating from the river. (8) According to the accepted version Martin again was wrong because timewise he couldn't have been with Custer that close to the river or saw his troops retreating and still, after reaching the ridge, have seen Major Reno's troops moving into the timber.

How do we know Martin was wrong? We know it because the writers either said he was and gave a twisted interpretation of his remarks, or they imply it by their battle scenarios. They said Martin received his message as he was going down Cedar Coulee, Godfrey's Gorge, or a mile and a half back from the river, which they then use to refute everything Martin said. What evidence do they have? They know this because Reno said Custer was planning on following him. The officers' agreed that this must have been Custer's plan because Adjutant Cooke went to the ford with Reno. The authorities accepted Girard's account that he gave a message to Cooke which said the Indians were coming down the valley in great numbers against Reno. We know this must have been true because Reno had sent McIlhargey with basically the same report. Custer remained along Reno Creek until he heard from Girard, after which he decided to flank the Indian village. By the time Custer reached the ridge Reno was already charging down the valley. Custer even saw Reno set up his skirmish line. Custer then went down Cedar Coulee or Godfrey's Gorge to Medicine Tail Coulee. What evidence do we have that Custer went down Cedar Coulee or Godfrey's Gorge? Remember Edgerly said he didn't see any signs of Custer going to Weir Point, so logic tells us he went down Cedar Coulee. Custer didn't know what lay behind Weir Point, and he could see that Cedar Coulee and Godfrey's Gorge were both clear. This proves that Martin was wrong since Custer could not have reached Medicine Tail Coulee, let alone Ford B, before Reno retreated. That proves Martin could not have received his message near Ford B and still have been on the ridge in time to see Reno move into the timber. In other words Martin lied and fabricated all those stories about where he got his message. Edgerly's story shows that you can't trust Martin because he told Benteen's troops that Custer was attacking the village and killing Indians right and left, and we know that wasn't true.

So the authorities have disclaimed Martin's remarks by ignoring, discrediting, distorting, or brushing them aside, and by doing so have failed to connect the essential dots.

Liddic:

> … That Martin was dispatched about ten minutes and a mile after Knipe, is confirmed by; the fact that Benteen only advanced about a mile from his meeting with Knipe before meeting the second messenger. Therefore, Martin couldn't have accompanied Custer into Medicine Tail and have enough time to ride back to join Benteen within a mile of the first messenger. Assuming Custer continued on at the same pace, Martin should have been dispatched no more than eight minutes or about a mile after Knipe in order for Benteen to meet Martin about ten minutes after he had met Knipe.[50]

Although one should question anything Benteen said, this timing seems to be about right. Gray, Liddic, and others attempt to restrict times to exact minutes. Judging riding time when we don't even know the different gaits that are used, or forgotten details concerning terrain and incidents that could have caused delays or increased speed, makes exact timing impossible. However, it is important to estimate times with location and events, but this, as I am attempting to point out, is not what Gray, Liddic, and the other authorities have done. I have used Kanipe's statements to indicate that he did not receive his message near Reno Hill but close to, at, or just beyond Weir Point. Martin should then have been only ten or fifteen minutes behind Kanipe. In fact rather than a condemnation of Martin's accounts, the evidence Liddic uses should be a confirmation of them.

In his attempt to discredit Martin, Liddic brings out the following:

> Benteen ordered the trumpeter to rejoin the company. But as Martin rode
> past 'D' to fall in with his company. Lieutenant Edgerly heard Martin telling
> the troopers that Reno had attacked the village and was "killing Indians and
> squaws right and left." Interestingly, at the Reno Court of Inquiry, Martin
> said Benteen ordered him to go to the pack train to bring the mules up and
> keep them together. But later Martin recanted this testimony and told Gra-
> ham he didn't speak English very well in 1879, and they misunderstood
> him, and it was a mistake, as he was never ordered to the pack train. He also
> told Graham another story about the wound his horse had suffered.... [51]

This is another good example of what I consider a lack of insight, failure to
connect the dots, or merely cursory thinking. Liddic describes the various white-
washings by officers and especially Benteen, but he doesn't apply any of it to an
analysis of Martin's statements. Might Edgerly be attempting to excuse their failure to "be quick" in going to aid Custer? Is it possible that Edgerly may have mistook what Kanipe said and thought it was Martin? It is odd that both couriers
would have used such language. The expression, if used, typifies my conception
of Kanipe more than that of Martin. Kanipe was more apt to have thought that
by the time he joined Benteen, this is what Custer's troops would have been
doing. Martin's statements of when he received his message, heard gunfire,
sighted Custer's troops retreating, and saw Reno moving into the timber, all connect timewise in contrast to Liddic's supposition. We should also recognize that
at the trial Martin, outside of knowing he wasn't expected to tell everything he
knew, was not aware of the officers' cover-ups.

The recanting to Graham, instead of a criticism of Martin, should be recognized as an indictment of the Court. The number of questions asked of Martin
concerning the packs makes one realize that there is no way Martin was misinterpreted.[52] Combine that with the knowledge that the packs and their arrival on
the hill was a central part of the Defense's cover-ups, and there should be no
question that the packs were close behind Benteen. This is another example of
the Court not accepting an enlisted man's testimony that went contrary to that of
an officer. The lack of intense questioning of officers indicates the Courts complicity with the Defense. The packs supposed late arrival was and has been one of
the time gap closures. Martin's later denial also illustrates the fact that the
enlisted men were not privy to the cover-ups, except in the off hand way as
expressed by Martin's realizing that he wasn't to say all that he knew. Afterwards,
Martin became aware of how his statements were damaging to Benteen, and so

(as a good and loyal soldier) recanted them. Possibly Lt. Gibson's remark was not so incredible,[53] or at least it makes Benteen's reference to the packs being some 7 miles behind indicative of a cover-up.

Liddic states how Benteen testified to doing little that he was ordered to do by Custer's message brought by Martin. However, Liddic excuses the Court's lack of follow up questions by saying that the Court was only impaneled to investigate Reno's conduct at the Little Big Horn, not Benteen's, and so they couldn't push the Captain any further. This, to me, is another excuse for the failure to probe into officer's actions. Since these orders were not only shown to Major Reno but should have been instrumental in judging the actions he took or didn't take, they were pertinent to an understanding of Reno's conduct. Certainly the packs and their location and arrival time was a major factor in Reno's Defense. In examining Reno's conduct, officers and their understanding of orders, time, actions, and other various elements should have been fair game. As Captain Carter said, the officers were not questioned in any way similar to the questioning that had taken place in other courts of inquiry and court—martials.[54]

Liddic points out Reno's reaction to questions concerning the Custer orders Benteen received and showed to Reno when arriving on the ridge:

> … The Recorder asked the Major if he had read Custer's order to Benteen? Reno replied he had and although he couldn't repeat the exact "phraseology" as he remembered, it said to come on, there was a big village and to bring the packs. Reno was asked if the message didn't have the words "be quick." Reno casually said, "Yes, I do, now that you called my attention to it." Reno had previously told the court about the "immense" number of Indians he had faced alone in the valley, and the Recorder asked: "From the number of Indians you saw around you and your estimate of the number that were there, did it occur to you at the time that, with only 225 men, he might need someone to 'be quick?'" The junior major of the 7th Cavalry looked at the Court and then at the Recorder, and answered, "It never occurred to me at all." No further comment is necessary on Benteen's and Reno's testimony regarding Custer's 'last message;' it defies coherent description.[55]

What to me defies coherent description is how the coterie still do not make the connection to the essential issues. They recognize how Benteen and Reno are able to shove off Custer's orders, and there is no third degree by the Recorder or the Court with all the violation of military protocol involved. They then accept without question Reno's and Benteen's version of Custer's orders and the change in time—elements that are vital to an accurate assessment of the battle. Liddic nor the others do not even attempt to bring out or examine the time differences, but accept without explanation times that vary from those given after the battle by three and more hours. And if they considered the majority of Indian accounts the time gap would be even greater. Many Indians have the battle taking place in the morning and the Custer portion being over by noon. Liddic has Reno's retreat taking place after 4 o'clock.[56] In other words, the authorities point out the discrepancies on minor issues but accept those on major ones.

Liddic then describes Major Reno's retreat and the difficulties the troops encountered. Reno's conduct is in general condemned. Liddic then submits his conception of Custer's action during this period:

> While Reno was giving the order to abandon the timber and retreat to the bluffs, Custer after speaking with his scouts, caught up with the head of the command which was riding towards Medicine Tail Coulee. After reaching Medicine Tail, the troops rode across the mouth of Cedar Coulee. From the point where Cedar Coulee joins Medicine Tail Coulee, it descends about a mile and a half before it meets a gap a half mile wide in the steep bluffs along the river's eastern banks. This break in the bluffs gave easy access to the Cheyenne camp circle at the upper end of the village and is called Ford 'B'. Custer was heading for this crossing point to cut off any fleeing Indians and to stop any movement to the north caused by Reno's attack. Custer had a good idea of the village's layout and its size from previous observations. In response to the couriers he had dispatched, the regiment would be concentrated shortly and Reno would have his support'. Shortly after crossing the mouth of Cedar Coulee, Custer halted the troops and his men rearranged themselves and tightened their saddles for the action ahead. During this brief halt Custer ordered Keogh's battalion of two companies forward to take the lead.... [57]

Without going back over all the reasons and material that I have presented, I will say that I disagree with Liddic. I will state some of the differences: Martin left Custer from 50 to 600 yds. from Ford B. After receiving his message, Martin went up Western Coulee or Middle Coulee to Weir Point. Two important things happened that wouldn't have if he had received his message in Cedar Coulee or Godfrey's Gorge before Custer reached Medicine Tail Coulee: (a) Martin wouldn't have heard firing coming from his right, and (b) he wouldn't have met Boston Custer half way up the coulee and still needed to tell Boston where Custer was. As long as we are on the subject of Boston, one might wonder why he didn't cross Ford A and follow Reno. I doubt if he was so well-versed in tracking that his following the trail to his right was just a matter of luck, but instead would have been because Custer's plan to flank the Indians was well known. It coordinates time-wise that Martin heard firing and when he reached the ridge saw Custer retreating from Ford B. The capping factor is that he saw Reno as he moved into the timber. Martin then went to where he met Benteen, and they still made it back just as Reno and his men were reaching the bluffs. Liddic may think Martin made up all of his accounts, but I think he was incapable of doing so, and that his record portrays a good honest soldier who wasn't in on the cover-ups.

Liddic is still taken in by the Crow's comments that they were told to remain behind, which was true up to a point. After hurrying to the bluffs on the heels of his Crow scouts, Custer signaled to his men who had just finished watering. The Crows were told to watch events unfolding in the valley while Custer crossed over what later became the Reno entrenchment area to meet his men. The Crows were not dismissed at that time. Custer, after briefing his company commanders, returned to the crest, at which time he waved to Reno's men who were reforming after they had crossed the ford and passed through the timber. Custer then went to Weir Point with his men following. Custer viewed a comparatively peaceful village, and began his move (via Western Coulee) to Medicine Tail Coulee. The Crows then went to the vicinity of Weir Point where Bouyer reported a similar peaceful village scene. The essence of which proves Custer was ahead of Reno's move down the valley. The sighting of Custer and his troops on the ridge by enlisted men only validates this observation. The Crows then followed along the bluff as Custer's troops moved down Western Coulee. Bouyer told Curley he should return to the packs. The three Crows went with Bouyer as he met Custer near Ford B. Bouyer informed Custer that Reno was now engaged, and that Benteen had not joined him. Martin was sent back. The Crows were then dismissed but went to Bouyer's Bluff and fired on the Indian village. Custer's troops went to the ford and began their retreat. Martin was now on the ridge, and when he looked back he saw the troops retreating. Martin moved to where he viewed Reno's men entering the timber. He then pushed on to where he met Benteen. As I said, these events coordinate time-wise, whereas Liddic and the authorities have to ignore Martin's accounts in order to support their scenario.

Most of the coterie have Custer's troops entering Medicine Tail Coulee from Cedar Coulee, or in Liddic's case Godfrey's Gorge, and they proceeded to ride across the mouth of Cedar Coulee. Custer, after stopping for the troops to check their mounts, moved toward Ford B. Liddic then makes an interesting statement as he says, "Custer had a good idea of the village's layout and its size from his previous observations."[58] His previous observations, according to Liddic, were near

Reno Hill and Sharpshooters' Ridge. From the Reno Hill area a few tepees may have been seen, and the same could be said for Sharpshooters' Ridge, but Custer would not have been aware of the size or extent of the village nor would he have seen enough of the village to have wondered where the warriors had gone. One might recall that Liddic said the Weir Peaks blocked their view, and since they didn't know what Indians might have been on the other side of Weir Point, they went down Cedar Coulee or Godfrey's Gorge because they were clear.[59] What I also like about Liddic's scenario is that after failing to move directly north but instead going down Godfrey's Gorge, Custer, because of the couriers he has sent, is sure that the "regiment would be concentrated shortly" and Reno would have his 'support.' I keep reminding myself that these writers know this is Custer, and they have undoubtedly stated, as Liddic has, that Custer operated under the maxim that attack and victory were synonymous. But what do they have Custer doing? According to their scenarios, he has seen Reno go into action. He now knows there is a large number of warriors, and that Benteen is back on the trail. Custer is noted for leading his troops, but is this what he does? No, he takes his time because he knows Reno can hold out against this overwhelming number of Indians. Does he lead a charge across Ford B and into the Indian village? No, he has Captain Keogh with two companies take the lead to the ford. And who should then arrive but Boston Custer. If Martin left when and from where Liddic and the other authorities believe, then Boston Custer should have caught up to Custer as he halted after reaching Medicine Tail. I wonder if the coterie even recognize the dots that need to be and can be connected.

SOURCES

1. Liddic, 81.

2. Curtis, *The Papers of Edward S. Curtis*, 99.

3. Reno Court, 390.

4. Ibid., 390.

5. Camp, 97.

6. Ibid., 97.

7. Carroll, 38.

8. Viola, *Little Big Horn Remembered,* 157.

9.   Liddic, 81.

10. Ibid., 84.

11. Camp, 97.

12. Reno Court, 397.

13. Liddic, 85.

14. Camp, 156.

15. Curtis, 101.

16. Maquire Map, Reno Court, Exhibit #2.

17. Liddic, 85.

18. Graham, 42.

19. Liddic, 86.

20. Taylor, 177.

21. Camp, 92, 93.

22. Ibid., 97.

23. Reno Court, 390.

24. Gray, 336, 337.

25. Miller, *Custer's Fall—The Indian Side of the Story*, 126, 127.

26. Graham, 19.

27. Ibid., 20.

28. Camp, 175.

29. Ibid., 178.

30. Ibid., 178.

31. Ibid., 162.

32. Ibid., 162.

33. Graham, 25.

34. Ibid., 23.

35. Ibid., 15.

36. Ibid., 13.

37. Ibid., 13.

38. Liddic, 89.

39. Camp, 101.

40. Graham, 42, 43.

41. Ibid., 162.

42. Taylor, 177.

43. Camp, 103.

44. Ibid., 104.

45. Ibid., 105.

46. Ibid., 103.

47. Ibid., 105.

48. Ibid., 103.

49. Pennington, *Curtis, Curley, Custer*, 138.

50. Liddic, 90.

51. Ibid., 90.

52. Reno Court, 391–392.

53. Liddic, 91.

54. Graham, 309.

55. Liddic, 91, 92.

56. Ibid., 92.

57. Ibid., 96.

58. Ibid., 97.

59. Ibid., 85.

8

CUSTER IN MEDICINE TAIL COULEE

Liddic writes about Boston Custer joining General Custer, and poses the question as to how he came to follow Custer's trail. The question is a good one, but as I previously mentioned, any officer should have known that Custer planned to take his five companies and flank the Indians. Boston Custer was probably aware of this from the division of the command. Benteen, on the other hand, might have hesitated because he had prior orders to cross the Little Big Horn and aid Reno, and he may have thought Custer was already fighting in the valley. From Kanipe's report[1] and Edgerly's story[2] that is what he could have expected. Liddic indicated that Half Yellow Face directed Benteen's troops to the bluffs where Reno's men were retreating. The Rees mention Half Yellow Face, who was still in the valley, but also refer to White Man Runs HIm as Half Yellow Face.

Liddic then describes Boston Custer meeting Martin on Sharpshooters' Ridge. Here Liddic puts his spin on what Martin said.

Martin to Camp:

> … Martin started back on trail before got up the hill (that is up to high point where whole command had halted) he heard heavy firing in the direction of his right. It might also have been Reno's fire that he heard as that would have been to his right. He afterward supposed was at Ford B. After this he met Boston Custer going to join the command. When Martin got to top of ridge he looked down in village and saw Indians charging like swarm of bees toward the ford waving buffalo hides. At the same time he saw Custer retreating up the open country in the direction of the battlefield.[3]

Martin said that before he got up the hill he heard heavy firing to his right. If Martin was going back by way of Cedar Coulee, Martin's Ridge, or Godfrey's Gorge, firing from his right would most likely not be coming from Reno, and he would not have been able to see Custer retreating. Martin said when he got to the top of the ridge he looked down on the village and saw Indians charging like swarm of bees toward the ford.... He couldn't have seen this from Sharpshooters' Ridge because Weir Point would have prevented it. The firing on his right from Custer's troops, the sighting of Custer retreating, and seeing Indians moving to the ford would have been possible if Martin had gone back to the high point by way of Western or Middle Coulee.

Liddic's statement that it was Keogh's battalion that was sent forward by Custer was supposedly verified by both DeRudio and Mclernand after the battle. I question anything either said concerning tracks. How many Indians on horseback had crossed the ford and went up Medicine Tail Coulee both during and after the battle? How many Indians took and rode cavalry horses? How many Indians went over the area on foot? And if shod hoof prints were seen couldn't they represent any of the five companies? I wouldn't consider DeRudio's and Mclernand's views to be verification.

Liddic discusses in detail various opinions as to how the five companies were divided and under whose command. My only concern, at this time, is that I can't see Custer failing to lead the way to the ford, and I believe what concrete evidence we have supports that he did. The primary question that should be investigated is why Custer didn't attack across Ford B.

Liddic's following report lacks congruity:

> With his brother beside him, Custer would have surely asked three important questions: 1) Did he see Benteen and/or the pack train? 2) Did he see any Indians on the back trail? 3) Did he see anything of the two messengers who had been dispatched? The answers Boston gave would have greatly reassured Custer and confirmed his next move.... Despite a lack of communication from Benteen, Custer was now assured the village he observed from Sharpshooters' Ridge was the main encampment, and there were no significant village to the south. He could base his tactical disposition of his own battalion on this current intelligence rather than on presumptions. This information would allow him the opportunity to formulate a more audacious plan. Custer did not have to relegate any of his wing for a reserve. In addition, by some extrapolations, Custer could determine about where Benteen and the pack train were on his back trail based on the time it took his inexperienced brother to reach the command.... Boston, by conveying this knowledge, had ratified that the dust Custer had seen from Sharpshooters' Ridge was from these units.

... spoke volumes about the location of all the Indians ... down in the valley, across the west side of the Little Big Horn River, and apparently unaware of his presence only a mile and a quarter from the north end of the village.... His idea of the village's location proved to be correct, ... It was 'Custer's Luck' indeed, to happen upon a standing village! ... Benteen's three companies would be coming over the bluffs or down the coulee in about thirty minutes....

... In all likelihood, Custer expected to chase after the noncombatants, wanted the regiment concentrated as soon as possible, and Benteen's troops, with or without the pack train, could be employed as a reserve force to occupy and/or destroy the village. This would free Custer to commit his entire five companies to the enterprise.... [4]

Custer was supposed to be receiving information on Benteen, the packs, the Indians, and his couriers from Boston Custer at the halt a mile and a half from the river. Boston Custer should not have reached Custer until he was retreating from the ford. For the sake of argument, I will assume Liddic is right and that Martin concocted his stories. Custer now knows Benteen is back on the trail and there are no Indian camps to the south. Custer, this daring attack-minded commander, will **now** be able to come up with an **audacious** plan. Really! Custer **now** knows the Indians are down in the valley. If Custer had gone to Weir Point earlier, he would have known where the Indians were, how large the village was, and gone down a coulee that would have enabled him to synchronize an **audacious** attack with that of Reno's. Since I'm supposedly agreeing with Liddic, why didn't Custer realize all of that from Sharpshooters' Ridge? If Custer could have seen the village, as Liddic claims, and Reno was already in action, what would Custer's priorities have been? Shouldn't he have attempted to find the quickest route to attack the village? Certainly that wouldn't have been by going down Cedar Coulee or Godfrey's Gorge. Weir Point would have blocked Custer's movement, so he would have gone around the peaks and straight north down middle or western coulee. This would have enabled him the quickest access to the village. If Custer couldn't see the full extent of the village, (which would have been impossible from Sharpshooters' Ridge), why wouldn't a competent commander have gone to Weir Point where he could have seen the entire village?

As I explain elsewhere, either the Ree scout Stabbed, the Sgt. Major, or Bouyer was responsible for notifying Custer that Benteen was back on the main trail. He would have received this information at or about the time Bouyer and the three Crows met Custer. Custer would then have wanted Benteen and the packs to hurry, "be quick," and join him. He then sent Martin with his message to Benteen. Martin would not have carried a message to Benteen as long as Custer still thought Benteen would be going to the valley and then moving in support of Reno. Sgt. Kanipe would have been sent back to Benteen if Custer had seen Benteen from Sharpshooters' Ridge.

Liddc said that, once Custer had heard from Boston Custer, he didn't need to relegate any of his wing to a reserve. Now that Custer knew this, he could concentrate all 5 companies on attacking the Indians in his newly formulated audacious plan. I haven't been able to figure out what this audacious plan was, and I am not aware of when it took place. Custer must have thought he had plenty of time to support Reno, so he decided to retreat from the ford and move to the north. Liddic doesn't believe Custer needed a reserve force, so he must believe that when Benteen and the packs arrived they could judge through the dust and smoke what Custer expects from them. Since Liddic believes Custer may have wanted Benteen to act as a reserve force and possibly occupy or destroy the village, it might have been wise for him to leave an informative reserve force.

Liddic continues on with what he considers a rational view and I consider an irrational one:

> … As to Custer going to Luce Ridge, I do not contradict these students that he went there, but it had nothing to do with waiting for reinforcements. Reinforcements, for what purpose? His command had yet to fire a shot, and from the army's past experience, a big village would run as quickly as a small village. Custer now knew the positions of his other units wereconfirmed, and he started for the low ridges to the northeast that rise above the coulee. These ridges offer a good overall view of the area about Ford 'B.' But, higher above these ridges is a rather steep promontory, traditionally known as Luce Ridge. Custer could have got a good view of the ford from the lower ridges, but if he wanted to see further up the valley beyond the ford he would have had to climb to the top of Luce Ridge. Custer would climb to the top of this ridge for just this purpose. However, from these lower ridges, Custer saw "a beehive of activity about a mile ahead on the eastern side of the river in the area of Ford B.
>
> In reaction to Reno's attack, the old men, women, and children from the other camp circles fled in the direction of the Cheyenne camp circle, as it was the nearest and fastest escape route.[5]

I agree with Liddic that Custer wouldn't have gone to Luce Ridge to wait for reinforcements. In fact I'm still wondering what his **audacious** plan was. I also wonder what happened with all of his great lookout views of the village, and why he would be going to still more lookout locations. Isn't this the courageous leader with whom attack and victory are synonymous? Custer knows Benteen did not go in support of Reno in the valley, and that Reno is now fighting in the valley and would be expecting the support Custer promised. What is Custer doing? Even though he hadn't felt it necessary to go to Weir Point where he would have had a complete view of the Indian village, now that he should be attacking the village as quickly as possible, does he? Not this attack-minded leader! He is going to Luce Ridge because there seems to be a lot of activity around the ford that is still about a mile ahead. Custer, if he did go up Sharpshooters' Ridge, would have known that the village lay in the valley northwest of Weir Point. However, according to Liddic, even though he couldn't see most of the village he wouldn't have gone to Weir Point, nor would he go around Weir Point to go down a coulee that came out a half mile from Ford B. No, the coulees leading away from the village that came into Medicine Tail Coulee roughly two miles from the Ford were clear, and since he couldn't see beyond Weir Point, he had to go down these other coulees. If I believed all this then the blame for the Little Big Horn debacle is clear—it was that stupid commander Custer.

Liddic believes that at this point Custer's concern centered around the non-combatants. Captain Keogh was now heading for the ford to begin the action. (It was about time.) Liddic asserts that there were two villages—he believes that the Indians moved their camps further north and west later that day. It's interesting that he says "the complete one which Custer saw from Sharpshooters' Ridge and later from Luce Ridge, and the camps were moved north about two miles following his defeat."[6] I agree on the movement, but not the sighting of a complete village from Sharpshooters' Ridge or from Luce Ridge. However, we're back to why Custer, if he had seen the complete village from Sharpshooter Ridge, would have gone away from the village down Godfrey's Gorge, why he would even halt to check equipment, and why he would have bothered to go up Luce Ridge. Time should have been of the essence. He then sends Keogh with two companies to the ford. But by now he knows Benteen and the packs should be coming to support him and that Reno may need his help. Custer knows he doesn't need to keep any companies in reserve, but what is he doing? He is going up Luce Ridge to observe. Shouldn't he be attacking, and wouldn't Custer himself be leading that attack? No, he needs to look at the village, and he is sending two companies to the ford to clear the way for an attack. Is this Custer?

Liddic again ignores contradictory sources and testimony. He has Bouyer coming down from a high peak to the southwest while Custer is still on Luce Ridge and Keogh has advanced to the ford. Liddic disregards Martin's testimony that when he received his message to take to Benteen, Mitch Bouyer was there and there were three Crows.[7] The timing evidence that Liddic also disregards is that Bouyer would have informed Custer that Reno had set up a skirmish line, not that he had retreated. Liddic again brushes off Martin's statement that after getting back on the ridge he saw Reno still fighting in the valley. Liddic doesn't really dismiss it but has it happening much earlier, after Martin left from Cedar Coulee or Godfrey's Gorge. Benteen's telling Martin that the place where Martin received his message was within 600 yards or so of the ford was just another case of Martin distorting the truth.

We now have Custer still climbing around Luce Ridge since he seemingly just can't get enough views of the village. Keogh was clearing noncombatants from the ford. Custer, seeing the movement in the ford and village area, felt the hostiles were all on the run. "With the information his brother brought him, Custer could now afford to play a bolder hand than before was possible. With definite knowledge of the conditions on his back trail, he could commit the entire battalion to the pursuit of the non-combatants."[8] Bouyer must have told Custer that Reno's men were retreating, but that the Indians had left him, otherwise Custer might have been afraid they would attack Benteen and the packs. No, I forget I'm still thinking Custer was a competent commander. Custer now believes he can commit Yates' Battalion to the pursuit … He no longer considered the village a target; his strategy had changed because of the information Boston Custer conveyed and his observations from Sharpshooters' Hill, confirmed from Luce Ridge.[9]

This shows Custer's versatility, for he is now conducting his command more like a general should, not in the manner Sgt. Ryan referred to, which was that he always took the lead.[10] He is acting more in the style of a Pershing or an Eisenhower rather than a Patton. Custer is not passing up viewing locations such as he did with Weir Point. He had sent Keogh to the ford to "secure the crossing in preparation for an attack by the rest of the wing."[11] Custer, from what he saw, became concerned with the noncombatants, and rather than dashing across the ford and cutting them off from the warriors, he decided to move to the north and then encircle all of the hostiles. Since Custer's forces had left the valley, hopefully the Indians would not change direction after seeing his movement to the north. Anyway, Custer was going to play a bolder hand now that he knew Reno retreated.

In order to support his view Liddic uses a portion of an interview with Crazy Horse.

Crazy Horse:

> When Custer made his charge the women, papooses, children, and in fact all that were not fighters made a stampede in a northerly direction. Custer, seeing so numerous a body, mistook them for the main body of Indians retreating and abandoning their village, and immediately gave pursuit.[12]

> It was after four o'clock when Keogh's battalion began moving down Medicine Tail Coulee … [13]

What is wrong with the above? First, Bouyer has already reported to Custer. He supposedly told him that Reno had retreated. Custer might have worried about the warriors then attacking Benteen and the packs, but maybe Bouyer told him they had left Reno and were coming back to attack him. Under Liddic's scenario it is questionable whether they were aware of Custer's troops, but again I will assume that they were. With all of the dust and smoke being created, plus the bluffs to Custer's right, it is unlikely that Custer could have seen much of the Indian movement. However, my main criticism of this scenario is the time wasted and the fact that Custer (even with his audacious plan) has not yet launched an attack. The village was in a near state of panic—when would there have been a better time to attack? Reno, according to Liddic, had been fighting for some time and had even retreated. Where is the support Custer promised?

The core ingredient for any analysis of this period is the relative positions of Reno and Custer. Was Reno ahead of Custer or was Custer ahead of Reno? In my other books and articles, as well as in this manuscript I have brought out my reasons for believing Custer was ahead of Reno. I am still waiting for any objective denial of the points I have made. The primary sources, those that were with Custer the longest, have him going along the ridge and not back from it. Those saying Custer did not go to Weir Point brush off the overwhelming evidence that he did. Evidence that is supported by common sense. When Custer is on the ridge he has to realize that Reno is moving, or will be, down the valley to attack the village. At that time he is hoping Benteen will be nearing the valley and will aid Reno. But time is the essential military factor. There is no way that he can see enough of the village from Sharpshooters' Ridge, plus he should still be looking for the quickest and best way to cross the Little Big Horn in his flanking attack. However, according to Liddic, and many of the authorities, he goes along on one side or another of Sharpshooters' Ridge and then goes away from the village down Cedar Coulee, and in Liddic's case Godfrey's Gorge. Rather than coming out a half mile from the river, Custer then comes out two miles away. He should have heard firing from Reno's troops by this time, but is he in a hurry or does he have an audacious plan? No, he wants his men to check their horses, which should have been done while they were watering back along Reno Creek or as he was observing the village from the ridge. Boston Custer has now joined him so he is informed that Benteen is back on the main trail. However, supposedly he already knew that from his sighting on Sharpshooters' Ridge. Custer is now able to make a bold plan, in which he sends Keogh and two companies to the ford. They have moved somewhat closer to the river, and Custer sees a high ridge to his right. He doesn't want to pass up that viewing location so he goes to it. Luce Ridge wouldn't really help because of the bluffs on both sides of Ford B along with the dust, smoke, tepees, trees, and movement, but Custer doesn't want to pass it up so he goes to it anyway.

Custer is now receiving all this evidence that the Indians are leaving their village, so the village is not his objective. Keogh has flushed the Indians from the ford area, and since Custer doesn't need any reserves he also commits Yates' battalion to this pursuit. Is it an attack? No, Custer believes that since the noncombatants are moving to the north, so he will also go across the bluffs to the north where he will find a crossing ford and he can then flank the Indians.

Custer now knows Reno has retreated, so shouldn't he be concerned about Benteen and the packs? No, because he realizes the warriors will come back to protect the noncombatants. Shouldn't he be afraid the Indians might scatter to the south and west? No, he would have captured the noncombatants and the warriors would give up. Since Custer has a clear path to Ford B and the village, shouldn't he launch an attack across Ford B where he could cut off the noncombatants from the warriors? I don't even have a weak excuse for not doing this one.

If you might remember, Liddic said Martin couldn't have seen Custer's column retreating because it was before 3:45 p.m. and Custer hadn't even reached Medicine Tail Coulee.[14] Now it was after 4 o'clock and Keogh's battalion began its march down Medicine Tail Coulee.[15] If there is anything that has bothered me with writers is that they ignore time differences, and do not even attempt to explain these differences except by referring to "old time" and "new time," or using different time zones, none of which are an explanation.

Liddic uses Crazy Horses' statement to support his claim that Custer moved to the north, but he does not mention that Crazy Horse said "an attack was made on the village by a strong force at 11 o'clock in the morning, at the upper end of the village. This was the force commanded by Major Reno, and very **shortly**

afterward (my emphasis) the lower end of the village was attacked by another strong force, that commanded by Custer."[16] It is hard for me to understand how "shortly afterward" can mean 4 hours later. I realize that the Indians didn't have watches, and their honest estimates would be based on pointing at the sun and the interpreter judging the time. What needs explaining is how or why Indian estimates as to time are more comparable to those early reports of the soldiers. Let's look at a few. One might note all of the "abouts."

> Major Reno in his official report: "About 8 a.m. the command was in the valley of one of the branches of the Little Big Horn."

> "As we approached a deserted village, and in which was standing one tepee, was about 11 a.m."

> "… about 12:30 a.m. [p.m.] when Lieutenant Cook, Adjutant, came to me and said the village was only two miles ahead and running away;"

> "I did not see him again [Captain Benteen] until about 2:30 p.m."

> "We joined forces and in a short time the pack train came up."[17]

◆   ◆   ◆

Low Dog: "I was asleep in my lodge at the time. The sun was about noon."18

◆   ◆   ◆

Left Hand: "The first attack was made at the south end of the village when the sun was there (9 a.m.) … When the sun was straight (about noon) we heard shooting at the lower end of the village, and knew it must be more soldiers."[19]

◆   ◆   ◆

Martin at the Reno Court:

Q. What time of day was it when you saw the Indian village where you and General Custer looked at it?

A. I judge it was about 12 o'clock.[20]

◆   ◆   ◆

Sgt. Kanipe: "Reno followed Benteen Creek down on main trail and forded Little Big Horn about noon."[21]

◆   ◆   ◆

Captain Benteen: "... the horses not having been watered since evening before, and this being along about one o'clock p.m. of a hot June day, they were needing it badly...."[22]

◆   ◆   ◆

Waterman: "At that time sun was there (position indicating 9 a.m.)"[23]

◆   ◆   ◆

Turtle Rib: "The fighting started against the camp of the Uncapapa. He was asleep when the soldiers were first reported ..."[24]

◆   ◆   ◆

Joseph White Bull: "It was not yet time for the midday watering when White Bull, watching his horses north of the camp, heard a man yelling the alarm.... "[In White Bull's Vestal account the fighting started around noon and lasted "only about an hour."]"[25]

◆　　　◆　　　◆

Henry Oscar One Bull: "At midday I went back to the pony herd and drove the horses to the river for the noon watering. Just then I heard shooting near the Hunkpapa camp circle.[26]

◆　　　◆　　　◆

Kate Bighead: "It was somewhere past the middle of the forenoon."[27]

◆　　　◆　　　◆

James Browndog sent a speech by Ghost Dog to John Collier, Commissioner of Indian Affairs, in 1940. In it, Ghost Dog, referring to the Little Big Horn Battle, said the following regarding time: "Now I will come to our great battle on Little Big Horn River.... The fighting took place before noon. And the entire regiment was destroyed by noon. I was sleeping in my tipis. When Custer fired into our camp ..." [28]

I don't think you can ignore or fail to explain remarks by both whites and Indians as to the earlier time of the fight. You certainly have to consider that both the Indians and the white people would not necessarily remember the exact times, but there is no way I can accept these discrepancies. You don't have Keogh moving down Medicine Tail Creek after 4 o'clock, and Indians having it over with by noon. Kate Bighead had the Cheyenne burying their dead in the afternoon.[29] And the authorities still don't recognize a timing cover-up. The question shouldn't be whether there was a timing cover-up, but why?

Considering what the authorities have Custer doing, another fundamental point that needs examining is the number of Indian warriors at Ford B when Custer was in a position to launch an attack (or should have been). White Cow Bull and Bobtail Horse said there were no more than ten.[30] He Dog said there were "fifteen or twenty."[31] J. L. Beardsley said, "some of the old chiefs say there were hardly ten warriors guarding the ford, at the point where Custer would have crossed, in the beginning."[32] Dr. Eastman was also told by the warriors that Custer's soldiers were upon the river's bank, but they discovered it wasn't possible to cross, and they: "began shooting into the camp;.... But suddenly the soldiers were pulling back from the ford … [33] Here again the question is why? This was Custer. The camp was concerned with Reno. From all reports it was in a near panic, yet Custer doesn't attack or press an attack?

Contrary to Liddic's assertions, Custer had gone to Weir Point while Reno was just beginning his move down the valley. He then went down Western Coulee, and moved toward the ford. Custer was never on Luce Ridge, but he could, should, and, I believe, did send Keogh in a reserve capacity to Luce Ridge. Keogh most likely fired on Wolf Tooth's band, and even sent a platoon after them as the band moved to the Last Stand area. Keogh's battalion then crossed Nye Cartwright while providing protective fire for Yates' retreating battalion. All of this doesn't explain why Custer didn't attack and why he retreated. Attempting to encircle noncombatants does not provide a logical answer to the question.

Several Indians brought out that they didn't believe Custer went to the ford, but they saw troops moving from Nye Cartwright to Calhoun Hill. There was little fighting at the ford, and many Indians did not arrive from attacking Reno in time to have seen any of the action that did occur, so this would have been a fairly common response. And there were a number that did refer to some fighting at the ford. There were also those that said if Custer had crossed the ford into the camp the troops could have gone right through the village. They realized that the village was in a near state of panic, and that most of the warriors were either attacking Reno or about to join in the attack. Many of the warriors that were the first to turn back to the ford knew there were not enough of them to have prevented the troops from charging through the village. Why Custer didn't is the primary question surrounding the battle. What the effect would have been is another question.

Indians arriving after the brief fighting at the ford would have seen Keogh's reserve force crossing Nye Cartwright, and firing in support of the retreating Yates' battalion. Yates' battalion would have been made up of three companies, led by Custer, that went to attack the village. To put the action in perspective: Near Ford B Martin received his message to take to Benteen, Martin then arrived on the ridge, heard firing, and looked back to see Custer's troops retreating. He then saw Reno still fighting in the valley. Some of Yates' battalion had already retreated to the north around the first cutbank, while others (already companies were becoming mixed) were further up Deep Coulee in a disorganized move to join the reserve group.

In opposition to my view you have Liddic's and the authorities "accepted" scenario. They have Custer holding back with three of his five companies, and sending two to the ford under either Yates or Keogh. In Liddic's case he has Keogh. The village is in a turmoil and the noncombatants are fleeing the village, so Custer decides that rather than attacking the village he will go to the north in an attempt to cut off the noncombatants. If he is able to accomplish this he believes the warriors will be willing to surrender, and move to the reservations which is the army's primary goal.

My theory is that Custer took three companies to the ford under his command. He placed two companies in reserve and sends Keogh to Luce Ridge. Keogh moves to Nye Cartwright and then to Calhoun Ridge in an attempt to protect the retreating companies. Custer must have been shot at the ford which stopped the attack, considering that with the number of warriors at the ford and the state of the village, Custer should and would have charged into the village. It wouldn't have mattered at that time if he had planned on attacking the warriors or cutting off the noncombatants, because either plan could have been best accomplished by an attack across Ford B. I'll just mention that if this was the Custer that I have read about, and the timing that I have used is correct, Custer, in an attempt to synchronize his attack with that of Reno, would have never retreated from the ford without a greater amount of fighting than indicated, and he wouldn't have moved to the north. In his attack, Custer would have used at least two of his companies to move against the warriors and possibly one to cordon off the noncombatants.

The authorities say that if Custer was shot at the ford, Keogh would have:

> ... assumed that role for the right wing. Cooke, as regimental adjutant, would have then accompanied him throughout the fight. This did not happen as Cooke's body was found with Custer on last stand knoll. In addition, Keogh as the commander of the wing would have probably opted for a defensive position while trying to determine what Custer's overall plan was or would have pulled back in the direction where Reno's command was last seen. It is also highly doubtful, in this situation, if he would have ordered an advance to the north away from his support where the main column was later found.[34]

The arguments presented are cursory and paradoxical. I have not found any compelling evidence that two companies were sent to the ford, whether under the command of Captain Keogh or Captain Yates. As I have tried to point out throughout my writings, this would be uncharacteristic of Custer, especially under the conditions that existed. Some have said that since Captain Keogh was the senior commander he would have been in charge of the two companies going to the ford to scout out the ford and village. I think to even accept a scenario like the one proposed by Liddic or other writers you have to admit they don't think Custer was much of a commander. If they admit this and bring out their reasons (not just using the actions they hypothetically attribute to him), then I will accept their scenario. I also am not going back through the timing distortions, but you may realize why I say the relative positions of Reno and Custer, after separating on Reno Creek, is an essential determination. And in rejecting my arguments you need to come right out and say Martin lied. Don't use Benteen's remark, as so many writers have, to dismiss Martin's statements. Benteen said Martin was "just as much cut out for a cavalryman as he was for a king." [35]

Why do I reject the Keogh/Cooke adjutant argument used to refute that Custer was shot at the ford? Their argument actually supports my theory of events and that Custer was shot at the ford. Keogh would not have gone to the ford ahead of, or with Custer; instead he was placed in charge of the reserve force that amongst other duties was waiting for Benteen and the packs to arrive. After Custer was shot, the retreat from the ford was disorganized. Keogh's reserve force attempted to aid the retreating troops, some of which moved to the north while other members fell back to Keogh's reserves. Adjutant Cooke would have stayed with a severely wounded Custer in a move to the north, thereby ending on Last Stand Hill.

The other major reason used to reject the claim that Custer was shot at Ford B was the state of Custer's body when found on Last Stand Hill. Custer had two gunshot wounds, one in the head and the other in the chest, both of which were considered to be fatal. However. it is said the one in the head had blood around it while the chest wound didn't. This is considered proof that Custer was already dead when the chest wound was inflicted. Consequently Custer was alive, and supposedly fighting until he was shot in the head. I would agree that if there was blood on Custer's head and none near the chest wound that he wasn't shot in the head at the ford for several reasons. (1)The head wound would have killed him immediately, so my theory that the movement to the north from Medicine Tail Coulee was triggered by an attempt to get Custer to the steamboat Far West would not have taken place. My theory is based on my believe that the only sound reason for failing to attack across Ford B would be to get a wounded Custer to the steamboat where he could receive better and safer medical attention. (2) The Lacotah, White Cow Bull and the Cheyenne, Bobtail Horse claimed the man leading the troops was shot in the chest, and then fell in the river. The chest wound would not have been immediately fatal. One could then reason that Dr. Lord, Tom Custer, and other officers would have felt Custer's only chance was to get him to the Far West. This for whatever reason was prevented and they ended up on Last Stand Hill. Custer would still have been alive but unable to defend himself. The head wound was more likely to have been fired by an officer than by an Indian in order to prevent a wounded Custer from being captured .

Several reasons could explain the lack of blood by the orifices of the chest wound. Bullets of that period were referred to as "hot" bullets. These bullets, in contrast to those of today, traveled in a straight line through the body rather than having a tumbling or twisting effect. The bullets were referred to as "hot" because of their cauterizing effect. The path of the bullet would have been important. The bleeding could also been affected by Custer falling in the water, and most likely Dr. Lord would have been called and he would have cleaned the wound while creating pressure on the orifices along with applying a cold compress. All of which combined with the time exposure the body suffered could have prevented any signs of bleeding.

If White Cow Bull or Bobtail Horse shot someone other than Custer, or if they were lying it still doesn't answer the primary question: If Custer hadn't been shot at the ford why didn't he launch an attack at Ford B? Why would Custer have moved to the north when time was essential. Noncombatants or the village location is not a logical answer.

Timing is important in any analysis, but considering the situation in the Indian camp, there is no sound reason why Custer is not leading an attack. To have him taking his time, going down coulees leading away from the village, passing up a key lookout, and then going out of his way to observe a ford crossing when time is of the essence, lacks logic. Would he lead an attack with two companies or would he use three? Is he expecting aid from Benteen and the packs? Yes, he is. Would Custer expect Benteen and the packs when they arrived to grasp the situation and what his plans were? No, I don't think Custer would think that, so I believe he would have placed one or two companies in reserve. Where would he have sent them and who would he have likely placed in charge of them with the information he would want Benteen and the packs to receive when they arrived? I believe there is more reason to assign your senior officer to that position then Captain Yates. Custer would be leading three or four companies to the ford, so it was not necessary to take the senior officer; in fact he should be placed in charge of the more independent command. Therefore if Custer was shot at the ford, Adjutant Cooke would have been in no position to align with Captain Keogh. This would be particularly true if the retreat was disorganized, as I believe it was. So again the main questions are: Why didn't Custer attack at Ford B? Why did they retreat as soon as they did? And why move to the north? I have already given my reasons why there were shell casings found at Luce Ridge and at Nye Cartwright Ridge.

Liddic, in attempting to refute my position says if Keogh was in charge he would not have moved to the north, but instead would have set up a defensive position or moved to the south to join up with his support. This actually confirms the position that I have taken. It is true that this is what he should have done if he took over command at the ford, in that same sense it is what Custer should have done. If he was still in command, why didn't he do it? Do you really think he would have gone to the north in an attempt to encircle the noncombatants? This, as I have continually attempted to point out, is one of the two major questions of the battle. What this indicates is that Keogh was not sent to the ford with two companies. Reno should have been fighting in the valley, and Custer should have been attempting to synchronize an attack in support of Reno. Custer's basic plan would be to defeat the Indians. Custer would have taken at least three companies, under his control, to the ford, and left Keogh with most likely two companies in a reserve capacity. In other words, the evidence they try to use to say that Custer was not shot at the ford and was still in command, actually proves the opposite. If the situation was as Liddic and the authorities believe, then Custer (assuming he was a good commander) would have done what Liddic says Keogh would have done.

Liddic says there were three major points of view concerning Custer's troop movement to the ford:

> 1) The soldiers didn't go near the river, but turned north out of Medicine Tail About a half mile from the ford. 2) The soldiers went right up to the river's eastern bank, but somehow were forced to retreat to the ridges where they were to die. 3) The soldiers rode to the river, and a number of them crossed over, engaged in a brief but light firefight with the Indians and pulled back the way they came…. I believe the majority of accounts both red and white, combined with physical evidence found in the area, support number three. [36]

I would both agree and disagree with Liddic. He mentions that there were numerous minor adjustments in different writers interpretations. I would be more apt to support number 2, and the inference that there was a brief firefight, and there might have been one or two soldiers that actually crossed, but not a number of them. In both 2 and 3 there is no real reason for the pull back.

Liddic then says, "But it wasn't the overwhelming number of Indians, along with their determination and fire power which caused the soldiers at the river's banks to move back: it was Custer, himself, who ordered their withdrawal."[37]

I would agree with Liddic that it wasn't the number of Indians at the ford. I think it was because Custer was shot which stopped their attack, and then the number of Indians now moving to the ford, plus officers' desire to aid Custer that caused a retreat, and like too many retreats became disorganized. I do wonder, in Liddic's version, how Custer got there from Luce Ridge to order the withdrawal.

Liddic brings out a number of Indian accounts of the action or lack of action around the ford. I like in particular his reference to Low Dog's remarks:

> … Low Dog knew it was not any action taken by the Indians at the ford which caused the white man to back away. The soldiers started to cross the river and were going to ride into the village but "Custer changed his mind and moved off." The Indian accounts further state there were few warriors at the ford when the troops arrived. It was only after the soldiers had left that the warriors were joined by many others who rode away from the Reno fight to meet the new threat posed by this second group of white men.[38]

There are several things I like about the Oglalla's remarks and Liddic's recognition that Indian accounts refer to only a few warriors at the ford when the troops arrive. One has to assume, at this time, by Liddic's accounts that Custer is at the ford and causes the troop withdrawal. He has had Custer at Luce Ridge, and as Liddic soon brings out he still does.

If one analyzes the above accounts it shows that Custer was retreating at the same time Reno would have been retreating. It wasn't until Reno retreated that the Indians attacking him would have left and they had several miles to go to reach the ford area. We should remember that in Martin's account he saw Custer retreating at the same time Reno was still fighting in the valley. Martin's remarks are brushed off but shouldn't be.

Liddic's reason for Custer's retreat can be summed up in his following statement:

> … and the commander had to use what force he had to chase after the fleeing village. Yates' battalion was now on traditional Luce Ridge with Custer. Custer ordered Yates to dismount a company and prepare to volley fire in

response to the Indians who were seen advancing from the hills to the south-west in the direction of where Reno retreated.… Custer then directed Yates' buglers to sound "recall" in preparation for the move against the non-combatants.[39]

Custer is not at the ford as he is still a mile back on Luce Ridge but he is able to stop the attack. Why does he stop the attack even though there are not too many warriors at the ford? He stops the attack because he can see through the smoke, tepees, trees, and cutbanks that the noncombatants are fleeing to the northwest. The rugged terrain to the north doesn't deter him for he knows that he will be able to find a ford and cut off the noncombatants. Shouldn't he be afraid, since, according to Liddic, Reno has retreated that the noncombatants will turn back to the southwest and join the warriors? Wouldn't it be better, since there weren't too many warriors at the ford, to charge through the village and cut the noncombatants off from the warriors? Wouldn't this be more apt to cause the warriors to surrender? And, isn't this the attack minded Custer?

You students provide the answers.

I maintain that Custer went to Weir Point, and that Reno would have been just starting down the valley. Custer went down Western Coulee to Medicine Tail Coulee, during which time Reno's troops went into action. Mitch Bouyer and the three Crows met Custer while Curley remained on the ridge. Martin was sent back with his message to Benteen. Custer would have gone to the ford with at least three companies. He would have kept one or two companies in reserve. As a consensus of Indians bring out there were not many warriors at the ford as his troops arrived. The village was in a turmoil. As firing began more warriors rushed to the ford. However, Custer could have charged through the village, as his initial plan was designed back at the division of the command. He would be supporting Reno who was still fighting in the valley, and at the same time he could have cut off the noncombatants from the warriors. This poses the main question concerning the battle. Why Custer didn't attack at Ford B? My only answer is that something happened to the commander.

Liddic brings out numerous Indian accounts and attempts to weave them into a coherent sequence. He has Custer leaving Luce Ridge:

… and was riding to the north to link up with Keogh's battalion, already occupying a high point to the north, to begin the pursuit of the noncomba-tants. Some of these noncombatants were fleeing west toward the Big Horn Mountains and others were moving to the north.… Custer led the troops to what we now call Blummer–(Nye) Cartwright Ridge.[40]

I'm afraid this doesn't make sense to me. I wondered how Custer stopped the attack, but I will assume by bugle calls or couriers he was able to. Considering the situation at the ford and the terrain to the north I cannot understand how he thought he would capture the noncombatants, and particularly since he already knew Reno had retreated, and Benteen and the packs should be joining him. The area west of the river was left to the Indians—wouldn't one think the warriors and the noncombatants would join up. The warriors would provide harassment to the crossing troops while the Indians did what Custer was afraid would happen—they would scatter. Custer still had to cross Nye-Cartwright, Deep Coulee, the bluffs and terrain to the north, find a ford and begin to chase or corner the Indians. The warriors would certainly have been waiting for him at any ford, as the movement west of the river was much easier to travel than that to the east. But this is the scenario the authorities have came up with.

I am also bothered by the fact that writers attempt to act as if the command is still intact and under the command of Custer and its officers. Is a sound defense set up which was easily recognized by Terry's and Reno's troops when they arrived? Not that I am aware of. From what John Stands In Timber said,[41] and others, they would have had time. Was there a tactical retreat attempted? Not that there was any physical signs of, or testimony by the Indians. In most cases as shown by Godfrey's company's ability to stop the Indians in Reno's retreat from Weir Point, if Custer's five companies were still under officers' control, it should have been able to have been accomplished. Why wasn't there signs of either a defense or a tactical retreat? When did the company commanders leave their companies to join Custer on Last Stand Hill? And the coterie still doesn't attempt to explain the time differences. Most Indian and white accounts would have had the Custer part of the battle over in two hours, but Liddic has Custer leaving Nye Cartwright and it is now about 5 o'clock"[42]

SOURCES

1.   Graham, 140

2.   Camp, 118.

3.   Ibid., 101.

4.   Liddic, 100, 101.

5.   Ibid., 101.

6. Ibid., 104.

7. Taylor, 177.

8. Liddic, 106.

9. Ibid., 106.

10. Barnard, *Ten Years With Custer—A 7th Cavalryman's Memoirs, 279.*

11. Liddic, 107.

12. Ibid., 107.

13. Ibd., 107.

14. Ibid., 89.

15. Ibid., 107.

16. Graham, 63.

17. Overfield II, 43, 44.

18. Graham, 75.

19. Ibid., 111.

20. Reno Court, 304.

21. Camp, 92.

22. Graham, 180.

23. Ibid., 110.

24. Camp, 201.

25. Vestal, *Warpath*, 191–195.

26. Miller, *American Heritage,* June1971.

27. Marquis, *She Watched Custer's Last Battle,* (Booklet).

28. Speech sent to John Collier, Commissioner of Indian Affairs, 1940.

29. Marquis, (Booklet).

30. Miller, *American Heritage,* June 1971, *Custer's Fall,* 124, 125.

31. Camp, 207.

32. J. L. Beardsley *Outdoor Life,* March, 1933.

33. Liddic, 109.

34. Ibid., 111.

35. Graham, 180.

36. Liddic, 111.

37. Ibid., 111.

38. Ibid., 112.

39. Ibid., 112.

40. Ibid., 112.

41. 41 John Stands In Timber, *Cheyenne Memories,* 199.

42. Liddic, 117.

9

BENTEEN JOINS RENO

Liddic does his usual fine work in bringing out the various questions and differing opinions that have faced battle enthusiasts once Benteen arrived on Reno Hill. Most of the questions are not important for this study. The conflicting views as to whether Benteen, after joining Reno, was still under direct orders from Custer or rather, having showed the orders to Reno he was no longer bound by the orders are questions that, as Liddic points out, military men differ on. We know that it was quite some time before either Reno or Benteen went to investigate the firing that they undoubtedly heard from the Custer battlefield. Even then it took an unordered movement by Captain Weir to instigate the overall attempt. Liddic brings out the differing testimony of the officers as to the actions taken on the hill before they made the move, but doesn't connect it to any central cover-up.

Essentially what writers have failed to do is recognize the need to cover-up the time period involved. There is no question that there should have been an immediate attempt to support Custer—even if they hadn't heard gunfire. They knew Custer was attempting to flank the Indians; any denial was mere rationalizing. Whether they would have helped save any of Custer's men or whether they would have all been wiped out was immaterial. That they should have made the attempt could not have been denied, whether from a military or humane standpoint.

Liddic's discourse on what transpired after Benteen joined Reno emphasizes what I consider to be the failure of the authorities who have written about the battle. There is no understanding that the time concerning the actions taken during this period needed to be changed, and this was the second major cover-up at the Reno Court. The orders Custer gave was the first and most important. Both the orders Reno and Benteen received and the time of events had to be covered-up in order to prevent a court-martial of Reno. The honor of the 7th Cavalry and the army was also at stake. This failure by the authorities to perceive these cover-ups and their effect on the established views of Custer and the battle is the reason for this book.

The reported time differences of individual actions on Reno Hill and their relation to the overall time gap cover-up need to be recognized. The major one is the time gap closure between when Reno retreated, Benteen arrived, when the packs did, and the time when they went to investigate the firing from the Custer battlefield. An essence of any study should be to account for the difference between the early time reports and those that were used at the Reno Court. It is necessary to be aware of the essential need to take up time, and to extend or manipulate certain actions. The times from the morning of the 25th until those used to investigate the firing needed to be altered. The times given for when they went to investigate the firing are essentially correct since there were too many participants who were aware the move took place late in the afternoon. This made it even more important to change the earlier times. Reno's move down the valley, his fighting time, Benteen's and the packs arrival all of these times had to be moved forward, and this was accomplished with the support of the three primary officers. For most officers it would simply be a matter of staying away from giving specific times, saying that they weren't sure or they didn't look at their watches, and as long as Reno, Benteen, and Wallace agreed on specific times the Court would accept their version. Acceptance was no problem since the Court desired an acquittal. An enlisted man, civilian, or scout might differ, but this wouldn't offset officer's testimony.

It is necessary to recognize the importance of these time changes for both Reno and Benteen. If it was only Reno alone the officers might not have supported a cover-up, but when you added Benteen to the mix along with the 7th Cavalry's image and the armies' self interests, then the officers would and did support the change.

There remains one constant, which is the approximate time that Reno's troops moved to investigate the firing heard from the Custer battlefield. You couldn't allow a two and a half to three hour time difference from Benteen's arrival to when this movement took place. Benteen's arrival time had to be changed from about 2:30 to a later time. Then you still needed to have the packs arrival time at a much later period in order to fill the gap.

Girard's testimony at the Reno Court must be called into question. He was the main witness that Whittaker and other critics of Reno were counting on. However, his testimony was subject to coercion and army pressure. This is indicated when he changed his time statements. It is unlikely that he failed to remember the time when he looked at his watch. His changing this time doesn't ring true since he would have had to go to the court officials and say he made a timing mistake, and that he was at least an hour off. I can't see him doing this. What it strongly implies is that the army went to him, and we know they had things they could hold over his head. I realize that the Recorder's brief depended on Girard's testimony. Lee's whole case rested on Reno's early flight from the valley which released the warriors in time to return and overwhelm Custer's troops. To establish any semblance of an argument it was necessary for Custer to have been recognized on the ridge but still far enough back that Reno's flight, along with the short period of time that Girard claimed Reno fought in the valley, enabled the warriors to return in overwhelming numbers to defeat Custer.

Girard was asked the following questions:

Q. What time of day was it when the command [Reno's] left the woods?

A. I should say about 1 o'clock.

Q. How do you know that?

A. I was sitting in the timber with Lieutenant DeRudio and the command had then been gone for some little time and I pulled out my watch and it was ten minutes past 1 o'clock.[1]

What time did Sgt. Kanipe remember Major Reno reaching Ford A? Wasn't it about 12 o'clock?[2] And don't forget the "abouts." What time did Trumpeter Martin say Custer saw the Indian village from the high point? Wasn't it about 12 o'clock?[3] What were the official times Reno gave in his report following the battle? Then in an earlier report Captain Benteen said he was at the morass about 1 o'clock.[4] He said his horse at the walk could cover 5 miles in an hour.[5] He should have been within 7 miles of Reno Hill. Would it have taken him until 3:30 to 4 p.m., as he later maintained to have reached Reno Hill?

Then one should apply to the general timing analysis Martin's statement that after receiving his message to take to Benteen, it took him about ten or fifteen minutes to get back to where Custer saw the village. Martin said that Benteen, when he pointed out where Martin received Custer's message, indicated that it was about 600 yards from Ford B.[6] Many have expressed the opinion that they doubted if Benteen ever said that, but I think it is substantiated by Benteen himself when, at the Reno Court, his answer to the question of whether Martin said on which side of the river General Custer's column was: "Not at that time. He did after we had reached that **highest point** (my emphasis) at the figure "7." He then pointed out the place from which he had been sent back."[7] The ten or fifteen minutes back to where Custer viewed the village would have enabled Martin to have reached Weir Point but not the lookout position on Sharpshooter's Ridge from where Liddic said Custer viewed the village. And is it really necessary to bring out all the references to the highest point as being Weir Point? Lest we forget, remember that Martin said he saw Reno still in action in the valley as he continued on in his search for Benteen. Where would that have placed Custer before Reno had established his skirmish line? Custer in order to see a peaceful village would have been ahead of Reno. One could also recall Dr. Paulding's letter to his mother, and Captain Thompson's to Attorney Goldin.

After the Defense had set a later time for when the regiment was divided, it then made Reno's "charge" to the bluffs and Benteen's arrival time later, but there was still too much of a gap before they went to check on Custer. It then became necessary to extend the packs arrival time. One method of doing this was to use the necessity of waiting for all of the packs to arrive. Major Reno stated this numerous times. The packs were under the protection of an enlarged company commanded by Captain McDougall, and once Reno's troopers had replenished their ammo, there shouldn't have been any excuse for them not going to aid Custer. However, as Liddic said, even the time the first ammo packs were sent for and when they arrived were subject to different interpretations. Liddic brings out whitewashes by the various officers and justifiably accuses Lt. Hare of his share. However, earlier reports along with non-pressure reports to Camp and others are more likely to be accurate than those that took place at the Reno Court.

The following is a good example of my criticism of Liddic and his failure to make connections between underlying reasons for the actions or statements reported at the Court:

> … As for Hare, he confused the chronology of events on Reno Hill by ignoring Reno's half hour absence, as he told Walter Camp, about ten minutes after Benteen came up, Reno sent him to the packs. His confusion (deliberate distortion?) becomes readily apparent when one reads what Reno, himself, told the Court of Inquiry. When asked what orders were sent to the pack train, Reno replied that after he returned from examining Hodgson's body, the pack train still wasn't up. "I could not make myself omnipresent. I sent him (Hare) to the pack train to hurry it up all he could. At the time, it was not in sight."[8]

One should add that Hare in his report to Camp said, "Benteen came up about 10 minutes after Reno got to top of bluffs …, about 10 minutes later Hare went for ammunition. Pack train about a mile from Reno Hill.[9] This correlates with testimony by the two orderlies, Martin and Davern.

The major officers were the ones being protected at the Reno Court, so I wouldn't be too quick to jump on testimony by the minor officers, especially statements that were not made at the Reno Court. And I certainly would be leery in using Reno's or Benteen's testimony to rebuff them. My conclusion is that Lt. Hare was correct in regards to the arrival of the packs, and the necessity to wait for them was part of the major timing cover-up. Here are some of my reasons.

According to both Reno and Benteen the packs were not in sight. Several times during his testimony Benteen said the packs were 7 miles back. They must not have left the morass. You have a fairly good view back along Reno Creek from Reno Hill, so the statement is odd in itself. However, I will ignore that, but what I don't think can be ignored or rejected by Liddic and others is the following testimony by Martin and Davern at the Reno Court. Martin's testimony:

Q. You say Captain Benteen gave you an order to go to Captain McDougall?

A. Yes sir.

Q. Did you start right off?

A. Yes, sir.

Q. How far did you go to find Captain McDougall?

A. About 150 yards.

Q. Captain McDougall himself was in front of his troops?

A. Yes sir.

Q. How were the packs?

A. They were pretty well together.

Q. What did you say to Captain McDougall?

A. I said Captain Benteen, sends his compliments and wanted him to bring up the packs, and not get too far behind, and to keep them well closed up.

Q. Then what did you do?

A. I went back to my company and took my position on the left of it.

Q. Did Captain McDougall close up the packs then?

A. Yes sir.

◆   ◆   ◆

Q. How fast were the packs moving when you went back to Captain McDougall?

A. Some walking, some running, and some trotting.

◆   ◆   ◆

Q. How long did you have to wait till the packs came up?

A. Probably ten or fifteen minutes. I mean the packs made a long string and in 15 minutes everything was up.

◆   ◆   ◆

Q. Can you tell how long it was after the packs moved up till the command moved down the river?

A. I think about an hour and a half. We waited for some men from the bottom, and then moved out together.[11]

Liddic attempts to discount Martin's testimony because after forty years he recanted his remarks to Colonel Graham. I am sure that when he heard that Benteen denied sending him back he would have claimed the Court misinterpreted what he said. Can anyone explain how the above questions and answers could have been misconstrued, particularly when what he said would have been antithetical to the Defenses and the Court's position? If there had been any probing into Martin's or the officers' testimony as to the packs' location, the Court would have had to charge Reno with a court martial offense. As I have said, the questioning of Martin was pathetic. There were no questions as to orders Custer gave, even to Reno let alone to Benteen.

Martin's pathetic questioning could only be matched by that of Private Davern, Reno's orderly. At first they used leading questions which attempted to make it appear that Lt. Wallace was by Reno's side when he received the orders from

Custer. Then there was continual questioning on matters of time, not to ascertain the correct time of events, but to make it appear that he had little actual knowledge concerning the time. Since Davern had said Cooke's orders to Reno indicated that Benteen would have similar orders and that he was to support Reno on his left, most of the questioning was to show that Davern was not really aware of any orders being sent to Benteen, and that he had no idea of where Benteen was. Reno's counsel in his summation used Davern's lack of knowledge of Benteen and his whereabouts to dismiss his remarks. (Note my addendum.) Why was it necessary to discount Davern's account? The following questions should provide an answer:

Q. Were you closer to Major Reno than Lieutenant Wallace was?

A. I don't know whether I was or not.

Q. Were not Lieutenants Wallace, Hodgson and Hare near enough to hear the order?

A. They might have been.

Q. Were they not as well placed to hear the order as you were?

A. They might have been.

Q. You saw no effort to carry the order to Captain Benteen?

A. No, sir.

◆   ◆   ◆

Q. What time do you think Major Reno's column reached the top of the hill from the bottom?

A. I think it was between two and three o'clock.

Q. Do you think it was before or after 3?

A. I think it was before.

Q. And remained there how long do you think?

A. They remained there about two hours.

Q. That would bring it to about 5 o'clock?

A. Yes, sir.

◆   ◆   ◆

Q. What time do you suppose Major Reno's command crossed the river to go to the timber?

A. About 1 o'clock, maybe after 1.

◆   ◆   ◆

Q. Could you see the pack train when you came on the hill?

A. Yes sir.

Q. How far off was it?

A. 50 or 100 yards. I went to speak to a sergeant of my company in charge of a part of the pack train.

[They then asked him questions if he had seen Lt. Hare go for the packs and he said he didn't.]

Q. Did you say the pack train reached there 15 minutes after Major Reno reached there?

A. No, sir.

◆   ◆   ◆

Q. Was Captain Benteen there when you came up?

A. Captain Weir was there I don't recollect Captain Benteen?

Q. The pack train was how far away?

A. The advance was on the hill when I got there.

◆   ◆   ◆

[As to when Captain Weir went to open communication with General Custer.]

Q. How long was that after the pack train came up?

A. Between one and two hours.

Q. Do you mean two hours after you crossed the stream, or two hours after you got on the hill?

A. Two hours after I got on the hill.[12]

Major Reno: "I went to the river after Benteen arrived … I was gone about a half hour. [To find Hodgson.] … In about an hour the packs arrived.[13]

As I have said when the highest point is brought out it refers to Weir Point. The following statements by Benteen illustrate this point:

Q. Was there any movement ordered from that position downstream after your arrival that afternoon? If so describe it.

A. No, sir, there was no movement ordered that I know of. I went down the same direction that Captain Weir had gone to the highest point of land and had the troops by file on the river bluffs,

◆   ◆   ◆

Q. Describe your movement to that point, the location of the country and everything you saw?

A. That was my first sight of the village after I arrived at that high point. That was the only point from which it could be seen and I saw, as I supposed, about 1800 tepees.

Q. When you joined Major Reno on the hill, state how far the pack train was away.

A. It was not then in sight. I suppose it was 7 or 8 miles off then.

Q. State how long after you joined him on the hill was it that the pack train or any part of it arrived?

A. I should think it was an hour and a quarter, or an hour and a half before it arrived.[14]

Can you really tell me that there was no attempt to cover-up time? And isn't it clear why the time had to be changed?

In his official report Reno had Benteen arriving about 2:30 p.m., "and in a short time the pack train came up," but at the Reno Court it was another hour and a quarter or hour and a half before the packs arrived. Even though the packers said the ammo boxes weren't opened,[15] Lt. Wallace said some were, so we, of course, know they were opened. The officers didn't distort the facts or lie. All of this took some time and when they were about ready to check on the firing they saw some men coming up from the valley so they waited for them. The hour and a half to two hour gap from when Benteen arrived is now taken care of. Reno had to wait for the packs before he went to check on the firing that had been heard some two hours before, which had ceased except for some sporadic firing.

What is frustrating with Liddic and other authorities is they are aware that in the case of the ammo, Reno's troops really did not need it. Liddic said: "This wait for ammunition is even more suspect because even with the availability of 4000 additional rounds, Reno still didn't order an advance, as now he decided to wait for the rest of the pack train. Culbertson said it was because of the wounded that Reno waited for the entire pack train to arrive. "The troops simply had no way to move the wounded who were not able to ride without blankets to carry them upon."[16] This rationalizing doesn't negate the fact that Custer had sent orders for their support, gunfire had been heard, the packs had arrived, and that going to find Hodgson body should not have taken precedence over the orders and gunfire. What does it take to recognize the Court was a cover-up? Colonel Merritt was right when he said that the officers wouldn't tell them anything, and Captain Carter was right that there was no probing questions or third degree directed at the officers by the Recorder and the Court officials.

Liddic makes the following appropriate remark, but again there is no connection with basic premises. He says of Benteen, "One guess is as good as another as to what Benteen really saw, heard or did during the campaign."[17] Liddic also mentions that "Weir moved out about five minutes before he was followed by his company, thus it was about quarter after five when 'D' started north."[18] Doesn't the evidence indicate that while Custer's troops were being slaughtered, Reno's and Benteen's forces were sitting on Reno Hill for at least two hours, for no good reason?

Liddic makes several interesting points. Liddic is not going to give up on Sharpshooters' Ridge being the high point that one goes to. He says:

> After Weir left Reno Hill, he moved to the first high ground in sight, which is Sharpshooters' Ridge, to try and see what was the situation to the north. After he saw what he could, which wasn't much, Weir noticed the tracks from Custer's battalion and followed them. About a quarter mile past this ridge, he saw the tracks changed from a company front and turned to the east. Weir and his orderly then rode for the high twin peaks which today bear his name.[19]

What is interesting is not only that Weir first goes to Sharpshooters' Ridge, but also that he couldn't see much. From what Liddic has said, he should have been able to see the village and the warriors moving to the ford and the noncombatants fleeing. Liddic, in putting down Mr. Sklenar's interpretation that Weir never went to the Weir Peaks, said:

> If one reads the testimony of Hare, he said that Weir's troops were on "the highest point around," which describes Weir Point, not Sharpshooters' Ridge.... DeRudio left no doubt as to Weir Point as "it was the highest point down the stream.[20]

We should remember Martin referring to the highest point. With all these references to it being the highest point, and that it was the only place you could see the full village, it is hard to imagine why Custer would not have gone there. Or is it possible that he did?

"It was a little after 5:45 PM when Edgerly led Company "D" up the slopes of Weir's Point, arriving up over the projection in front of Weir as he was on the "second peak farthest north."[21]

Liddic spends the rest of his Chapter 9, *The Trip To Weir Point*, on who ordered the retreat, and the fighting that occurred until they set up their defense at Reno Hill. The basic question during this period is whether Custer was still fighting at the time Reno's command arrived on and below Weir Point. The consensus of Liddic's remarks would indicate that the fighting would have ended. I would certainly agree. I think it is apparent, not only by the officers' denials, but by a study of Indian accounts. Indians indicate that not only was the fighting over, but that the fighting did not last over an hour or two. The differences would usually depend on when the particular Indian joined the battle. I would accept Kate Bighead's statement that the Cheyenne took care of their dead that afternoon.

My main reasoning would center around the timing cover-ups. As I have brought out Custer was retreating while Reno was still fighting in the valley. You add an hour to two hours on to that and the Custer battle would have been over. I would question Benteen's remarks on any subject, but I would have to agree with him that I don't think there was any evidence of a defensive stand. Neither the physical signs or the Indian accounts do not indicate that there was one.

Liddic has added to my conception of one person, even though it is somewhat reversed from Liddic's. The person is Lt. Hare. I have thought it was interesting that Hare, after the battle, never wanted to talk to anybody about the battle, even years afterwards. I have surmised that it was because he was aware of the orders Custer sent to Benteen by way of the Sgt. Major and the Indian Stabbed. However, Liddic has made me realize the part he played in the Reno Court cover-ups. After the killing of Reno's Adjutant Hodgson, Lt. Hare took over that position. He was involved then in the orders or lack of orders Reno gave. Reno's Defense placed him along with Wallace and Hodgson next to Reno when he received his orders from Custer. Yet according to Lt. Varnum both Hare and Wallace were with him as they moved down the valley ahead of Reno. As his testimony to Camp brought out he would have lied at the Reno Court as to the essential timing cover-up with the packs. He was the one other officer besides Wallace who would have known that Custer had sent orders to Benteen by way of the Sgt. Major and he undoubtedly assigned Stabbed to go with Sharrow. I now believe Hare had to have been in on the Defenses' strategy sessions along with at least Reno, Benteen, and Wallace.

The two most important question still stand out. Why didn't Custer attack across Ford B, and why did his command move to the North?

SOURCES

1. Reno Court, 96.

2. Camp, 92.

3. Reno Court, 304.

4. Graham, 180.

5. Reno Court 432.

6.   Camp, 105.

7.   Reno Court, 432.

8.   Liddic, 123.

9.   Camp, 66.

10. Reno Court, 391, 392.

11. Ibid., 361, 362, 363, 364.

12. Ibid., 563, 566.

13. Ibid., 408, 409.

14. Ibid., 407, 408.

15. Liddic, 124.

16. Ibid., 125.

17. Ibid., 126.

18. Ibid., 131.

10

THE FINAL STAGE

What happened in the final stages of the battle that resulted in the destruction of Custer's five companies is primarily a matter of conjecture. I will try to summarize the main points of Liddic's version of why Custer moved to the north and why he failed to obtain his objectives. Liddic's view is similar to the accepted view of the main writers:

> Custer's command arrived at the Last Stand area under their own volition for a specific purpose; the main column was intact, had suffered very few casualties, and the companies were under the control of their officers and non-commissioned officers.

> It was before five o'clock when Custer arrived in the vicinity of Calhoun Hill. It had been about 45 minutes since he had dispatched Keogh's battalion to Ford B. Custer had seen nothing during that charge, the subsequent recall, or his own action on Nye (Blummer)-Cartwright Ridge that indicated that the warriors had changed or even threatened to change, to an aggressive posture. It still appeared the warriors were only interested in delaying his movements so the noncombatants could escape.[1]

I have already given my reasons for disagreeing with Liddic's scenario as stated above, so I will only briefly state my differences here. Timing is off, and this constitutes a major cover-up. Custer led at least three companies to Ford B in order to attack the village, support Reno, and cut off the noncombatants. Statements by the last of the primary sources to have been with Custer, along with a consensus of remarks by scouts and warriors, support this premise. It is also backed by an analysis of Custer's psyche and his military intelligence.

If the following conjectural scenario of Custer's Last Stand, as portrayed by Liddic and many of the authorities, was to stand up to any rational analysis, I would have to accept the fact that Custer was a stupid (I can't get away from that word) commander.

The following is my summary and critique of the scenario presented by Liddic: Custer sends Keogh and two companies to Ford B. There are only a few Indians at the ford; the village is in an uproar; women are looking for their children, those that have found theirs, along with other noncombatants, are taking down tepees, grabbing belongings, and fleeing to the northwest. Warriors have left to attack Reno and many are still preparing or just on their way. Reno has retreated. However, Custer, according to Liddic, has seen nothing "that indicated that the warriors had changed or even threatened to change, to an aggressive posture."[2] In support of this view Foolish Elk, an Oglalla, recalled that most of the Indians were still catching their horses when Custer moved back from the ford.[3]

Even though there were not many Indians at the ford and they were not in an aggressive mood, the attack-minded Custer decides to retreat. Custer does this because from Nye Cartwright Ridge he can see that the village is being evacuated. There then is no sense in attacking the warriors that are still there, for as Foolish Elk said most of the Indians were still catching their horses, nor should they attempt to separate them from the noncombatants that are fleeing to the northwest

What I find intriguing is that Reno had already retreated, and yet the Indians were not in an aggressive mood. The Indians were either awfully slow in going to attack Reno, or Reno must not have even bothered to set up a skirmish line. Wouldn't Foolish Elks' statement be more likely to indicate that Reno was still fighting in the valley?

Custer's troops have now retreated to the Calhoun Hill location and Custer has his officers assemble. It is now that he informs his officers that encircling the noncombatants will be his objective. This assembling of the officers brings out that the regiment was still intact and under officer control. The only person that I know of that indicated an officer meeting was the Crow scout Curley. I have spent some time in bringing out, not only a map by Curley presented to Richard Upton from Michael Reynolds, but statements which indicate that he would not have been around in order to see any meeting near Calhoun Hill. The meeting he mentions would have taken place near Ford B by some officers after Mitch Bouyer came down from the bluffs and explained that Reno had now gone into action. Bouyer had already dismissed Curley, and Custer now allowed the other Crow scouts to be released. The Crows would have gone to Bouyer's Bluff and fired on the Indians as Custer moved to the ford. When Custer retreated they then fled back to where they met Benteen. Reno was retreating at that time.

Liddic now states that Custer probably didn't understand the nuances of the terrain to the north and west, which made it very formidable.[4] This brings out

Custer's military brilliance: instead of moving down a comparably open terrain to the best ford in the area, with few warriors to protect it, he retreats a mile and then moves across an unsuitable terrain that he has little knowledge of in order to cut off some noncombatants which he could have done an hour earlier.

> Custer's plan was both offensive and defensive. He was going to use Calhoun Hill as his base. This would give him the position to hold a corridor open for Benteen. Custer's overriding concern was the escape of the Indians, especially the noncombatants. And to this end, Custer remained committed to offensive operations until he realized how wrong his judgment was in both the temperament, determination, and number of his foe.[5]

What is nice to know is that his five companies are still intact and while Keogh and Calhoun are holding the base at Calhoun Hill, Custer is taking Yates' battalion and going after the noncombatants. However, Custer hasn't judged the determination and number of his foe. If Custer had only gone to Weir Point he could have been aware of the size of the village, and if, as Liddic and most of the authorities believe, Reno was already in action (Martin and the Crows must have distorted or lied about Custer having seen a peaceful village), Custer then should have been aware of the number of Indians he would be facing.

> Bouyer had probably told Custer about the ford near the present iron railroad bridge … (Ford D.) These advanced troopers now met up with heavy resistance from the Indians who had raced ahead … Custer finally realized he had misread the situation. It wasn't just the noncombatants who were this far north of the village, but also hundreds of warriors who had rushed downstream to oppose his movement.[6]

Really! I thought that when Keogh was at the ford Custer had decided to go after the noncombatants and that is why he had Keogh retreat. At that time, according to Liddic, he knew Reno had retreated, and many of the warriors were still preparing to fight Reno. Custer's plans, after he heard from Girard via Cooke, was to support Reno by flanking the Indians. When Custer heard that Benteen was back on the trail he expected, or should have, that the Indians attacking Reno would leave when they heard of his threat to their village. This then was where the main battle would take place, and that is why he wanted Benteen and the packs to hurry to aid him, instead of following his original plan which had Benteen crossing the Little Big Horn and being on Reno's left.

I differ with Liddic and others who believe that Custer's plan is now to cut off the noncombatants. I am sure Custer wanted to separate the warriors from the noncombatants, but I would surmise that he would have used one company to accomplish this while using two to attack the warriors. This is why he wanted Benteen to hurry to aid him, and why he would have left one or two companies in reserve. Considering the action that followed, I think he would have left two companies under the command of Captain Keogh. Custer, if he was the commander I believe he was and not the one described by Liddic and others, he would have left plans for Benteen with Keogh as to the part he wanted him to play in his offense, and where he wanted the packs.

Getting back to the situation Liddic is describing: Custer is trying to cut off the noncombatants in order to get the warriors to surrender so they will then go to the reservations. Since Reno has retreated there are now no soldiers west of the river, but Custer doesn't think the warriors would be moving to the north to protect the noncombatants. I want to go back to the beginning of this treatise where I said there were two maxims that were continually mentioned by practically all writers, yet they failed to apply them in their scenarios. One was that to Custer "attack and victory were synonymous," and the other was the fear the Indians would scatter once they were aware of troops moving against them. Does Custer attack at Ford B under ideal conditions? No, he retreats to an unknown and imposing looking terrain to launch an attack that he never does. Then he is afraid the Indians will scatter, but, according to Liddic. Reno has retreated so this leaves the whole area south and west of the Little Big Horn open. The Indians are now in a position to scatter while he moves on the east side of the Little Big Horn to the north. If they didn't scatter the warriors should be waiting for him at any crossing. And yet he is surprised that the warriors are there. This to me portrays Custer as—no I won't use that word again. Since I don't believe that word applies to Custer, is it any wonder that I think something happened back at Ford B to the commander? And if these companies were under the control of their commanders, when and why did they leave and end up on Last Stand Hill?

> It was before six o'clock. The forty some men on Last Stand Hill would be dead in fifteen minutes. It had only been less than two hours since Keogh had advanced so confidently towards Ford B....

> Both Gall and Rain in the Face related how the soldiers got shells stuck in their guns and then just discarded them. This might account for some Indian stories which mentioned the soldiers appeared panic stricken.....

> It was a little after six o'clock.

The troopers on the hill, who were still able to move, abandoned their wounded and dying comrades and fled towards the river. Hare later confided to Camp, he thought Custer's men had been struck in a panic, and they didn't fight very well. There were perhaps twenty-eight of these men.... These Indians shot a number of them, and the rest were forced into this ravine where the soldiers were all killed.... Black Elk was even more graphic. He said they were so scared that they didn't know what they were doing.[7]

I have always found it interesting how this movement to the north finds the 5 companies organized and under the control of their officers, but outside of some sign of an organized defense on Calhoun Hill there is no substantial claim by any observer at the time, nor physical evidence that a defense was established, nor a tactical retreat or any retreat to where they could have expected help. I think this signifies that "I" and "L" companies were placed in reserve; three companies were sent to the ford; there was an unorganized retreat from Ford B; and that some of the retreating troops attempted to join up with Keogh's two companies. I believe the only thing that would have caused the retreat from the ford before an attack even took place was the shooting of Custer. I can only conjecture that the move to the north was an attempt to get Custer to the Far West. In conjunction with the shooting of Custer, an unorganized retreat developed and the commanders were unable to regain control of their companies. They went with those troops aiding Custer and ended up with him on Last Stand Hill. After moving to the present cemetery area, for whatever reason, those with the wounded Custer were prevented from continuing. Then after a brief spell they attempted to come together with Keogh's companies, but they could get no further than Last Stand Hill. The main body of Indians had moved up from Ford B and were able to overwhelm Calhoun's defenses, and for most of his troops a retreat succumbed to panic. Since so many of the Indians moving to the ridge were hidden, there were attempts to escape to the river, as indicated by the 28 mentioned.

All of this is speculation; however, the two theories I have presented concerning orders and time constitute the two basic cover-ups associated with the battle, and are not conjectural but can be ascertained by sound analysis. The facts are known and only need to be connected. Then the major premise as to what or who caused the debacle can be determined.

Liddic and so many others when describing the Custer part of the battle cannot bring themselves to admit that the troops became panicky and many committed suicide. I don't consider acknowledging this as casting aspersions on any trooper, whether a new recruit or an old veteran. They knew of the torture they would suffer if captured, whether they were wounded or not. This wasn't the Civil War. Liddic believes that when they weren't able to reject the shell casings the soldiers threw their carbines away, and the Indians mistook this for panic. It is all right to mention panic in referring to Reno's flight from the valley or the troops from Weir Point, but not by Custer's men until the very last minutes. And contrary to the view that they were under officers' control until the last, the lack of defense, the failure to establish a tactical retreat, and the company officers found on Last Stand Hill indicates that the troops were not under officer control long before the final stage at Last Stand Hill. This doesn't rule out determined fighting at various locations. Although Wooden Leg's and Kate Bighead's testimony is used, nothing is said about their referring to suicides or the number of them that they claim took place.

Too often failures to analyze "off limits" or "unpatriotic" aspects of a subject limits ones analytical objectivity. We believe that we have to project an accepted or what can be called a patriotic view of the battle, as the one expressed by the Recorder, 1st Lt. Jesse Lee in his summation:

> The well-known capacity, tenacity and bravery of General Custer and the officers and men who died with him forbid the supposition of a panic and a rout. There was a desperate sanguinary struggle, in which the Indians must have suffered heavily. From the evidence that has been spread before this Court it is manifest that General Custer and his comrades died a death so heroic that it has but few parallels in history. Fighting to the last and against overwhelming odds, they fell on the field of glory. Let no stigma of rout and panic tarnish their bloodbought fame. Their deeds of heroism will ever live in the hearts of the American people and the painter and the poet will via with each other in commemorating the worldwide fame of Custer and his men.[8]

How long did the action on Custer field last? I would be inclined to agree with Liddic, except for the time of day:

> … This reconstruction portrays the Custer fight lasting about two hours, from the time Custer descended into Medicine Tail Coulee until the last few troopers were overrun on Last Stand Knoll, after 6:15 p.m. The action on Custer field itself, from Finley Hill to Last Stand Knoll, in my opinion, was a little over an hour's duration.… [Indians] they estimated it was about two hours before the last soldiers were killed. Other Indians said the action didn't

last anywhere near that long. Gall said the fight was over in about thirty minutes, maybe a little longer.[9]

♦   ♦   ♦

The testimony at the Reno Court of Inquiry indicates the officers tended to use the shorter time estimates. It would be to their advantage to believe and so state that the Custer fight was over in forty-five minutes; Wallace said Custer was heavily engaged by the time Reno reached the bluffs or a little after 4 o'clock, in this he was seconded by Varnum. Edgerly, who would have been in one of the best positions to know, said it was all over in twenty minutes or a half hour at most, Benteen said Custer was probably finished in a half hour, but on a guess, an hour at the very most. However, the scouts said the fight lasted much longer. Girard stated the action lasted until about dark; Herendeen said it was more than an hour. That the shooting continued until about dark as reported by Girard, could have been the sporadic shooting the Indians conducted while looting the battlefield.[10]

Liddic doesn't mention that many of the Indians stated that the battle started before noon and was over by noon. Kate Bighead said the Cheyenne took care of their dead that afternoon.[11] Liddic also doesn't dwell on the question that if the battle didn't get over until 6 o'clock, when Major Reno's forces arrived on Weir Point they should have been aware that there was still fighting. It is one thing to cover-up orders and time and another to cover-up that a battle was still going on. If Custer's troops were still engaged, there would have been no acceptable military excuse for not attempting to aid them, even if the number of Indians appeared to be too many.

Liddic rightly points out that the officers tended to use the shorter time period in order to show that they would not have been successful even if they had responded earlier. It certainly accentuates the questions as to why a command under officer control did not establish a recognizable defense, why the fight didn't last longer, and why a tactical retreat didn't take place. This would not have excused Reno, and is an indication of the cover-up.

Girard's account that the fight lasted much longer is understandable, as I have previously indicated, Girard was the main witness for Jason Lee the Recorder or Mr. Whitaker. (I am sure Mr. Whitaker played a part in the prosecution—I have no idea to what extent.) The time Girard first gave at the Reno Court when he said he looked at his watch would have been near the correct time since it coincides with so many of the earlier reports by both whites and Indians. This time went against the time that the officers were then presenting. The Recorder, Whitaker, Girard, or any of Reno's critics certainly would have realized that there testimony could not offset the officers. Either the army, Jason Lee, or Whitaker was responsible for Girard's time change. The army was in a position to coerce and intimidate Girard into changing his time so it would not be damaging to Reno. However, it is quite possible that Lee or Whitaker or both persuaded Girard to change the time in order to present a brief that would coincide, up to a point, with that of the Defense, thus making it more acceptable. Because of their need to present a case against Reno, and since the Defense had Reno ahead of Custer, I am sure that at first the Recorder meant to use this against Reno. They then may have realized this would not be effective, either because Lee also represented the army or just the fact that they knew they couldn't offset the officers' testimony that Reno moved down the valley before Custer went to the ridge. The Recorder laid the basis for their brief by taking advantage of Reno's contention that Adjutant Cooke had gone to the ford. This along with Reno's excuse to hide McIlhargey's mission by claiming he was sent to Custer to inform him the Indians were strong in his front enabled Girard to say the Rees told him there were all these Indians moving against Reno—which we know there weren't. Girard, after informing Reno, was going to warn Custer, implying that Reno should then have known Custer would be supporting him even if not from behind so he shouldn't have fled the valley. As part of the script, when Reno was setting up his skirmish line, Girard saw Custer back on the ridge near Reno Hill. Custer then couldn't have reached Ford B in time to create a recognized support for Reno. But knowing that Custer would be supporting him, Reno should have remained on his skirmish line or in the timber and not have fled to the bluffs as quickly as he did. The warriors were then able to leave Reno and get back in time to overwhelm Custer. Reno's flight was then responsible for Custer's defeat. There was no way this was going to bring a court-marital charge against Reno as long as the officers stuck together on the basic issues of orders and time.

Which of these ploys came first or whether they were worked out between the Defense and the Recorder I wouldn't know. However, to assume these distortions were honest conception errors when coupled with the other cover-ups has to be more than a mere coincidence. These ploys by both sides have been responsible for much of the misconception surrounding the battle. Adjutant Cooke did not go to the ford with Reno, and we should know that neither Reno, or the Rees saw, at that time, Indians moving against Reno. That was not the message McIlhargey took to Custer. Reno's concern was his support that he was expecting from Benteen, and whether he should wait for it.

Once Custer gave Reno and Benteen orders to attack the village (and he would have given both of them attack orders) he would have gone to the ridge and proceeded in his plan to flank the village. Reno's counsel recognized the need to keep Reno ahead of Custer in order to sustain Reno's claim that he only expected Custer to be following him. They then used Varnum's sighting of the Gray Horse Troop on the ridge close to Weir Point in order to show that Custer had plenty of time to have attacked the village in support of Reno. Since Reno saw no evidence of that support, he was justified in retreating to the bluffs. To support their script the Prosecution needed Girard to say he saw Custer near what became Reno's entrenchment area, and that he could only have reached the vicinity of Weir Point before Reno retreated. The sighting contradictions have not been questioned.

The only thing the Recorder's script accomplished was to present a case against Reno that would appear in the media and continue to nourish Reno's critics. The main effect was that it prevented an accurate assessment of the events leading to the move to the north of Medicine Tail Coulee by Custer's troops. I don't know whether this is a true portrayal of behind the scenes intrigue, but to believe there were no moves, countermoves, and back room strategy, is naive. The evidence substantiates that Custer was ahead of Reno, and the time used at the Reno Court was a cover-up.

Liddic in his summation on the Custer battle expresses the following:

> I have questioned many of the acts of commission and omission of Custer's subordinate officers, especially Reno and Benteen. This is not meant to gloss over the decisions and actions of Lieutenant Colonel George A Custer. As commanding officer, he was predominantly responsible for the situation he found himself late on the afternoon of June 25th. This accountability extends to not only his own violent death, but also to the total destruction of the five companies of his beloved regiment.[12]

It is true that Liddic has brought out many acts of commission and omission on the part of Custer's subordinate officers, especially Reno and Benteen. However, Liddic (along with the other writers over the years) fail to connect these acts to the cover-ups of the major premises—those of orders, time, and their connection to the defeat of the 7th Cavalry. Liddic doesn't seem to understand this failure, and that he and the other authorities are actually condemning Custer.

Any competent commander would have sent attack orders to Benteen even before sending them to Reno. Since Custer hadn't heard from Benteen he would have expected Benteen to be following his previous orders to move to the valley. His attack orders would have Benteen when reaching the valley to move in support of Reno.

I don't attempt to present time in the precise way that Gray and others have done because there are too many ephemeral factors. However, I will make a general comparison of times.

It would have been 5 a.m. according to Reno's and Benteen's after the battle report of when the regiment moved from Halt 1. Custer had already gone to the Crow's Nest that by accepted measures was some 4 miles away. The regiment was approximately 20 miles away from the Indian encampment. According to most authorities Custer didn't contact the Indians until 4 p.m. In other words it took 11 hours from the time the regiment moved from Halt 1 to when Custer with his five companies first met the Indians. Using walking time of 3 miles an hour they should have covered the 20 miles by 12 noon, but according to the authorities it took four more hours. Keep in mind that time was of the essence as Custer was still hoping for an element of surprise. Then we should factor in that the overall movement was more apt to have averaged out to a trot. At a trot they should have covered 20 miles in 3 1/2 hours. Without any stops they should have arrived by 8:30 a.m. Maybe the Arapaho warrior Waterman was right that it was about 9 a.m. when the first attack took place. We know (should know) Custer left for the Crow's Nest before the regiment moved which means that he should have met them at Halt 2 by 6 a.m. Halt 3, where he divided his command, should have definitely taken place by 8 a.m. as first brought out by Reno. This should have left about 16 more miles. The gait for this 16 miles should certainly have averaged a trot. By 11 a.m. Custer should have been in a position to have launched an attack at Ford B. For good measure lets add another hour and say 12 noon. How do these times compare to Crazy Horses' time? Kate Bigheads' time? White Man Runs Him's time? Left Hand's time? James Browndog's time? Low Dog's time inference? And many other Indians. At about what time did Sgt. Kanipe have Major Reno crossing Ford A? About what time did Trumpeter Martin have Custer sighting the Indian village? In other words by 12:30 p.m. Custer could have been attacking the Indian village at Ford B. And is it still necessary to emphasize the importance of time, or bring out that to any military commander synchronizing his attack with Reno, and still hopefully Benteen, should have been of uppermost importance. And, for good measure, let's throw in the Custer maxim that attack and victory were synonymous.

Authorities have to recognize the need for not only Reno but Benteen to cover-up the orders they received, and the time of events. Authorities must also connect and understand why the Court and the officers went along with the cover-ups. Writers seemingly do not realize that by accepting the Reno Court cover-ups they have made Custer out to be an inane, inept commander, and even one that was lacking in courage.

SOURCES

1. Liddic, 141.

2. Ibid., 141.

3. Ibid., 142.

4. Ibid., 144.

5. Ibid., 144.

6. Ibid., 146.

7. Ibid., 157.

8. Reno Court, 624.

9. Liddic, 164.

10. Ibid. 165.

11. Marquis, *She Watched Custer's Last Battle,* (booklet).

CRITIQUE:

Custer's Last Fight: The Story of The Little Big Horn, By David C. Evans

Evan's book was interesting and well written. He brought out testimony I wasn't aware of, and his inclusion of the Washita and Rosebud battles along with the appendices helped to provide an important background perspective as well as a follow-up to the Battle of the Little Big Horn. I thought his general analysis of Major Reno, Captain Benteen, and Lt. Colonel Custer was very good. I haven't attempted, in any detail, to examine the conduct of Generals Crook and Terry, or Colonel Gibbon, so I thought his account was enlightening.

I didn't find Evans' answers satisfactory in explaining my basic question as to why Custer did not attack with his five companies, or why he would have moved to the north of Medicine Tail Coulee. I do not believe there is any real evidence that any coordinated tactical defensive plans were made or executed after the movement to the north of Deep Coulee, either Evan's timing was wrong or you have an extremely inactive commander. Evans gave a good explanation as to how the Reno Court was not attempting to charge Major Reno or indict Captain Benteen, and that Reno's fellow officers in their testimony changed their opinion of Reno's conduct from prior accounts. His failure was not to apply this understanding to areas other than Reno's conduct.

What is very difficult for me to understand is how Evans can (as he does on pages 416–417) believe that Custer failed to do what Evans recognizes he should have done. Since you recognize cover-ups at the Reno Court, shouldn't you ask: What if Custer didn't foul up? What if he did inform his subordinates of his plans? What if Custer didn't go against what we believe was his very nature? What if he did what we thought an intelligent cavalry officer would have done? What if he planned to attack at Ford B? Since Custer should have recognized the need to coordinate his attack with Reno's, and we know he didn't trust Benteen, what if he didn't plan on waiting for Benteen before launching his attack at Ford B? Wouldn't Custer's psyche be a strong motive for believing he wouldn't have waited for Benteen? In other words, what if he did the things Evans believed he should have done? Essentially this means that, after viewing the Indian camp from Weir Point, why wouldn't Custer have launched an attack within twenty minutes on the Indian village at Ford B? Is there any evidence that Custer moved to the ford with the intention of attacking the Indian encampment? Since there is (Crow, Lacotah, and Cheyenne accounts), then the main question should be: Why didn't he attempt an attack at Ford B? What could have stopped such an effort? I think there is only one answer, but the questions should be asked, not ignored or brushed off, and sound reasons be given, even though they would be conjectural.

This brings me to my main point as to why I didn't find Evans' answer satisfactory in explaining why Custer did not attack with his five companies. Evans fails to recognize the main cover-ups which have made Custer and the actions he took appear to be that of an incompetent cavalry commander. The most important cover-up concerns the orders Custer gave. Custer's failure to have informed Benteen through his messages via Trumpeter Voss, Sgt. Major Sharrow, Sgt. Kanipe, and Trumpeter Martin that he was planning on flanking the Indians indicates, to me, that they already knew his plans. We should also consider that what we know of Trumpeter Voss's and Sgt. Major Sharrow's messages came from Captain Benteen. Cover-ups should then come to mind. What might Benteen need to have covered-up? Could it be that Custer did send him orders which indicated his plans to attack the Indians, and what part he wanted Benteen to play in that offense? Why would Benteen want to hide such knowledge? Walter Camp attempted to justify Benteen's account of not rushing across country to aid Custer, because Custer didn't say where he was, and that he only said, "to come on." I believe the reason Custer didn't specify where he would be is that he realized Benteen and Reno knew through his prior statements and orders that he was planning on flanking the Indians. The questioning of Martin by the court clearly indicates their concern that questions not be asked pertaining to the orders Custer gave to either Benteen or Reno. Why? The only answer seems to be the Court's fear that they would reveal Reno's and Benteen's knowledge of Custer's plan to flank the Indians.

I cannot agree in any way with Evans' essential view of the battle and the actions Custer followed. (Page 400) I cannot see Custer moving to the north of Medicine Tail Coulee in order to cut off the noncombatants, nor do I see any sound evidence of a south skirmish line, whether from Indian testimony or artifactual evidence. Evans fails to analyze either the Crows, the Sioux, or the Cheyenne accounts that differ from his view. His differences with Trumpeter Martin's on the orders Custer gave, as well as his objections to the theory presented by White Cow Bull, lack sound reasoning. The belief that Custer, having seen Reno go into action, would still have seen a sleeping village and think that he had caught the Indians napping, is not explained in any objective or realistic way.

Did the Crows fire on the village from Buoyer's Bluff, and if so were they the ones that met Benteen? Evans indicated they fired from Bouyer's Bluff and did meet Benteen. But how could they have done so if Captain Yates did not reach Ford B until Reno's troops had fled to the ridge? It is highly unlikely the Crows would have fired on the Indian village with troops still back on Luce Ridge.

Why would Custer attempt to hide his troops from the Indians by having them go down Cedar Coulee, move to Luce Ridge where they could be seen, and then send Captain Yates to Ford B with just two companies to make a feint at the Indian village in order to draw them away from Reno's troops? Did Custer know of the Crazy Horse Ford when he decided to move north in order to capture the noncombatants? Wouldn't it have been more effective to have cut them off from the warriors by attacking at Ford B? If you don't believe the Cheyenne village was just off from Deep Coulee Ford, you should explain why you are not willing to accept the conclusion of Dr. Marquis, Dr. Kuhlman, Gregory Michno, and others that it was—particularly when you bring out the Indians' account of moving their villages after a warrior's death. Why didn't Custer, if his aim was to capture the noncombatants that were fleeing to the north and west, move across the Crazy Horse Ford to accomplish his objective? Custer surely would have known that warriors would be waiting for him at any ford crossing. For Custer to believe he would have to wait for reinforcements in order to be able to attempt this crossing, and still expect to capture the noncombatants is, in my opinion, absurd. If an attempt had been made it would have been brought out by the Indians. Although I believe John Stands In Timber is correct that soldiers moved to the present cemetery area, there is no other account of a tactical troop movement to the Crazy Horse Ford vicinity. John Stands In Timber's account, although indicating a move to the present cemetery location, does not suggest the troops were there some two hours after Wolf Tooth's band fired on them, most likely in the vicinity of Luce or Nye Cartwright Ridge.

Let's take a closer look at the reasoning Evans is using. On page 266 he describes how Custer, watching from Weir Point, saw Reno on his skirmish line, and thought he had caught the Indians napping. It would have been impossible for Custer to have seen a seemingly deserted village and think the Indians were "napping." Nor could Mitch Bouyer, as reported by Curley, have wondered where the warriors had gone. This at a time warriors would have been moving to attack Reno, and others preparing to do so. Indian women would still have been taking down tepees and searching for their children. The villages would have been in a state of bedlam.

Evans believes the Crow scouts fired on the villages from Bouyer's Bluff. I agree, since there is testimony from the Crows, a Lakota, and Cheyenne that they did. However, they then would not have been released at the time Evans says they were, nor would they have been able to make it back to Benteen while Reno's troops were still fleeing from the valley. The importance is that their firing from

Bouyer's Bluff indicates Custer's troops were at Ford B while Reno was still in the valley.

(Page 267) We do not know what Boston Custer said when he joined Custer's five companies, and since he had no reason to know just how far back Captain Benteen was, it is doubtful that he said that Benteen was close behind. Actually (besides the fact that I believe Custer was already shot), Boston Custer should not have met Custer's troops until they were already retreating. This can be deduced by Martin's account of looking back from the ridge and seeing Custer retreating just after he had passed Boston Custer. One should also remember that Martin then saw Reno just moving into the timber from his skirmish line. Custer's prior knowledge that Benteen was already back on the main trail is illustrated by the fact that Martin was sent back to Benteen in contrast to Kanipe, who had been sent with a message to the packs. The fact that Martin didn't mention Boston Custer at the Reno Court doesn't signify anything (although that he wasn't asked about it might indicate something).

Evans, in basing his scenario on Custer planning to move to the north end of the Indian encampment, should explain why he doesn't agree with not only Marquis, Kuhlman, and Michno, but Indian testimony by Wooden Leg, Kate Bighead, White Cow Bull, and others that the Cheyenne village was just to the north of Deep Coulee Ford. I can think of no sound military reason for Custer to move north into an unknown area when a synchronized attack with that of Reno's troops should have been his main military objective.

Evans should give more logical reasons as to why the offense-minded Custer would not have attacked at Ford B at the only time he might have been successful. Instead, according to Evans and others, he sends two companies to the ford, and they don't arrive until forty-five minutes after Custer viewed the villages from Weir Point. The two companies under Captain Yates "demonstrate" for twenty minutes at the ford while Custer waits on Luce Ridge. Yates is pressured into retreating. Custer is not able to clear the Indians from Medicine Tail Coulee so he moves to Calhoun Hill to meet with the retreating Captain Yates. According to Evans' time-motion analysis, an hour and twenty five minutes has gone by since Custer viewed the Indian camps from Weir Point. Custer hears that the noncombatants are fleeing to the northwest from the Indian encampment, so he decides to move to the north and find a ford which he can cross to capture the noncombatants. Custer believes the warriors will then surrender in order to save the elderly, and the women and children. He takes another forty minutes to look for a ford. When he finds it there are warriors there (which he should have expected) so Custer fails again to attack, and decides to go on the defensive. By that time it is too late, since the full strength of the Indians are concentrating on his troops.

Evans believes that Custer was forced to move to Calhoun Hill when Yates' two companies retreated from the ford because he couldn't dislodge the Indians from Medicine Tail Coulee. However, according to Evans, the Indians Custer couldn't dislodge were not pressing his command too closely. Custer, knowing the noncombatants were fleeing from the village, decides to look for a ford downstream that he can cross in order to capture them. By that time Custer should have had a good idea of the size of the Indian encampment and the number of warriors he was up against. From Luce Ridge he should have realized that Benteen wasn't that close behind, so why, if he was afraid to launch an attack, didn't he decide to fall back, or even set up a defense around Luce Ridge or Weir Point? Custer then leaves Keogh's battalion to face the Indians coming across South Medicine Tail and up Deep Coulee, while he spends the next forty minutes moving northwest looking for a ford. He then is "surprised" that there are Indians at the ford so he goes on the defensive. And we criticize Reno and Benteen.

Evans then portrays a hard fought fight until Custer is finally overwhelmed by the Indians. I have not found any substantial evidence that the soldiers put up such a strong resistance during the "defensive" battle that then took place.

(Page 304) Evans' analysis of both Lt. Edgerly's account and that of Lt. Varnum's is misleading. It is used in order to support his contention that Custer's troops were still engaged when Company D went beyond Weir Point. Edgerly's statement that they were out there two hours should be questioned. This is a period when a major timing cover-up took place. At the Reno Court they needed to show that there was a movement to check on the firing heard from the Custer battlefield in an acceptable period of time. There had been the official time given for the meeting between Benteen and Reno as having taken place around two-thirty, yet the movement to Weir Point by the main body didn't take place until at least 5 p.m. This necessitated a division time change so as to be able to extend the 2:30 arrival time as initially stated by Reno. The packs time was also extended as can be determined by not only Reno's initial comments but also that of enlisted men. Edgerly's statement could be part of that cover-up, or it may have encompassed the full time they were gone. As Varnum reported, they probably did fire from long distance for some time, but all this does is substantiate the longer period of time from when Custer's troops had been wiped out.

Evans' statement (page 306) that unless Captain Weir waited well over an hour after Benteen's junction with Reno before proceeding downstream, Custer's troops would still have been in action, disregards substantial evidence that they did wait that long. The extensions previously mentioned bring that out. Evans' reasoning is also based on his time-motion analysis which has Custer doing nothing of an attack nature for some two and a half hours after having sighted Reno on his skirmish line. He dismisses Captain Godfrey's comment that it was some two hours after Benteen joined Reno before they made a movement downstream, because he was the lone dissenting officer and the majority of accounts have Weir and D company moving soon after the juncture. By this reasoning, Evans ignores not only his own analysis of officers' testimony but also Walter Camp's view, as well as those of enlisted men such as Davern, Taylor, and Martin. He certainly fails to recognize the need and the necessity at the Reno Court that such a delay not be pointed out by the officers. It becomes difficult for me to understand when writers knowing the court is bent on dismissing the charges against Major Reno, and that officers have reversed prior views of Reno's conduct, they fail to question officers' accounts on other issues that, if known and brought out, would have definitely necessitated a court martial for both Reno and Benteen.

Evans believes it is meaningless to attempt to establish the time of day for certain events by an analysis of day or watch time statements (page 505); however, he then establishes his theory on a time-motion analysis starting with Reno receiving his attack orders just beyond the Lone Tepee. I believe this can only lead to faulty analysis as time and motion depend on too many interpolating transitory and ephemeral remembrances, including topographical locations. One should recognize that the deviations in time stated by the officers and men raise questions that need examination and are essential for understanding and developing a logical sequence of events.

Evans recognizes that the Reno Court was a cover-up for Major Reno's conduct, and how by appealing to the officers' *esprit de corps* the Court could get the officers to go against their previous statements and support Reno. Since he also realizes that the court was willing to let the blame fall on Custer, it would then seem Evans might have asked what else would need to have been covered-up in order to prevent Major Reno, and possibly Captain Benteen, from being blamed for the debacle that occurred.

Shouldn't the following be natural questions for Evans to have asked: If Reno and Benteen knew that Custer planned on flanking the Indians, what knowledge and action would they need to cover-up? Wouldn't an essential examination, for Evans and other writers, be to find out if the early sightings of Custer on the ridge by Ree scouts and Reno's men were valid? If they were, wouldn't it be hard to deny that Reno wasn't aware of those sightings, and therefore he would have known that Custer was attempting to flank the Indians? Shouldn't Evans examine that possibility, and if he had, wouldn't he consider that Custer might have been on the ridge before Reno started down the valley? Wouldn't such a contention be supported by Custer saying he had caught the Indians napping? Finally, what if there had been at least a two hour wait after the juncture of Reno and Benteen before moving downstream, as not only Godfrey, but Taylor, Davern, Martin, Herendeen, and others brought out? If these questions had been asked at the Reno Court, what effect would that have had on the courts decision for not only Reno but Benteen?

Evans, ignoring actual time accounts because of the numerous deviations, instead relies on creating a scenario using his time-motion estimates. In so doing, let us remember that we are attempting to determine the actions and movements of Lt. Colonel Custer and his five companies, and that Evans, as practically all writers do, assumes that he is overly impetuous and attack-minded. We then have Evans setting up the following time estimates: First Reno receives his attack orders 5 minutes after leaving the Lone Tepee. (We should remember that the exact whereabouts of the Lone Tepee varies with different writers.) Eighty minutes later Reno establishes his skirmish line. He supposedly has traveled three or four miles to the river, checked it out, crossed in a column of twos, and his horses drank as they crossed. He has gone through 50 yards or more of timber, sent at least one messenger, waited for an answer, reformed, moved two miles down the valley, and established his skirmish line. Reno does this in eighty minutes. Custer, after giving Reno his attack orders, travels three miles towards the Little Big Horn (using Evans' account), waters his horses in Reno Creek or the North Fork, continues about 300 yards, and then goes to the ridge, roughly a mile and a quarter away. Here, at what Evans refers to as Wooden Leg Lookout, he sees Reno on his skirmish line. According to both Sgt. Kanipe and Trumpeter Martin, Custer traveled at a fast trot or gallop. Custer probably was able to have watered his horses in line (not as they crossed a river in a column of twos), and overall, traveled four and a half miles to his first lookout. We might also speculate that Custer, since he attempted to send two Crows, and then had the other four Crows and Buoyer go to the ridge, would have gone to the ridge ahead of his men (as any competent commander should do). Reno, however, even though traveling farther and from accounts having more difficulty, has been able to establish his skirmish line in eighty minutes while it has taken Custer eighty-five minutes to reach his first lookout near what would later become Benteen's H Company entrenchment location. Custer then moves a mile to Weir Point, which along with his observation of the village, takes another fifteen minutes. He believes he has caught the Indians "napping." Without reiterating (under Evans' scenario) what a stupid statement this would have been, Custer now attempts to conceal his troops by sending them down Cedar Coulee. Custer, upon reaching Medicine Tail Coulee, must have changed his mind about concealment because he then goes to Luce Ridge. Supposedly Boston Custer joins him and tells him that Benteen is not far behind. Although concerned about Reno, Custer waits for a time, and then decides to send Captain Yates and two companies to Ford B to demonstrate in order to draw the Indians away from Reno. They reach the ford forty-five minutes after Custer had been on Weir Point. Custer could have launched an attack at the ford some twenty minutes earlier (using Evans' time-motion analysis up to this point), but he believes he must wait for reinforcements. After 20 minutes at the Ford, Yates retreats. Custer is not able to clear Medicine Tail Coulee of Indians so he meets Yates at Calhoun HIll. This uniting takes place forty minutes after Yates had gone to Ford B. Since the Indians are not pressuring Custer too much at this point (even though he wasn't able to clear them out of Medicine Tail Coulee), and Custer had seen the village "napping" an hour and twenty-five minutes earlier, Custer realizes it must have been because the noncombatants had left and are moving to the north and west. Custer knows there must be a ford to the north which will enable him to encircle the villages and capture these noncombatants, thereby causing the warriors to surrender. He leaves Captain Keogh's battalion along Calhoun Ridge, then takes another forty minutes to find this ford, but since there are Indian warriors there Custer decides to go on the defensive. It is now 2 hours and 20 minutes since he saw Reno on his skirmish line, but the great offense-minded Custer hasn't yet attacked the Indians. I assume there are too many Indians by this time, so Custer is never able to establish a tactical retreat in order to meet Benteen.

Personally, I can't accept this scenario. I don't agree with any scenario that has Custer arriving on the ridge after Reno has set up his skirmish line. Nor can I imagine how any commander would not realize and attempt to coordinate his flanking movement and attack on the village with Reno's attack in the valley. I can't believe Custer would not attempt to launch this attack within twenty or at the most thirty minutes from when he viewed the Indian village from the ridge. After Reno's initial firing, there is no way that Custer would have believed he had caught the Indians napping or that their village was deserted. If Custer had still been fighting at the time Major Reno's troops moved downstream beyond Weir Point, this would have been common knowledge, not only during the night of the 25th but after the battle. Instead of Indian accounts indicating the Custer battle was over before they moved against Reno and Benteen, there would be numerous statements that while still attacking Custer some warriors went to attack the other soldiers.

Evans does magnificent work in bringing out a myriad of facts and testimony, but my overall criticism is that he fails to connect those facts and testimony to the underlying essentials. He has a cavalry commander that has been recognized throughout his career as being daring and courageous to such an extent that many consider it to be his major fault, and he realizes that the Court of Inquiry, from its officials down to the officers it has called to testify, are in favor of dismissing the charges against Major Reno. And if those charges were enacted they would also indict Captain Benteen, possibly others, and open pandora's box. However, Evans' ignores conflicting testimony, common sense, Custer's psyche, and logic, while creating a scenario which, seemingly without realizing it, ends up condemning Custer.

Evans criticizes timing because of its variation, but instead of analyzing why, sets up his own time schedule based on an initial time cover-up by Lt. Wallace. This time (12:05 p.m. for the division of the command) was accepted by officers, officials, and writers ever since. The question is why the variation in times from earlier official reports. Indian correlating times are ignored or glossed over. Early times given by Reno and Benteen are similar to times given by enlisted men such as Kanipe, Davern, and Martin. Evans ignores timing differences and uses cover-up testimony by officers to support his own time-motion analysis. Evans and others do not seem to understand how a time change was necessary in order to cover-up the late move of Weir, Benteen, and Reno to investigate the firing that had been heard from the Custer battlefield. To develop a proper time picture you need to connect the early official time given by Reno and Benteen with the time expressed by enlisted men, civilians, and Indians.

In making this connection you must not fall back into accepting officers' accounts just because they were officers. An understanding of the position they were in is absolutely necessary. Evans uses a varied and impressive number of statements to support his view of the battle. This is to be expected, but in doing so he accepts the officers' accounts and rejects those of enlisted men, scouts, civilians, and Indians. The diversity in Indian accounts needs to be factored in with an understanding of their fear of reprisals, along with a tendency to support what they recognize as the interviewer's conception of events. One example of this is Evans' failure to analyze the contradicting statements by Wooden Leg. Wooden Leg recanted his earlier accounts of suicides on the part of the soldiers. Yet Wooden Leg had stressed the anger of whites when Indians mentioned suicides. This anger and refusal by whites to accept suicides can be seen in the early rejection of Dr. Marquis writings, and even today the failure of writers to even approach the subject. Is it so hard to imagine an interview in which Wooden Leg, rather than confronting the white mans' anger, shrugged off his earlier statements and said the suicides didn't happen. One should recall the old frontier saying that if you were faced with capture by Indians you should save one bullet for yourself, or the various statements by men that they would shoot their wives or daughters before allowing them to fall into the hands of the Indians. Do you really think the Cheyenne would lie to Dr. Marquis? And one should give sound reasons, not just summarily reject Kate Bighead's statements on suicides, and her inference to what was most likely members of E Troop. I don't know how many suicides there may have been, but to deny suicides and present a picture of the troops valiantly fighting to the end may appear patriotic, but it is representative of an unrealistic American tendency in reporting historical events.

I question the tactical defensive locations Evans has Custer establishing or attempting to establish—such as the South Skirmish LIne. There should have been time to set up defensive positions, but if they had been established there should be more Indian testimony as to how they were overran. The statements following the battle by the men viewing the battle scene also do not report evidence of defensive stands outside of the Calhoun Hill location. The archaeological studies that have been made only show where men or groups of men had fallen. The evidence appears to reveal more of disorganized actions, rather than the overrunning of an officer established military defense.

Evans' book is certainly well written and provides a wide source of information. My objection is that although he recognized and blames Reno and Benteen for their actions and rationalizations, he still accepts their testimony to substantiate his theory of the battle, and discredits or dismisses remarks by enlisted men that conflict with the officers.

I will use a prime example. Martin is the one person who could have clarified much of what is still being questioned and considered controversial. To my knowledge he was never taken back to the battlefield to point out specific locations. He was not asked at the time of the Reno Court what Custer's orders to Reno were. He was never asked if Custer sent orders to Benteen, or when the Sgt. Major was sent to Benteen. Martin had to be a witness at the Reno Court, but he was never asked the questions he should have been. He was then summarily dismissed. Evans and others accept Benteen' remarks concerning Martin's "skidaddling," and Edgerly's comment that Martin when he joined the troops, said, "... Reno was charging it [village] and killing everyone, men, women and children." Evans recognizes cover-ups, but where it is apparent, as in this case, that the statement is being used as an excuse for Benteen not to have hurried, they are accepted. One should question why Martin, who had seen the Indians forcing Reno into the timber, would have made such remarks. Might the remarks have been made by Sgt. Kanipe? He was credited with making similar comments, and at the time that he left with his message, this is what he could have thought would be taking place.

Evans accepts Benteen's denial of sending Martin to the packs. He supports this by using the fact that Martin later told Colonel Graham that the Court must have mistook what he said, and that he hadn't gone back to the packs. This should raise questions. Considering the questions that were asked of Martin at the Court concerning his going to the packs, there is no way they could have been misconstrued. Wouldn't this be a good example of how Martin, aware that he wasn't to tell everything he knew, realized that he had said more than he should? Martin was a good soldier. Don't you think that later, when he realized Benteen denied sending him, Martin would attempt to reject what he said in order to protect his commanding officer? The location of the packs was a major cover-up. Instead of going along with Benteen, Evans should recognize this as prima facie evidence that the packs were close behind, and that Benteen was lying. Then by questioning why Benteen needed to deny the Martin message that he sent to Captain McDougall, a great deal of the mystery surrounding the Little Big Horn Battle would be solved.

Why was Martin not asked questions on when and what were the orders Custer gave to Sgt. Major Sharrow? What were the orders he gave to Reno? These are prime examples of the questions that I accuse early writers of not asking, and later writers of not raising and examining. Although realizing "whitewashes" by officers, they still accept their remarks over those of enlisted men and others.

Another example of something that should be questioned is the location as to where he left Custer that Martin is said to have pointed out on the Maquire Map. If Martin had received his orders close to Ford B, as he and others have reported, where would this place Custer's move to the ridge in relation to Reno's trip down the valley? Custer couldn't have came within 50 to 600 yards from the ford, and have Martin, after moving back to the ridge, see Custer retreating and Reno still in the valley. This would be especially true if Custer had gone down Cedar Coulee, moved to Luce Ridge and then sent two troops to the ford. Wouldn't it mean Custer had preceded Reno? Since the Defenses argument was that Reno, not only didn't know Custer was flanking the Indians, but that he looked for support that didn't come so he then fled to the ridge. Would this have sounded reasonable if Martin had received his orders fifty yards from the ford as the Crow's told

Michael Reynolds. This would open a number of questions that they did not want opened. Wouldn't this mean Custer accepted his scouts' reports at the Crow's Nest, or saw for himself the location of the Indian villages? Wouldn't he then have formulated plans, at the division of his command, as to how he would attack the Indian encampment? Wouldn't Reno and Benteen have been aware of his plans? Wouldn't Custer's orders been more extensive and correlate with those stated by the two orderlies? Reno should then have stayed in the valley and Benteen should have hurried to Custer's aid.

Cover-ups to protect Reno, Benteen, the 7th Cavalry, and the Army give that strict impression that Custer made unsound military decisions. The purpose of this manuscript has been to prove Custer's knowledge and his tactics were correct and reflected those of a competent commander until he moved to the north of Medicine Tail Coulee. Since that movement has no reasonable or sound military reason, it has led to my conclusion that something must have happened to Custer at Ford B.

CRITIQUE:

The Little Big Horn, By Robert Nightengale

Robert Nightengale has asked an Army Board to find that Lieutenant Colonel George Armstrong Custer was not negligent at the Battle of the Little Bighorn, that he followed accepted military practice, and that he did not violate orders. Nightengale also wants the Board to find Major Marcus Reno and Captain Frederick Benteen guilty of presenting wrongful testimony at the Reno Court of Inquiry. The most controversial aspect of the charges Nightengale and others are attempting to bring is that Captain Weir and Captain Benteen would have seen Custer either retreating from the Indian encampment or while deploying his men at Last Stand Hill, depending on their respective arrival time on the Weir Peaks, and Benteen failed to go to his aid. In this same context they want the Board to recognize that Lieutenant Colonel Custer was able to see Benteen's troops at Weir Point, and consequently extended his men south along Battleridge in an attempt to facilitate Benteen's movements in coming to his aid. Benteen's retreat and the over extension of Custer's defensive perimeter then enabled the Indians to overwhelm Custer's forces.

I certainly support Nightengale's attempt to have the Army Board review the official military record of the battle, and the Reno Court of Inquiry. The evidence Nightengale uses to substantiate the distortions, cover-ups, and actual lies made by Major Reno and Captain Benteen at the Reno Court are well presented and I believe undeniable. I would also accept his general view that Custer did not violate his orders, however, I cannot support the actions he credits Custer with nor the evidence used to formulate his major premise. Nightengale maintains that Reno and Benteen abandoned Custer. I can agree in the general sense with this part of his supposition but not with two vital contentions that the Army Board, I believe, would have to rule on in determining whether there should be a change in the official records. The first is their judgmental assessment of Custer's personal decisions and actions. The second is whether there is any substantial verification that Benteen, when moving to Weir Point, would have seen Custer's forces along Battleridge. Concerning the first assessment, I think the Army Board would condemn the military decisions made by Custer as presented by Nightengale, and would not find adequate basis for the second.

Nightengale's other charges encompass Major Reno's action in the valley. He believes Custer sent Reno to create a diversionary action in order for him to attack the Indian center. This would have divided the Indian forces and enabled Custer to achieve a victory. However, Reno did not carry out his orders and became demoralized with the death of Bloody Knife next to him. This created a retreat which was disorganized and Reno remained in an incapacitated condition, and was never able to effectively maintain control of his command.

Robert Nightengale's charges levied against Major Reno concerning his disorientation and lack of judgment in his retreat from the valley can, I believe, be substantiated. But, although I agree that there is certainly evidence that Reno remained incapacitated, I do not think that it is sufficient to make a firm decision against him.

My overriding criticism of Nightengale, as with many other Custer defenders, is that they still make Custer's military operation out to be inept. Consequently, if I was on the Army Board, and although I would acknowledge many of the basic points made by Nightengale against Major Reno and Captain Benteen, I could not affirm his account of Custer's military tactics as being sound.

I would like to examine the main charges Nightengale makes that I, and most likely the Army Board, would question. As previously stated, I agree with his charges that Major Reno and Captain Benteen distorted facts and essentially covered up their actions. There is no doubt that they did not follow orders, to what extent is the question. In my estimation there is ample evidence for the charge that Major Reno and Captain Benteen would have either heard or had reported to them the sound of gunfire downstream, which would have necessitated an immediate move to investigate. They would have had to know the gunfire came from Custer's battalions. Custer's orders to come to his aid were explicit, and I think they would have overridden any other countermanding battlefield orders or problems, and would have necessitated, at least on Benteen's part, an immediate move downstream. Although Reno's and Benteen's testimony indicated they did not hear gunfire and their attempt to aid Custer was as quick as they deemed expedient, their lies and distortions at the Reno Court, as brought out by Nightengale, should enter into any decision by the Army Board. Consequently, I believe, the Army Board would accept this charge by Nightengale as justified. At the time of the Reno Court such a charge could have resulted in a court-martial for Major Reno and an indictment of Captain Benteen.

In my view, the following charges made by Nightengale would be questioned and rejected by the Army Board:

1. That Custer's orders to Major Reno to cross the Little Bighorn and attack the Indian camp from the south were purely a diversionary action to enable Custer to attack the encampment at the center with the object being to divide the Indian forces and cause their dispersal.

2. That Major Reno and Captain Benteen and many other troops, once Reno had retreated and been joined by Benteen, realized that Custer was attacking *within* the Indian camps.

3. That after reaching Weir Peaks, Major Reno's forces led by Captain Benteen would have been able to see Custer's troops retreating or deployed on Last Stand Hill, and that instead of going to Custer's aid, Benteen would have retreated back to Reno Hill.

4. That Lieutenant Colonel Custer saw these forces on Weir Peaks and this caused him to extend several of his companies along the ridgeline in expectation that Benteen's troops would continue to move north in support of him.

My reasons for believing the Army Board would reject the above four charges include the following major points:

Point One: Nightengale's claim that Major Reno's orders were to create a diversionary attack. A diversionary attack, in contrast to a full-fledged assault, would have allowed Major Reno to feint an attack at the Indian villages in order to draw their warriors out of the camps. Then Reno could have set up a defensive position or retreated in an effort to lure them away from where the main attack was to take place.

I disagree. I think Custer's plan was for a full-fledged attack on the Indian encampment from the south. However, what Nightengale's charge does encompass, and which I agree with, is that Reno realized Custer was planning on flanking the Indians, instead of expecting support only from the rear, as he professed at the Reno Court. By the time of the Court, Reno and his Defense knew that if he said his orders were to create either a diversionary or a full fledged attack on the Indians at the time Custer was attempting a flanking move there would be little justification for not, at least, remaining in the timber, and none at all for not attempting to go directly to Custer's aid once Reno had retreated to the ridge and been joined by Captain Benteen. The knowledge of Custer's move to flank the Indians, coupled with Benteen's instructions to "be quick", would have made an immediate move to find and assist Custer mandatory. This is why Custer's orders should be classified as the major cover-up at the Reno Court. Misrepresenting them was necessary in order to prevent a court-martial of Major Reno. This has also had an effect on the historical view of Custer's actions and military tactics.

My belief is that Major Reno was to launch an attack against the encampment, and that Custer had ordered Captain Benteen to move in support of Reno once he reached the Little Bighorn. However, Nightengale does not indicate any particular plans for Benteen at this juncture. He accuses Custer of sending Benteen on a "useless mission" to the left, which was done primarily for spite in order to take Benteen "down a few notches." Since any sound military strategy on the part of Custer should have included Benteen in the attack on the Indian villages, this can therefore be considered a condemnation of Custer which would effect the Army Board's decision in judging Custer's military tactics.

Point Two: The second part of Nightengale's charges that I question has to do with Reno retreating to the ridge and being joined by Benteen, then hearing gunfire, and in viewing the village realizes that Custer has attacked and is actually fighting in the Indian encampment. At this point Nightengale's portrayal of Custer's five companies attacking and entering the village must correlate not only with the time he believes the officers and troops would have sighted Custer, but also with Indian accounts of the events. Outside of only a few, we know that the Indians attacking Major Reno did not follow him to the ridge. They turned back, not only when they received reports of Custer's move against the village, but also when troops were sighted on Luce or Nye Cartwright Ridge. Nightengale must account timewise for the dichotomy between having Custer's five companies in the village at the same time troops are seen on Luce or Nye Cartwright Ridge, and not merely ignore those accounts. Most of the Indians returning to their villages after attacking Reno would still have been on their way at the time of the reported gunfire and sighting by the troops on Reno Hill, yet I know of no accounts by them, nor do I know of any by the Indian warriors that had not left the village, of any Indian reaction to Custer's entry, the damage the troops created, or how they forced him to retreat.

The following are questions the Army Board should ask, and Nightengale needs to be able to provide an answer for:

Why wasn't the testimony from those Indians that had not gone to fight Reno filled with accounts of Custer's entry into their villages? Why didn't the Indians returning from fighting Major Reno (who should have been arriving during or shortly after the sightings by the soldiers from Reno Hill) describe how they aided in driving the soldiers from their encampment? Why does Kate Bighead say she saw Reno's troops retreating across the Little Bighorn and then ran back to her village, but never mentions Custer's soldiers invading the villages? Why don't the Cheyennes—whether those that had been fighting Reno or those that had not left the encampment—describe the fighting and action that must have taken place in the camps to their friend Dr. Marquis? Most of the Indians fighting Reno did not believe that Custer even came as far as the ford. Nightengale must explain these paradoxes.

Nightengale does attempt to use Indian as well as soldier testimony to substantiate his claim that Custer entered the village. Indian testimony that he uses came mainly from Chief Gall, Chief Red Horse, Kill Eagle, and a Sioux woman, Moving Robe Woman, a Hunkpapa.

Chief Gall reported that his two squaws and three children were killed. One would assume that since Gall was a Hunkpapa and their camp was closest to where Reno attacked, that the killings were a result of fire from Reno's troops.

Red Horse referred to the two attacks and said that one party charged right into the camp.

Red Horse's story as told to Assistant Surgeon McChesney stated:

> The soldiers got into camp and set fire to some of the lodges. The soldiers came on the trail made by the Sioux camp in moving, and crossed the Little Bighorn River above where the Sioux crossed, and attacked the lodges of the Uncpapas, farther up the river. The women and children ran down the Little Big horn River.... The soldiers set fire to the lodges. All the Sioux now charged the soldiers and drove them in confusion across the Little Bighorn River, which was very rapid, several soldiers drowned in it. On a hill the soldiers stopped and the Sioux surrounded them. A Sioux man came and said that a different party of soldiers had all the women and children prisoners ...[1]

Red Horse is certainly describing Major Reno's attack and not that of Custer. By "different soldiers," McChesney said Red Horse "always means the battalion immediately commanded by General Custer, his mode of distinction being that they were a different body from the first encountered." Red Horse goes on to say "as soon as we killed all the different soldiers the Sioux went back to kill the soldiers on the hill."[2] This indicates the Custer phase of the battle was over by the time they sighted and then went to attack the troops on Weir Point.

Kill Eagle said, "Before retiring across the creek, the soldiers got into camp and set fire to some of the lodges."[3] Moving Robe Woman, a Hunkpapa, stated, "The soldiers began firing into our camp ... I heard a terrific volley of carbines. The bullets shattered the tepee poles ..."[4]

The Kill Eagle report is inconclusive, it could be used to support either Reno's or Custer's entry into the villages, but since it sounds similar to Red Horse's account, which referred to Reno one would assume that it reflects camp stories of Reno's attack. Being a Hunkpapa and without any other evidence, Moving Robe Woman's statements would appear to relate to the firing by Reno's soldiers. The shattering of tepee poles could explain how some fires got started. There are also reports of several of Reno's soldiers who couldn't control their horses, which ran into the Indian camp where the soldiers were killed. This could account for the belief that troops got into the villages. Nightengale uses an account by Sitting Bull which doesn't state that Custer's troops were actually in the camps. A statement by Thunder Hawk claims that Custer did cross the river and moved down the west side firing into the tepees. Since this is the only Indian account that positively indicates Custer's troops crossed the river, and is contrary to all other testimony that I have read, I do not believe this is sufficient grounds to support the allegation that Custer's battalions entered the Indian village.

What is the evidence used by Nightengale to substantiate his charge that certain of Reno's and Benteen's officers and troops saw General Custer in the Indian encampment shortly after arriving on the ridge? Nightengale's contention is that if they were aware of it, then Reno and Benteen, although denying any knowledge, should have moved immediately to aid Custer. The testimony Nightengale uses came mainly from Sergeant Davern, Lieutenant Edgerly, and Lieutenant Mathey. They observed Indians circling in the bottom downstream. They also heard firing which they realized had to have come from Custer's troops. Mathey said that he looked through glasses but didn't see any soldiers. Since there should have been a good deal of smoke and dust as well as action in the Indian camp, at the time of the sighting the Indians could have been moving their camps to the west and north along the Little Bighorn which they did after Custer's troops were defeated. It is difficult to judge just when this sighting would have taken place. I believe the timing implication that is being used is wrong. It is hard for me to consider this adequate confirmation to support the theory that Custer actually invaded the middle of the Indian encampment, and I certainly could not construe it from Indian accounts. I do believe Custer went to the ford, and it is certainly possible that some of his troops crossed the ford into Indian camps. If this was true, then it was more apt to be associated with the difficulty some soldiers had in controlling their horses, rather than part of a full fledged attack across Ford B. Again, timing would not correlate, since Custer should have entered the camps shortly after Reno attacked in the valley, and if he was still in the village at the time Reno and Benteen reached Reno Hill (as previously stated), those Indians returning should have been full of stories of the Custer invasion of their camps, and how he was driven out. If there was consternation and panic associated with Reno's attack, then Custer's penetration of the village would have created bedlam. There should also be a better account (even though speculative) on how Custer was able to accomplish an organized retreat and then possibly have sent Yates' battalion downstream. In addition, there would still need to be an explanation for the troops that were seen on Nye Cartwright Ridge.

There are several other considerations that one should recognize in examining Nightengale's reports of the soldiers hearing gunfire downstream in the bottom, and believing that the action they had seen resulted from Custer's crossing and fighting within the villages. First, I think one can assume that following the battle, with the recognition of what happened to Custer's troops, the soldiers on Reno Hill realized that they had done nothing to save their comrades at a time when they should have attempted to go to the sound of gunfire. This must have created strong guilt feelings.

Second, at the time, the soldiers believed that Custer moved to the ford and was intent on crossing and attacking the Indian encampment, it seem natural that they would associate the gunfire they heard and the Indian movement on the bottom as coming from Custer's troops fighting in the village.

Third, I believe that the evidence does support the fact that Custer and part of his battalion moved to the ford. They should have been in the process of retreating at the time the gunfire was heard. There would have been gunfire from the Indians crossing the ford and from the troops in the following locations: North Medicine Tail Coulee (Deep Coulee), Greasy Grass and Calhoun Ridge. At this time the firing would not have been coming from Last Stand Hill.

Fourth, it is likely that those asked (except for Major Reno, Captain Benteen, and I would include Lieutenant Wallace, since he was probably in on the cover-ups), felt compelled from their own psychological guilt feelings to have mentioned hearing gunfire, and how they associated it with Custer. However, because of the effect it would have had on the courts decision whether to bring court martial charges against Reno, and which could have resulted in an indictment of Benteen, along with their recognition that the military officials did not want to bring charges against either of them, most of the men would have deliberately tempered their statements. I think this is especially reflected in statements concerning the length of time before they moved to investigate the sound of gunfire that they heard.

Point Three: The third matter that the Army Board would or should reject is Nightengale's charges against Captain Benteen that after reaching Weir Point, he would have seen Custer retreating or about to be engaged on Last Stand Hill, but instead of going to his aid, Benteen retreated back to Reno Hill. This accusation by Nightengale"s is really the quintessence of those he is making in order to have the Army Board change the official records; therefore, I will attempt to examine the main testimony and rationale used by Nightengale to support this scenario, and why I disagree with it.

The following postulate by Nightengale can be considered the center piece for his belief that Captain Benteen would have realized Custer's troops were still alive:

Those on the Weir Peaks would have made no mistake had they been viewing the Custer battlefield during the battle or after the soldiers had been destroyed. The smoke and dust would have hung over Custer Hill "like a mountain." When the soldiers on the Weir Peaks looked over at Custer Hill the evidence indicates that Custer and his men were still alive.[5]

Nightengale brings out the point how at that time gunpowder was made from a black powder, and since there was little wind that day, the black smoke would have hung heavy over the battle area even if the fighting had taken place earlier. This, along with the dust raised, would have caused such a covering, that the testimony of those on Weir Point would have mentioned it, and they could not have been able to identify the Indians as they did, and the firing that many had noted. This means then, that they realized the final battle had not yet occurred.

That these soldiers on Weir Peaks would have been able to see what was going on around Battleridge appears to be the primary consideration that Nightengale believes proves his charge against Captain Benteen. To support his contention he uses Indian testimony that indicates the density of the smoke and dust that hung over the battlefield during the fighting. I am sure that no one would oppose such Indian statements.

Nightengale's testimony, therefore, is used to bring out the ability of those on the Weir Peaks to observe the action or the lack of action taking place on and around Battleridge. One should note the following in examining the statements used: Who did the soldiers attribute the gunfire to—whites, Indians, or both? And did the troops on Weir Point mention seeing Custer's soldiers?

Timing is the other major component one must consider in supporting or rejecting Robert Nightengale's charge that Custer's troops were still alive when Captain Benteen reached Weir Point.

From his interview with Lieutenant Hare, Walter Camp wrote that Hare said, "While out in advance with Company D, the Indians were thick over on Custer ridge and were firing ... at that moment (Hare) thought Custer was fighting them."[6]

This would appear to be a natural statement. Company D was attempting to find out what happened to General Custer; consequently, seeing Indians on a hill some distance away that were firing their guns, one would at first expect they were shooting at Custer's troops. Hare does say it was at that first moment when seeing them—the inference being that he then realized there was not a battle taking place. However, he was able to see firing but does not report the black smoke and dust that would be present if a battle was taking place. One should then ask, if there was not a battle going on, who were the Indians firing at? Was it Custer's troops as they were deploying along Custer Hill? If so, why was there no mention of seeing the troops? If they were firing at the troops, wouldn't the troops have been firing back? If both sides were firing, and since we might assume that the Indians were circling, shouldn't there be a good deal of dust and smoke that would have been mentioned by some of Benteen's men?

Private Edward Pigford, in an interview with Walter Camp, stated:

> ... at first when looked toward Custer ridge the Indians were firing from a big circle, but it gradually closed until they seemed to converge into a large black mass on the side hill toward the river and all along the ridge. He thinks what he saw was the last stage of the fight.[7]

Private Pigford's account does not support Nightengale's premise that the main battle had not yet begun. If this had coincided with the statements of others, one might assume that the last phase of the battle was taking place; but since it does not, it raises several questions. Where was the black smoke that should have been hanging over the battlefield and would have made his observance questionable? Might this not represent the large mass of noncombatants that we know moved onto the battlefield following the end of the fighting? Wouldn't the ability to have seen what was going on indicate an earlier end to the battle, rather than the battle just ending or not having started? Wouldn't Pigford have seen some signs of soldiers, unless the battle had been over for some time?

Lieutenant Godfrey said, in an article in the *Century* magazine:

> Looking toward Custer field, on a hill two miles away, we saw a large assemblage ... we heard occasional shots, most which seemed to be a great distance off, beyond the large groups on the hill.[8]

This would not indicate either a retreat or a battle going on at the time. If the battle had not yet started and Custer's men were establishing or had established a defensive position, wouldn't there be more firing by both sides around Custer Hill?

At the Reno Court of Inquiry, Lieutenant Godfrey was questioned as to what he saw from Weir Peaks:

> Q. At the same time you moved down to Captain Weir's position to the point known as Weir's Hill did you look at the direction of the place of the massacre?
>
> A. Yes, sir.
>
> Q. Could you see it?

A. I could see the general lay of the ground, but could not see any bodies or persons except Indians.

Q. Was there anything in the way of fighting going on there at that time?

A. No, sir, I don't think there was. I saw no evidence of fighting at that time.[9]

Here again, Indians but no soldiers seen or battle reported. This would support Nightengale's supposition except for its specious logic. Personally, I can't envision the scene. Supposedly Custer's men are being deployed in defensive positions, or had already established them. Custer's eyes are riveted to Weir Point for any signs of Captain Benteen. He then sees the troops on Weir Point. However, at this time, though the Indians are firing some shots at his troops, they are not firing back. Consequently, there is little smoke or dust hanging over the area to prevent those on Weir Point from seeing Custer, or for Custer from seeing them. Yet there are no reports of the troops on Weir Point seeing soldiers, guidons, or even hearing bugle calls. Wouldn't you think that perhaps Custer might have his troops fire several volleys? I realize that one needs to be very leery of officers' statements, particularly at the Reno Court, for they could have been warned by higher ranking officials to avoid any such acknowledgments, especially since it could be considered a natural criticism of their own actions; but, both the officers' and the troopers' statements—even those taken from before the Reno Court—seem to be consistent; the sighting of Indians, some Indian firing, and no reports of soldiers. Sergeant Windolph later reported:"Way off to the north you could see what looked to be groups of mounted Indians. There was plenty of firing going on."[10]

He doesn't describe seeing soldiers. At that time, one could have expected to see mounted Indians and to have heard a certain amount of gunfire. We know the Indians, after the battle, fired into wounded and even dead soldiers—if for no other reason than to test the new weapons that they had acquired. "Plenty of firing" is a relative term.

Lieutenant Wallace at the Reno Court of Inquiry:

I went to a point where I could see where General Custer's battle took place. Indians were all over the country but no firing was going on. There was no particular disturbance, all was quiet.[11]

Although in the one sense this account supports Robert Nightengale's theory, the basic questions still remain: If the battle took place right after the retreat by

Captain Benteen's troops on Weir Point, why wasn't there firing during this time by both the Indians and the soldiers? The Indians should have been moving and circling so there would be plenty of dust being raised. There would have been a great deal of firing throughout the period leading up to the soldiers reaching Custer Hill. From their own standpoint, it is true that both Captain Benteen and Major Reno would have wanted the fighting to have been over for some time—this is evident from Benteen's testimony at the Reno Court. However, we also know that there was still firing from the Indians, as evidenced by the testimony Nightengale uses as well as that of the Indians referring to such after the battle was over. Lieutenant Wallace's account supports my belief that he was the third and probably the only other major officer in on the cover-ups that took place at the Reno Court.

Lieutenant Varnum at the Reno Court of Inquiry:

I went to the position of Captain Weir's company at the far point of the ridge downstream. At that time I could see all over the plain towards where I afterwards knew the Custer battlefield had been, and it was covered with Indians in all directions coming back toward us.[12]

How can this testimony support Nightengale's position? My imagination cannot picture a scenario where if Custer's men are on Custer Hill at this time, they would not have been aware of it. I don't believe that Varnum or all of the others would cover-up such action. Black smoke would have been hanging over the landscape.

Walter Camp noted in an interview with Lieutenant Edgerly:

… Edgerly said that when he looked over toward Custer battlefield he saw Indians shooting as though at objects on theground and one part of the hill on Custer battlefield was black with Indians.[13]

Although Edgerly believed the Indians appeared to be shooting at something on the ground, in no way does he indicate that a battle was still in progress. Considering the number of Indians that moved to the battlefield, they could appear as a black mass. One would assume that any shooting was at objects (soldiers) on the ground. This would not support Nightengale's view that the battle had not started.

George Wylie was a trooper with the soldiers on the Weir Peaks and, when interviewed by Mr. Camp, made some various curious statements: [RN]

> Seeing many horsemen over on distant ridge with guidons flying. Weir said, "That is Custer over there,"and mounted up ready to go over, when Sergeant Flanagan said "Here Captain, you had better take a look through the glasses. I think those are Indians." Weir did and changed his mind.[14]

I don't believe this a curious statement on the part of George Wylie, but a very explanatory one. We know that following the battle the Indians took clothes, weapons and guidons, and had been taking horses. We also know that they then dressed themselves in these clothes. Some were reported to have attempted to scare the noncombatants by faking a soldier attack on them. We also know that one of the criticisms made of the troops on Reno Hill is that they said they had no idea what happened to Custer, when there is ample testimony that during the fighting on Reno Hill they saw Indians dressed in cavalry uniforms, carrying guidons and riding cavalry horses. So, as other writers have pointed out, there should have been no question what happened to Custer.

My analysis of the above testimony would not indicate a retreat, a battle in progress, or that soldiers were holding out and in comparatively good shape at that time. Considering our knowledge of what the Indians did following the Custer battle, this testimony would signify that the battle had been over for some time.

I think the "black smoke" hypothesis presented by Robert Nightengale doesn't prove his charges at all, but actually destroys them. On the retreat from the Indian encampment or when deploying his men on Custer Hill—and as Nightengale says," … surrounded by thousands of Indians …"[15]—would you expect the Indians to be the only ones firing, or would Custer's men also be shooting back? Would there be a good deal of dust being created by the Indians and the soldiers? Since testimony indicates only a comparatively small amount of gunfire—none associated with the soldiers—and no great amount of black smoke or dust, would you say this is more apt to signify a battle about to start, or one that had ended some time before?

According to Nightengale, Custer's eyes were glued to Weir Point, and after seeing Benteen's soldiers there, he sent several companies in that direction. This supposedly caused the early demise of his men. I would assume from Nightengale's account, that Custer's troops were in fairly good condition and under officer control. If this was the case, and with several thousand Indians surrounding you, what would you imagine Custer would do? He sees Benteen's men several miles away, so would you expect him to send several companies in his direction? If so, were they to go on horseback or on foot? Would you expect the several thousand Indians to attack these companies or let them proceed? Instead of sending those companies down the ridgeline, do you think it might be better for Custer to signal the forces on Weir Peak by waving guidons, firing volleys, and blowing bugles? If this seems logical, don't you believe that Custer might have thought so too?

The third ingredient which has to be considered in analyzing the testimony already given is timing. I believe that timing is one component that should be recognized as being inaccurate in this scenario. For various reasons—ranging from understanding how there was the need to lie to protect and rationalize their actions or the fact that no one kept an accurate account—time was the last thing that any of them were concerned with. One should realize the necessity and importance for Major Reno and Captain Benteen to portray, at the very least, a comparatively fast move to aid Custer. The changing of the official time and the distance the packs were traveling behind Benteen were all a part of this cover-up. Testimony attests to the fact that the move to find Custer took place around five o'clock. I have gone along with this estimate, but actually believe it was later. I will get back to this point.

Under the generally accepted time, one must realize that if Custer had moved to the ford or attacked the Indian encampment, he would have been driven out by the time the Indians returned from engaging Major Reno. Any analysis of the time lapse from when the packs arrived on the hill to when Weir and then the rest of the troops moved to Weir Peaks, shows from one and a half to at least two hours in that interim. I know of no Indian testimony that portrays the battle lasting over an hour from when the warriors attacking Reno returned and moved against Custer. From a time standpoint, I cannot visualize Custer still battling the Indians when Weir or Benteen got to Weir Peaks.

From my analysis of the battle, I would be more apt too support the testimony of Sergeant Davern at the Reno Court as being closer to the actual time lapse between hearing gunfire and the time when Captain Weir and then Captain Benteen with the other companies moved to Weir Point.

Sergeant Davern at the Reno Court:

Q. Where did Captain Weir go about the time you spoke to him as you stated?

["… as you stated" concerned Davern's answer used by Robert Nightengale in reference to hearing gunfire downstream and believing it came from Lt. Colonel Custer.]

A. Nowhere.

Q. Do you remember whether Captain Weir moved his command down the stream?

A. Not at that time. He did later in the evening. [This supports my contention that the official time was changed in order to narrow the time period before they moved to investigate the gunfire.]

Q. How soon after the pack train came up did the whole command move down?

A. About two hours after the advance of the pack train came up.16

I would consider three hours must have gone by from the time all of Captain Benteen's battalion arrived on Reno Hill, saw the Indians leave, heard gunfire from around Ford B, the packs came up, Captain Weir went to find Custer, Lieutenant Edgerly summons D Troop and moves after Captain Weir, followed by Major Reno or Captain Benteen then deciding to follow D Company. Captain McDougall indicated that when he arrived with the packs, the troops on the hill had not formed a skirmish line, which he then did. This was at a time when officers and troops were not only worried about Indians, but were dealing with wounded and panicky men. When the ammunition packs came up there are reports of their being opened, and others that they weren't. From the picture that I have been able to gather from various testimony, there would have been an intermingling of troops and overall confusion. We know military movements are not automatic. In my mind, between the time Captain Benteen arrived on Reno Hill and when his companies reached Weir Point, it would have been at least three hours if not longer. Custer's troops should have been retreating from the ford at the time Reno was retreating from the valley. The gunfire reported on Reno Hill could have been heard from Ford B, Greasy Grass and/or the Deep Coulee area. Within the next hour or hour and a half from the time Custer's troops retreated from Ford B the battle would have been over. Captain Weir would not have reached a position where he could see the battlefield for at least another hour and a half to two hours. Benteen's arrival time could be encompassed in this period or have been even later. Noncombatants, along with warriors would have been moving over the battlefield. Some firing would have been taking place; no soldiers would have been seen. This corresponds to the testimony of those on and around Weir Point.

In my estimation, the gun smoke evidence brought out by Nightengale refutes the supposition he is attempting to make, and it clearly shows the battle was over.

The smoke, for all practical purposes, had to have cleared. As Kate Bighead said, the Cheyenne buried their dead that afternoon. Her statements indicate that the battle had been over for sometime before the soldiers reached Weir Point. I cannot see the Army Board believing that Nightengale has presented any compelling evidence or adequate corroboration to support his charge that Custer's troops were still intact when Benteen and Reno's companies reached Weir Point.

However, I do believe the Army Board would find sufficient evidence to support charges by Robert Nightengale and others as to the following:

1. There were cover-ups by Major Reno and Captain Benteen concerning orders, timing, and knowledge of Custer's plans and the action taken by him.

2. Reno and Benteen failed to move as quickly as they should have to aid Lt. Colonel Custer.

3. Custer's orders to Benteen to come quickly would transcend any problems or counter-orders by Reno.

4. From evidence that Robert Nightengale and W. Kent King have presented, the Board should realize that there had been changes in the maps used at the Reno Court from those of earlier maps.

5. That the Reno-Benteen promotion petition was primarily a cover-up.

6. That Lt. Colonel Custer did not violate orders from General Terry.

The following charges, which constitute the primary ones being levied by Robert Nightengale, I do not believe an Army Board would or should substantiate:

1. The five companies under Lieutenant Colonel Custer's command entered the Indians' main encampment.

2. Major Reno's forces, when reaching Weir Point, saw Custer's troops and that they were still alive.

3. Rejection of Number 2 would mean that Lt. Colonel Custer's troops were already defeated at the time Major Reno's forces reached Weir Point.

4. Lt. Colonel Custer's military decisions and tactics, as portrayed by Robert Nightengale, would not be considered sound

What Nightengale and those bringing the charges before the Army Board desire is an exoneration of Custer's decisions and tactics based on blaming Major Reno and Captain Benteen for his defeat. Yet the tactics they credit Custer with making only denigrates the military image of Lt. Colonel Custer.

I cannot see how the following Custer actions, as portrayed by Nightengale, can be considered sound military tactics:

1. The sending of Benteen's battalion on a "useless mission" primarily for the purpose of taking him "down a notch or two." This on a day Custer knew they would be attacking the Indian encampment.

2. Not having any initial plans to include Benteen's battalion on the attack of the Indian villages.

3. Sending Major Reno on a diversionary attack with only three inexperienced companies, and a commander he did not trust against an Indian camp that (contrary to some views) Custer realized contained at least fifteen hundred warriors.

4. Assuming Nightengale was correct and Custer and his five companies were in a comparatively secure defensive position around Last Stand Hill, that he was waiting for reinforcements from Captain Benteen, he then sees Major Reno's forces at Weir Point some two miles away, and, with supposedly thousands of Indians surrounding him, Custer sends several of his companies down the "ridgeline." One can infer from the charges Nightengale is making, that by the breaking up of his defensive positions, Custer enable the Indians to cut through his lines, separate his forces, and annihilate his command.

These actions and tactical decisions certainly would not allow me to credit Custer with exhibiting sound military judgment. Though one should condemn the late move by Major Reno and Captain Benteen to investigate gunfire and to find and support Custer, the effect of such an earlier movement cannot be determined. Even given the fact that one can find other actions by both Reno and Benteen that can be criticized, there is not sufficient evidence, as presented, to blame them for the military debacle that encompassed Custer's five companies.

I hope, if the Army Board is convened, that they would combine and insert the reasonable aspects of Robert Nightengale's discourse with other scenarios. Ones which recognize and credit Lt. Colonel Custer's decisions and actions during the battle with what would be expected from the courageous military genius Custer portrayed on numerous occasions throughout his illustrious career.

SOURCES

1. Nightengale, Robert, *Little Big Horn*, p. 111.

2. Graham, *The Custer Myth*, pp. 61, 62.

3. Nightengale, *Little Big Horn*, p. 112.

4. Ibid., p. 112.

5. Ibid., p. 190.

6. Ibid., p. 184.

7. Ibid., p. 184.

8. 8 Ibid., p. 184.

9. 9 Ibid., p. 184.

10. 10. Ibid., p. 184.

11. Ibid., p. 185.

12. Ibid., p. 185.

13. Ibid., p. 185.

14. Ibid., p. 185.

15. Ibid., p. 191.

16. Nichols, Ronald H.,ed., *Reno Court of Inquiry*, p. 353.

CONCLUSION

In my preface I said the purpose of writing this book was to reveal how testimony at the Reno Court of Inquiry affected writers' assessment of the battle, and how it created a framework for the battle that placed the blame for the defeat of the 7th Cavalry primarily on decisions of the commander, Lt. Colonel George Armstrong Custer. The two main conspirators at the Court, Major Reno and Captain Benteen, placed the blame on the splitting of the command, and Custer's failure to inform them of his plans. In order to prevent a Reno court-martial, officers' compliance clouded the picture so that even now Custer buffs are mislead, and seemingly without realizing it they allow the blame to be concentrated on Custer. Although I vindicate Custer of those charges, I don't think there should be any question that the debacle was due to a combination of events.

Let's look at the actions of the three major officers, Custer, Reno and Benteen. I will look at Reno's first.

Reno concealed the fact that he had received orders from Custer which said his support from behind was to come from Captain Benteen, while Custer would be attacking the Indians from the north. After sending messages to Custer to find out if he should wait for Benteen, and after seeing Custer's troops on the ridge (neither of which he admitted to), Reno attempted to follow his orders to move against the Indians. He was expecting support from Benteen and Custer. When this support didn't appear and the situation in the valley became serious, he made a panicky flight to the bluffs. Should he have remained in the valley? Yes, he should have. Would it have changed the outcome? It is doubtful. Should he have made a tactical retreat from the timber? Yes, he should have. When he was joined by Benteen on the bluffs, should he have immediately attempted to go to the aid of Custer? Yes, because it might have saved some of Custer's men, although it may also have brought about the destruction of the 7th Cavalry. Should it have been attempted? Yes, it should have. Did Reno cover-up why he didn't move immediately after Benteen joined him on the bluff? Yes, he and his Defense closed the time gap by changing the time and twisting the actions that took place on the bluffs so that it appeared Reno moved as quickly as possible to investigate the firing that had been heard from the Custer battlefield. Was this time delay and its cover-up a court-martial offense? Yes, it was.

Captain Benteen also covered-up not only Custer's recognition of where the village was located, but the orders he received and when he received them. After Lt. Gibson informed Benteen that there were no Indians or camps to the south of the known camp, should Benteen have crossed Ridge C and gone on to the Little Big Horn valley as ordered? He should have, but it is understandable why he didn't. He knew there were no Indians or villages to the south, and the way to the main trail by Valley 3 was clear of any obstacles. Should he have informed Custer that he hadn't seen and didn't believe there were any Indians or their camps to the south of the known camp? Yes, he should have, and, unless he expected Sgt. Major Sharrow to do so, I know of no acceptable excuse for why he didn't. Did he lie about the message he received from the Sgt. Major and when it was received? Yes, he did. Should he have hurried faster on his reconnaissance to the left? This is hard to say since we cannot judge accurately the terrain, the gait, or the exact path he would have taken. It appears that he did not hurry at any time, and his excuse was that he needed to save the horses. If he had moved faster and had reached the Little Big Horn in time to join Reno while Reno was still in the valley, would that have changed the outcome? Too many factors come into play, so one cannot make a sound prediction. Should Benteen, after joining with Reno, have insisted on their immediate move to follow his orders to aid Custer?

Yes, he should have.

Too many writers have accepted Reno's and Benteen's rationalizing in regard to their lack of knowledge of Custer's plans. This has placed the blame for the defeat on Custer. Most writers have concentrated on the image of Custer and his valiant forces fighting to the last, but in the end succumbing to the overwhelming number of Indians. By doing this they have prevented an accurate assessment of the battle.

Because of Custer's death, and since there were no survivors from his five companies, the officers' feelings about him would not have been sufficient for them to betray the living (particularly the two major officers, Reno and Benteen), the regiment's image, and the army's desire to prevent any official investigations from continuing. The officers went along with the cover-ups even though they recognized the damage it was doing to Custer's image.

Custer, from the Crow's Nest, recognized the location of the village and made plans to attack. When he neared the Little Big Horn he sent orders to both Reno and Benteen. Reno and Benteen had to cover-up these orders because of their failure to follow them, which would have constituted court-martial offenses. Custer's initial plan, as outlined by the two orderlies, had Reno and Benteen attacking from the south while Custer came in from the north.

Reno didn't get the support that he expected from Benteen, nor from Custer. He certainly panicked and fled prematurely from the valley, and his retreat was not organized, but he couldn't be blamed completely. Benteen should have hurried. I don't know of any of Benteen's horses that didn't make it, and if he had been quick enough to support Reno, as Custer planned, things might have been different. Benteen, in going back to the main trail, did what he thought was justified. However, his failure to notify Custer and follow the orders he received from Custer by way of Martin, cannot be excused, but responsibility can be shared with Reno. The lies, distortions, and cover-ups that Benteen used following the battle, along with the slowness of his response during the battle which prevented Custer's original plans from being carried out, places the blame for the defeat of the 7th more on Benteen than on Reno. Reno's panic retreat cannot be excused from a military standpoint, even though from the overall picture the early retreat may have been a good thing.

The real key to the debacle revolves around Custer's failure to attack a camp that was in turmoil, at a time when Reno was still fighting in the valley. When Custer heard Benteen was back on the main trail, he realized that Benteen and the packs should come in support of him. Custer knew his attack would increase the fear of the noncombatants that had been created by Reno's attack, and most of the warriors would leave Reno to protect the village. Custer realized that this is where the main battle would take place, and it is why he wanted Benteen and the packs to move to aid him. The fact that there are no signs or testimony that a major attack took place at Ford B remains the greatest mystery surrounding the Battle of the Little Big Horn. If this was not Custer you might come up with satisfying answers, but the only explanation that has made sense to me, is that Custer was shot at the ford. And there is testimony to support this theory. His getting shot, along with the size of the village, the warriors rushing to the ford, and the realization of what would happen if captured, were all elements that created an unorganized retreat. Were there pockets of stubborn resistance? Yes, there undoubtedly was. Did the Indians report panic on the part of some troopers? Yes, they did. Could it have been expected? Yes, it should have been. Were there signs of the five companies setting up a defense? No, there weren't. Were there signs of an organized retreat? No, there weren't. The two essential questions continue to be: Why didn't Custer attack at Ford B, and why did he move to the north?

Custer's plan was a sound one. Benteen's slowness and his move to the main trail prevented Custer's plan from taking place. If Benteen had crossed Ridge C and hurried to the valley he could have joined Reno. Reno's crossing Ford A, passing through timber, reforming, and waiting for his messengers to return, all would have taken longer than portrayed. Benteen would have been able to join Reno in attacking the village. However, Custer's failure to mount a flanking attack at Ford B was the deciding factor. If that attack had been made, Custer would have charged through the village cutting off the noncombatants and forcing the warriors that were still preparing to fight, back toward Reno and Benteen. The warriors would not have offered a coordinated attack on either front, and would have been defeated, or they would have scattered.

When Custer heard that Benteen was back on the main trail, at a time Reno was already attacking, he ordered Benteen to come to his support. Custer knew Reno should be able to hold on his skirmish line (reported by Bouyer) until Custer launched his attack. The warriors would then rush back to defend their village. Custer would want his main force to support his attack. Reno would have stayed in the valley and constituted a threat. If Benteen had hurried and followed orders he would have been able to join the two companies Custer had left in reserve. They would have supported Custer's attack on the warriors and the cordoning off of the noncombatants. As the packs and their enlarged company came on the scene it would have added to the confusion of the warriors, and they would have either scattered, been defeated, or surrendered in order to protect the noncombatants. Which brings us back to the main question. Why didn't Custer attack at Ford B? This was Custer's plan, and an attack at Ford B was a necessity if the 7th Cavalry was to be successful.

The accepted reasons for Custer's failure to attack and his move to the north are (1) Custer moved to the north to capture the noncombatants that had fled to the north. (2) The village extended further north, so Custer attempted to encircle it.

Are these sound reasons? No, they aren't. Here's why: (1) The noncombatants could have been more effectively cut off by crossing Ford B. The terrain to the north was not that inviting. The Indians were now aware of Custer's troops, and they would have moved to support the noncombatants. They would have been waiting for Custer at any crossing. (2) There is enough evidence from writers such as Marquis and Kuhlman along with the Indian accounts as expressed by Michno to accept the fact that after the Custer battle, and for that matter during it, the Indians moved their village to the north and west. Even if the village extended further north it would not have justified a Custer move to the north into an unknown area. Time was of the essence, particularly once Custer knew Benteen was not aiding Reno. He had called for Benteen and the packs to come quickly. His move further north would certainly not have helped, nor would

Custer have wanted to rely on Benteen to assess the situation when he arrived and be able to make a reliable military judgment.

I would then say that the failure to attack at Ford B was the underlying reason for Custer's defeat. An attack led by Custer with Reno still in the valley and Benteen coming on, even if somewhat slowly, should have enabled the 7th Cavalry to defeat the Indians. At the time Custer would have attacked at Ford B, the Indians were rattled and the village was in a state of confusion. The Indians would have attempted a harassing attack, but not a coordinated attack. The purpose of the harassing attack would have been to allow the various tribal units to scatter. The result of this action is conjectural, but the 7th Cavalry would have proclaimed success. Generals Sheridan, Terry, and the hierarchy might not have.

SUMMARY

I want to conclude with a summary which illustrates that Custer's actions were those of a competent commander until his five companies moved north of Medicine Tail Coulee. And that this substantiates my hypothesis that something had to have happened to Custer at Ford B. I will use an exemplifying criticism by an author in whose failure to connect recognized facts places the blame for the movement and the debacle that followed on Custer. The criticism was made by a famous Custer authority about a J. L. Beardsley's article in a 1933 magazine, *Outdoor Life*. The writer, whom I will leave nameless, said the article contained "many erroneous statements, but no new facts or theories." I don't know just what erroneous statements he attributed to Beardsley's article, but it is true the facts and theories presented were and are well known. The question is whether they were sound or not. I believe they were, and that they are indicative of the failure that the writer and others have shown in not connecting these facts and theories with Custer's knowledge and actions.

The significant facts and theories found in the article are: (1) Beardsley said, "Like all successful Indian fighters, Custer had learned that to surprise a body of Indians from two or more sides was the only successful method of defeating them, regardless of numbers. A large village will scatter as easily as a small one." (2) "They knew troops were near, but the accounts of the Indians all tell of the great confusion in the camp, trying to get armed and mounted, and what was more important to get on their war paint, all of which took time." (3) [If Reno had remained in the valley and continued to attack, and Custer had attacked across Ford B] "They (the Indians) would have been split into two bodies and unable to concentrate against either or muster their full strength ..." (4) "Some of the old chiefs say there were hardly ten warriors guarding the ford, at the point where Custer would have crossed," and that if he had it was entirely possible that he would have been successful.

Although I was not aware of Beardsley's article when forming my conception of the battle, my analysis of Custer's actions revolve around Custer's recognition of the elements Beardsley brought out.

The following is a brief summary of my supposition, which those facts and theories underlie:

191

General Terry, Colonel Gibbon, and Lt. Colonel Custer met on the 21st of June on the steamboat Far West. From scouting reports they had ascertained that: (1) The Indians would most likely be found along the Little Big Horn. (2) The number of warriors could be 1500 or more. As Custer moved to the Little Big Horn there would have been nothing that repudiated these reports.

Custer's 7th Cavalry on the morning of the 25th were at what is known as Halt 1, along Davis Creek. Lt. Varnum sent back a message from the Crow's Nest, carried by Red Star, that the scouts had seen the Indian village. Custer hurried to the Crow's Nest. According to the initial reports by Major Reno and Captain Benteen, the regiment moved from Halt 1 by 5 a.m. After going several miles they were met by Custer. Contrary to Benteen's cover-up accounts, Custer told them that the Indian village was located on the western side of the Little Big Horn. Assuming that the regiment walked the several miles to where they met Custer (Halt 2), the time should have been around 6 a.m. In an hour cavalry should, at a walk, be able to go 3 or more miles. Benteen said he had a fast walking horse that could cover 5 miles. They then went ahead several more miles before Custer halted and divided the command (Halt 3). They had now crossed the divide and were in the vicinity of Reno Creek. According to Reno's early official report the time was <u>about</u> 8 a.m. This time appears to be approximately correct.

Custer would have realized that Reno Creek led into the Little Big Horn, and the Indian village was somewhat to the north of the confluence. He would have known this from his prior knowledge of the region and from his own scouting reports.

Custer was planning to attack the village that day because of his fear that the Indians were aware of his troops. This fear would have prompted him to send a battalion to the bluffs on his left to make sure Indians were not waiting to ambush his troops and that there were no other villages to the south of the known village.

Although Custer had to be concerned that the Indians were aware of his troops, he also would recognize the need to formulate a plan to attack the known village. This would be, as Beardsley brought out, an attempt to strike the village from two sides. This also brings up why an analysis of time is so important. According to Benteen they would have moved about four to six miles from Halt 1, which they left by 5 a.m., to the division at Halt 3. The 8 a.m. registered by Reno is probably late, but we can use it as the approximate time of the division. They are roughly 12 miles from Ford A. It should be fairly accurate to say that even with stops the average gait then taken in estimating the time would have been a trot. This means that Reno could have reached Ford A by 10 a.m. These times then coincide with Indian accounts which have Reno's attack taking place before or by noon. We should remember Girard's watch time, Sgt. Kanipe's time for when Reno reached Ford A, and Martin's time for when Custer saw a peaceful village. We shouldn't dismiss these times, particularly since the later times used at the Reno Court and afterwards were initially needed to prevent Reno's court-martial.

Custer's dividing of the command also support Beardsley's known fact of the importance of a two sided attack. We know, or should know, that Custer needed to make sure there were no Indians south of the known camp. You don't send a scout to determine this because you need enough men that could attack or put up a defense against a large number of warriors. So you send three companies, and as we know, Captain Benteen was given that assignment. Custer would plan to attack the village from the south. He then assigned three companies to his second in command, Major Reno, who was to lead the attack. If Benteen didn't find any Indians he would cross the Little Big Horn and move in support of Major Reno. Custer certainly needed to worry about the packs so he provided Captain McDougall with an enlarged company to protect them. This left 5 companies under his command. We know he was afraid the Indians would scatter, so there is no way he would have his five companies trailing Major Reno's three companies. Since he believes in an enveloping two-sided attack he would plan for those five companies to lead a flanking attack from the north.

As Custer proceeds down Reno Creek his main concerns are: (1) Whether the Indians are aware of his troops, and whether Benteen is going to meet a large number of warriors and need help. (2) Will the 7th Cavalry be in time to prevent the Indians from scattering? As Custer nears the Little Big Horn he knows he must initiate his attack on the Indian village. He hasn't heard from Benteen, but his scouts have not seen any signs of Indians to the south, and there has been no firing from Benteen's direction. Custer then sends his attack orders to Reno by Adjutant Cooke, and he sends Sgt. Major Sharrow, and the Indian scout Stabbed to locate and give Benteen his orders.

Reno's orders were those as expressed by Reno's orderly Davern, and by Custer's orderly Martin. Reno was to cross the Little Big Horn and move against the Indian village. He would be supported by the whole regiment. Benteen would be on his left and Custer would go to the other end of the village and attack from the north.

Benteen's orders were that when reaching the Little Big Horn he was to cross and move in support of Reno. Custer would be taking his five companies in an attempt to flank the Indians

Custer's objective was to coordinate his attack with Major Reno's. As Beardsley said, the confusion in the camp would be aided by the warriors attempt to get armed and mounted, and to put on their war paint. The warriors would split into two bodies and not be able to concentrate against either or muster their full strength. This is why Custer would have realized the importance of coordinating his attack with Major Reno. Custer is not going to waste the valuable time that most writers have him doing. He wants to have six companies attacking from the south and five companies from the north—in a synchronized attack.

After sending Reno and Benteen their orders, Custer would have wasted no time in going to the ridge in order to observe the Indian village and decide how best to attack it with his five companies. The four Crow scouts and Mitch Bouyer led the way. After arriving on the ridge Custer sees Reno's men either crossing Ford A or moving through the timber. The time is around 11 a.m. Custer's five companies have been allowed to water their horses. Custer now signals to them and crosses over the later Reno entrenchment area to meet them. He then goes back to the crest to check on events in the valley. Reno's troops are reforming after passing through the timber. Custer waves to them. He goes on to Weir Point where he can get a better view of the Indian village. As Martin said, they see a comparatively peaceful village.

Reno is concerned about where Benteen's support is, and whether he should wait for him. He sends two messengers to Custer, but does not receive a reply. He then follows his orders to move against the village.

Benteen, hearing from Lt. Gibson that there are no Indians or camps to the south, moves back to the main trail. He receives or has received Custer's initial attack orders carried by Sgt. Major Sharrow. He arrives on the trail just ahead of the packs. According to Benteen's early report it is now **about** 1 p.m. Seeing the situation in the village from Weir Point, Custer realizes he will want the packs to support him. Captain Tom Custer sends Sgt. Kanipe to the packs with those orders. If Kanipe sees Benteen he should give him the same message.

Custer then moves down western coulee to Medicine Tail Coulee. The four Crows and Mitch Bouyer follow along the bluffs. They see Reno establish his skirmish line. Bouyer, knowing the battle is commencing, dismisses Curley and tells him to go back to the packs. Bouyer and the three Crows go down and meet with Custer. Custer hears that Benteen is back on the main trail. He receives this news either from Bouyer, Stabbed via the rear guard, or the Sgt. Major who has just returned from taking his attack orders to Benteen. This caused Custer to send Martin back to Benteen with his new orders. The Crow scouts were released, but went to Bouyer's Bluff where they fired on what few Indians were at Ford B. Custer moved to the ford, and then his troops retreated. Martin, who had reached the bluffs near Weir Point, saw Custer's troops retreating. Martin then saw Reno's men moving into the timber. He went on to meet Benteen.

Custer's troops moved to the north from Deep Coulee where his 5 companies were wiped out. The time would have been close to 3 p.m.

We are faced with the two major questions: (1) Why didn't Custer attack across Ford B? and (2) Why move north from Deep Coulee? There was never an offensive attack by Custer's five companies, nor a tactical retreat or an established defense. Why wasn't there? My answer has been that Custer was shot at Ford B and that is what stopped the attack. This incident along with other factors caused an unorganized retreat. Why, if Custer was in command, didn't that retreat move back to where Custer expected aid from Benteen and the packs? Why move further north? There, panic accompanied by the overwhelming number of Indians brought a quick end to Custer's five companies.

Known facts, theories and testimony accompanied by a need for, and a recognition of the cover-ups made at the Reno Court show Custer's plans and actions were sound until he reached Ford B, and it is at that point that the unanswered questions arise.

In my primary study, Liddic's *Vanishing Victory: Custer's Last March,* I have analyzed and explained why I reject the "accepted" version that has dominated the view of the battle for a hundred and thirty years.

Evans' in his book, *Custer's Last Fight,* and Nightengale in his book, *Little Big Horn,* do not differ with the accepted version. Neither recognizes the timing cover-ups or the need and basis for them. Both assume Reno's move down the valley preceded Custer's move to the ridge, and that Reno was establishing his skirmish line at the time Custer arrived at his first lookout.

Evans recognizes the difficulty of accepting an exact time for events, and believes that it is meaningless in comparison to determining where each of the major elements were in relation to specific events. I totally agree in the abstract, but not when necessary time statements are ignored, brushed off and left out of your analysis. I consider time the second primary cover-up, and a failure to comprehend it as such prevents any rational conclusion. I will again mention several essential statements of actions that definitely counter Evans' and Nightengale's description of events, and which they need to counter in order to support their hypothesis: (1) After Custer gave Reno his orders to attack he would have had to remain along Reno Creek or North Fork for over an hour, according to Evans' time table. Let's remember this is Custer; the Indian village lies beyond the bluffs; Custer has sent Major Reno to attack this village; yet Custer did not go to the ridge to reconnoiter until receiving a message from striker McIlhargey and Interpreter Girard. According to the accepted version Custer planned to follow Reno until McIlhargey's and Girard's messages made him decide to flank the Indians. (2) There are reports, by Reno's soldiers and some Ree scouts, of seeing Custer on the ridge while Reno was reforming his troops after passing through Ford A, and reports of seeing Custer on the ridge while moving down the valley. However, these reports are dismissed because timewise Reno is preceding Custer. (3) From a time standpoint, Martin's report of seeing Reno, while he was on his way to Benteen with Custer's message to "be quick" is ignored, along with the recognition that Reno was just retreating when Benteen (with Martin) reached the ridge. This would mean that no matter where Martin received his message to take to Benteen, Custer should have been able to launch an attack at Ford B while Reno was still in the valley. Lt. Varnum's sighting of E Company also supports that analysis. Wouldn't a competent commander have felt such an attack was necessary in order to aid Reno, defeat the Indians, or capture the noncombatants? Did Custer really trust Benteen? Since he wasn't sure Martin made it to Benteen, do you really think he would have waited for Benteen?

The failure by Evans and Nightengale to recognize Lt. Wallace's cover-up of the initial time of the division of the command, and the reason it was necessary, has led to their belief that at the time Captain Weir and Captain Benteen moved to Weir Point, they saw the Custer fight about to begin (Nightengale) or as it was ending. (Evans)

If Martin saw Reno in the valley while he was on his way to Benteen, and they returned at a time Reno's troops were retreating, shouldn't Custer's troops have been retreating during that same time? Gunfire could be heard by Reno's and Benteen's forces from firing by Custer's troops along Deep Coulee, but not the Last Stand Hill area.

The next important analysis is the time Reno and Benteen remained on Reno Hill before moving to Weir Point to investigate the firing that had been heard. At the Reno Court, wouldn't it be imperative for Reno and Benteen to attempt to show how they would have moved as soon as expedient to investigate the gunfire that had been heard from the Custer battlefield? How does the officers' testimony compare with the orderlies, Davern and Martin, as to the time they remained on Reno Hill before moving to investigate the firing? Whose testimony do you think might be more reliable?

To me you either have a competent commander whose actions had to be covered-up, or you have, not only an egotistical, self-glorifying commander, but one that is also inept and lacks courage.

My maxim for viewing Custer and the Battle is: If Custer was shot at Ford B he wasn't to blame for what took place; if he wasn't shot until Last Stand Hill he was to blame. In other word, Custer should have launched an attack at Ford B, which he could have done while Reno was still in the valley, but if he was shot at the ford and the movement to the north was an attempt by part of his force to move him to the Far West, and the rest of the soldiers became disorganized and retreated to the north and east, then Custer was not to blame for the defeat that followed. However, if he decided to move north for whatever reason and he wasn't shot until Last Stand Hill, then he was to blame. I don't believe Custer's background or psyche would have allowed him to not attempt an attack at Ford B, or that there were any sound reasons for him to have moved north of Deep Coulee; consequently I believe he was shot at Ford B. This caused a disorganized retreat that never came under officer control. There then was no tactical defense established or retreat to where they could have expected aid. This became an ideal setup for Indian warfare, and the battle did not last long. Custer's troops were annihilated, most likely two hours before Weir or Benteen reached Weir Point.

APPENDIX A

EXAMINING A TIME ANALYSIS

The following is a time analysis that has been used to justify the contention that Reno's movement down the valley was ahead of Custer's on the ridge, and that the three Crow scouts (White Man Runs Him, Hairy Moccasin, Goes Ahead) were not with Custer in Medicine Tail Coulee nor did they go to Bouyers' Bluff. Walter Camp used the following to justify the Crow scout Goes Ahead's assertion that they were not with Custer after he left the ridge: "They would have met Benteen's and Reno's commands together when they went back south along the bluffs, instead of Benteen's only, as they certainly did."[1]

This is a timing analysis in which I take a different perspective. I believe the evidence indicates that the three Crows were with Custer in Medicine Tail Coulee, then went to Bouyer's Bluff, and when Custer's troops retreated they fled back to Reno Creek where they met Benteen's forces. The three Crows—White Man Runs Him, Hairy Moccasin, and Goes Ahead—then directed Benteen to the ridge. This is an important timing recognition as it is evidence that Custer's forces were ahead of Reno's and that Custer's battalions were retreating even before Reno's three companies.

You can read practically any position into the Crows' varying accounts, so it is necessary to establish a relationship with other testimony. It is essential to use Martin's accounts as a primary source. Many writers use Camp's reasoning to say that Martin could not have received his message to take to Benteen in Medicine Tail Coulee, but instead would have had to have been in Cedar Coulee or near Weir Point. They say that is why Martin was able to see Reno fighting in the valley, reach Benteen, and still join Reno right after he had fled from the valley. This enables writers to use it to form or support their contention that Reno had established his skirmish line while Custer was still on his way to Medicine Tail Coulee—usually by way of Cedar Coulee. Martin is then sent back from Cedar

Coulee or at some point before Custer could have neared Ford B. To accept this position one has to discard Martin's testimony. This is an important hypothesis which effects ones view of Custer and the battle.

In contrast to this version of Camp's analysis, I believe that the Crows meeting Benteen at the time Reno's troops were retreating supports the supposition that Martin received his message to Benteen within 600 yards of Ford B, and that the three Crows and Mitch Bouyer were with Custer at the time. Curley, after Bouyer told him he was too young and should return to the packs, had remained on the ridge north of Weir Point. Custer then permitted the three Crows to leave. They would have gone to Bouyer's Bluff expecting or hoping that Custer would be successful in his attack on the Indian village. After a small amount of firing, Custer's troops retreated and the Crow's fled back to Reno Creek.

During this time Martin, who was on his way to Benteen, had reached the ridge near Weir Point. He heard firing and looking back saw Custer's troops retreating from the ford. I believe conjecturally (in contrast to the prevailing views) that C Company was the lead company when Custer went to the ford, then F and E. Michael Reynolds was with his father (the Crow Agent), Edward Curtis, General Woodruff, and the Crow scouts, White Man Runs Him, Hairy Moccasin, and Goes Ahead, when they retraced Custer's route. Michael said a platoon of C Company was with Custer within fifty yards of Ford B at the time Martin received his message to take to Benteen.[2] Benteen mentioned there were few C Company horses found on the battlefield. I believe this was because they initially got off their horses when Custer fell at the ford crossing. They did some firing, but were not able to hold onto their horses so many were retrieved by the Indians. Although some troopers attempted to join Keogh's two companies they were not a part of his reserve battalion.

Getting back to Martin, the following testimony would have had to be discarded if Camp's analysis was correct. (1) Martin's reference that after receiving his message he moved along Middle Coulee on his way to Weir Point.[3] (2) Martin then heard firing and when he looked back he saw Custer's troops retreating.[4] (3) As Martin moved on he saw Reno fighting in the valley.[5] None of this would have happened if he had received his message in Cedar Coulee, nor would he have had to tell Boston Custer where Custer was.

At the time Martin looked back and saw Custer retreating, the Crows had begun their flight back to Reno Creek. Curley mentioned passing some Rees with captured horses.[6] This was undoubtedly Little Sioux and the Rees that had captured Indian ponies in the flat and were now driving them up the ridge. Reno may have begun his retreat, which might account for White Man Runs Him's rationalized story to Curtis that he fired at Indians who were after several of Reno's men at the time Custer was sitting at Weir Point. His firing enabled them to reach the ridge. It would have been easy for White Man Runs Him to have thrown in something that actually happened into his Curtis story. Be that as it may, we now have Martin with Benteen. The Crows while on their way to Reno Creek, see Reno's men retreating.

There are two related reports that should be mentioned, the one by the scout Herendeen and the other by Girard. Herendeen's would be fairly accurate while Girard's would indicate his attempt to charge Reno with a court-martial offense.

Herendeen, wo remained in the timber following Reno's retreat, said that about twenty minutes after Reno retreated he heard volley firing from the Custer battlefield. This should have been from Calhoun's and Keogh's companies. When asked how long the firing lasted he said, "it might have lasted an hour, I think not over an hour."[7] He said that he didn't believe there had been any fighting at the ford because he hadn't heard any and he would have since that was behind his location and not that far away.[8]

Herendeen believed the firing he heard took place less than a half hour after Reno had fled the timber.[9] His failure to hear firing at Ford B is understandable. It illustrates not only the short period of firing at the ford, but actually fits into the timing picture. The firing at the ford coincides with Reno's action on the skirmish line. Herendeen would have been preoccupied, and the firing from the skirmish line should have prevented his hearing the firing at Ford B. Shortly after this Martin passed along the ridge and saw Reno's troops. The Crows were on their way back. Keogh's men were firing from Nye-Cartwright in support of Custer's retreating troops. Keogh's two companies then moved to Calhoun Hill, set up a defense, and volley fired. This firing was heard by Herendeen and by Reno's and Benteen's battalions who were now together. Herendeen continues to hear firing for possibly the next hour from the Custer sector. What this establishes is that there was no real tactical defense set up except for a temporary one at Calhoun Hill. The fighting at other locations was not due to an established defense but to necessity, including that at Last Stand Hill.

Outside of the initial skirmish line firing, the fighting by Reno's troops in the valley portrays a panic retreat from the timber by most officers and men. The panic effect should be applied to the fighting in the Custer sector. One should also associate the lack of bodies at Ford B with the fact that until Reno's retreat from the timber they had only suffered a few casualties. Earlier firing on west Calhoun Ridge and Nye Cartwright was heard by Little Sioux, Red Star, Strikes

Two, and Boy Chief as they drove the captured ponies along the flat. At the same time they heard Reno's men firing on their skirmish line.

All of these times coordinate, and what they should prove to students of the battle are: (1) Custer had plans to attack the village from both the south and the north. (2) These plans were known by Reno, Benteen, and the other officers, but were covered-up at the Reno Court. (3) Reno had sent McIlhargey not to tell Custer the Indians were strong in front of him, but to ask if he should wait for Benteen to support him. (4) Custer saw a peaceful village at the time Reno was reforming after crossing Ford A. (5) Girard's statement that the Rees said the hostiles were moving against Reno was a ploy used in Whittaker's attempt to create a script for the Recorder in order to bring court-martial charges against Reno. This is further illustrated by Girard's saying he saw Custer back by Reno's entrenchment at the time Reno set up his skirmish line.

The Crow's did fire on the Indian village from Bouyer's Bluff. They fled back beyond Reno Hill where Curley left them to go to the Little Big Horn, either to obtain water or to find his brother White Swan. The three Crows then met Benteen and pointed out Reno's troops that had reached the ridge.

This substantiates that Custer moved to the ridge while Reno was crossing Ford A. At the time Reno was reforming after crossing Ford A Custer saw a peaceful village. He then moved to Medicine Tail Coulee by way of Western Coulee. He heard Benteen was back on the main trail. Custer sent Martin with his message to Benteen. Custer reached Ford B during the time Reno was on his skirmish line. We are now back to the time coordinates that we previously established.

This should definitely confirm that Custer had planned to attack the village from both the south and north. Reno and Benteen were aware of his plans, and they knew an offense was underway. This means that there should have been no hesitation in going to support Custer. It also indicates that something happened at Ford B which prevented Custer's attack. It supports Benteen's contention that outside of a defense set up initially by Lt. Calhoun and Captain Keogh, there was no organized deployment by Custer's five companies. And finally, it shows why they needed to formulate a timing cover-up in order to close the gap from when Reno and Benteen met and when they went to check on and support Custer.

SOURCES

1.   Hutchins, *The Papers of Edward S. Curtis*, p.143.

2.   Michael Reynolds speech given to the Western Writers of America in 1975.

3. Hammer, (ed.) *Custer in 76*, p. 104.

4. Ibid., 101.

5. Ibid., 103.

6. Graham, *The Custer Myth*, p. 14.

7. Nichols, (ed.) *Reno Court of Inquiry*, p. 257.

8. Ibid., 269.

9. Ibid., 257.

APPENDIX B

THE MEANING OF BENTEEN'S ORDERS

Orders are the basis for the primary cover-up that took place at the Reno Court. Custer's initial attack orders as expressed by the orderlies are the most important ones that need to be recognized and analyzed. However, there has also been a minor dispute over whether the orders carried by Martin actually excused Benteen from going to aid Custer. Walter Camp raised this question, and it has been discussed by others, most recently Don Horn, a noted Little Big Horn authority.

The written order carried by Martin: "Benteen come on Big Village be quick Bring Packs W.W.Cooke P.S. Bring Pack."

Adjutant Cooke gave Martin the following verbal message: "Orderly, I want you to take a message to Captain Benteen. Take the same trail as you came down. If you have time, and there is no danger come back; otherwise stay with your company."

Walter Camp, others, and now Don Horn in a 2005 Little Big Horn Newsletter have suggested that the above orders do not direct Captain Benteen to hurry to aid Custer, but only to hurry and join the regiment. This view excuses Benteen's failure to go immediately in support of Custer.

At the division of the command Benteen was expected to reconnoiter the bluffs to the left of Reno Creek and go to the valley. He was to "pitch into" any Indians that he saw. Custer (contrary to Benteen's statements) did accept the scout's sighting of the Indian encampment in the valley of the Little Big Horn, and had to assume his regiment had been spotted by the Indians. He then planned how to attack the Indians. This plan depended on whether Benteen found any Indians or saw any camps to the south of the known camp. As he approached the Little Big Horn, Custer knew he had to launch his attack even though he had not heard from Benteen. Custer expected Benteen to be moving to his left on a somewhat parallel course to the valley. He then sent attack messages to Reno and Benteen as expressed by Reno's orderly Davern and Custer's orderly Martin. Benteen, when he reached the valley, would move in support of Reno and be on his left. Custer would attempt to encircle the Indian village.

Lt. Gibson, who was sent to scout in advance of Benteen, would have seen from Ridge C not only the valley but that there were no Indians or Indian camps to the south of the known camp. Benteen, being in Valley 3 when he received Gibson's report, continued on to the main trail. Somewhere along Valley 3, or after he had reached the main trail, he was met by Sgt. Major Sharrow with his attack orders. The orders said that when he reached the valley he was to move in support of Reno. He would be on Reno's left and in the center of the attack. In his flanking attack Custer expected to move his five companies to the southwest in an enveloping move.

After having viewed the Indian situation from the ridge. Custer would not have wanted the packs to follow Reno across the Little Big Horn. Instead, Custer wanted them to be in a position to support what he now realized would be the main offensive—an attack across the LBH into the village, splitting the noncombatants who would be fleeing the village from the warriors attacking or preparing to move against Reno. Kanipe was sent to take a message to the packs to hurry and follow him to Custer.

If he saw Benteen he was to tell him what can be assumed were the same orders—hurry, a big village, go to Custer, in other words, Custer was countermanding his orders that had Benteen moving in support of Reno.

As Custer neared Ford B, Bouyer reported to him. He undoubtedly told Custer that Reno had established a skirmish line and was in no immediate danger, but that Benteen had not joined him. Custer then heard that Benteen was back on the main trail. He received this information from either Bouyer; or a message from the Sgt. Major delivered by the Ree scout Stabbed to Custer's rear guard or to the last of his troops to leave the ridge; or the Sgt. Major returning from delivering his attack message to Benteen. Custer then sent Martin with his message to Benteen. Custer, as he had with the packs, now wanted Benteen to support him rather than Reno. Once Custer had viewed the Indian village from the ridge, he would not have wanted his initial orders carried out. Reno could hold out on his skirmish line until Custer's attack drew the warriors away from Reno in order to save the noncombatants. Custer wanted Benteen to bring the ammo packs in support of his main attack. He would have left several companies in reserve under the command of a senior officer with instructions for the packs and Benteen when they arrived.

Don Horn raised three basic points to support his position that Benteen was only expected to hurry and join the rest of the regiment:

(1) The instructions to Martin said: "Orderly, I want you to take a message to Captain Benteen. Ride as fast as you can and tell him to hurry. Tell him it's a big village and I want him to be quick and to bring the ammunition packs." Adjutant Cooke then gave Martin verbal instructions; "Now orderly, ride as fast as you can to Colonel Benteen. Take the same trail as we came down. If you have time, and there is no danger, come back; otherwise stay with your company." Horn believes that if Cooke was expecting Benteen to come directly to Custer, the safest place for Martin to have been was with the Benteen column, yet Cooke tells Martin to come back only if it is safe to do so. Horn thinks this clearly indicates that the Benteen column was not expected to come to Custer and, if Martin was to return to the Custer column, he would have to do it on his own and alone.

I disagree with Horn. I think a prerequisite for any analysis is to recognize two key factors that Benteen and Reno had to cover-up. First, that Custer, when at the Crow's Nest, recognized or accepted the Indian scouts' location of the Indians encampment. Second, that the orderlies were correct in saying that Benteen was sent attack orders along with Reno. Those orders indicated that Benteen was to aid Reno and that Custer would flank the Indians. Custer would not have sent an insignificant order by way of the Sgt. Major at the time Benteen professed to having received one, but not have sent him an order when he was about to initiate his attack. Reno and Benteen needed to cover-up the fact that they received such orders from Custer and consequently were aware that an offense was underway. At the Reno Court, Reno's orderly Davern, and later Custer's orderly Martin in his letter to Colonel Graham, had no reason to cover-up their remembrance of the orders, and those orders did indicate that Benteen was to aid Reno and that an offense was underway.

One also needs to realize that Custer would have been moving to Ford B to begin his attack at the time he gave Martin his orders to Benteen. Custer would have just heard that Benteen was back on the main trail but still some distance from Ford A. Custer would then have wanted Benteen, as he had the packs, to move to assist him and be in a position to aid the main attack. As previously stated, Custer would have heard from Bouyer that Reno had established a skirmish line, and he would believe that Reno could hold that line for the short time before his attack brought the warriors rushing back (as they did) to concentrate on Custer's troops. As Horn said, just the sight of Benteen's battalion along with the packs could have been a deciding factor.

Horn's belief that the message given to Martin from Cooke would not have had Martin staying with Benteen unless there was no danger, and that this clearly tells us that Benteen's column was not expected to come to Custer, represents non sequitur reasoning. Martin was an orderly sent with a message for Benteen, and after delivering his message he would be expected to return to the officer that had sent him. An orderly could be expected to carry a return message, and as in this case, would move faster than Benteen's battalion. Cooke would have realized that although they had just passed through the area without encountering any Indians, a battle would now be in progress and it may no longer have been safe. Cooke merely informed Martin that it was not necessary to attempt to return if conditions were not safe. Considering these orders, and since Martin's horse had been shot and he had been sent back to the packs with a message (contrary to Benteen's and later Martin's accounts), he would have continued on with Benteen.

(2) Horn's second sustaining point is that Custer was only expecting Benteen to come quickly in order to get into the fight and not to come directly to Custer. This means that Custer was leaving it up to Benteen as to where he would enter the battle and how he could be the most effective.

Again I disagree. You have a battle now in progress. This battle, in Custer's mind, would be taking place in the valley, behind bluffs, and with the main offensive being launched by Custer across Ford B. Benteen when nearing the Little Big Horn, would have had to decide whether to cross at Ford A or to move to the ridge. He would have had to go to the ridge in order to determine what and where would be the most effective deployment of his battalion and the packs. These decisions and actions would have taken time when time was of the essence.

In no way can I see Custer, the commander, leaving such decisions up to Benteen. Custer knew where the main attack was taking place, and this is where he would have wanted Benteen to come and bring the packs. He would have left one of his battalion commanders in a reserve role with instructions for Benteen and the packs. This officer would know Custer's plans as well as the current situation.

(3) Horn's third point is that Custer would have been in the village long before Benteen could join him, so this indicates that Cooke did not expect Martin to lead the Benteen column to Custer. This is hard for me to follow. Custer is launching an attack on an immense village (that he has seen) which by most accounts had several thousand warriors, yet Custer would have assumed or recognized the possibility that he might need additional troops to defeat these warriors. In fact, this might even be the reason he said in his message that it was a "big village" and to "be quick."

One general question not answered by the proponents of Horn's theory is why Benteen didn't use it to justify his failure to go immediately to aid Custer.

This leaves unanswered the main questions concerning the battle. Why didn't Custer attack across Ford B, and why did his command move further north?

APPENDIX C

CUSTER'S ORDERS ACCORDING TO DAVERN AND MARTIN

Custer's order should have been the requisite investigation at the Reno Court of Inquiry. If Reno's orders had been more explicit and extensive than he reported, and were then violated, it would have constituted an inescapable court-martial offense.

At the Reno Court, Davern (Reno's orderly) stated the orders given to Major Reno from General Custer. The following were the questions asked and his answers:

Q. State whether you heard Adjutant Cooke give any orders to Major Reno when he was moving toward the Little Big Horn River?

A. I heard Adjutant Cooke give him an order.

Q. Tell what that order was and where you were when it was given?

A. "Girard comes back and reports the Indian village three miles ahead and moving. The General directs you to take your three companies and drive everything before you." Those I believe were his exact words.

Q. Was anything else said?

A. Yes, sir: "Colonel Benteen will be on your left and will have the same instructions."

Reno's counsel in his summation discredited and dismissed Davern's answers (p. 599, Reno Court of Inquiry, edited by Ron Nichols). Reno's counsel:

At this point Reno received an order from General Custer, as commanding officer, which governed his future action. It has been stated in several ways,

211

but all of them unite in declaring that he was to charge the Indians, who had already been discovered in the bottom on the left side of the Little Big Horn, under a promise of support from General Custer's command. At the same time that Reno received this order he was accompanied by Lieutenant Wallace, whose testimony the Court has heard, and by Lieutenant Hodgson who so bravely died in this charge.

One should keep in mind what Lt. Varnum said in the book recounting his reminiscences, how he kidded Lt. Wallace, who was by the side of General Custer, not to stay back with the "coffee coolers." General Custer laughed and told Wallace he could go with Varnum. This doesn't sound like he would have been by Reno's side. Why might Reno's defense have wanted to put Wallace with Reno?

Reno's counsel goes on:

> An orderly, by the name of Davern, at that time a private soldier, who was in the rear of Major Reno, has testified to a recollection that is different from that of either Major Reno or of Lieutenant Wallace, and which is also different from the recollection of Captain Benteen. [In other words don't take Davern's word—instead take the word of those who would be facing court-martial charges if Davern was right.] He has sought to convey the impression that at the time this order was communicated, a statement was made that Colonel Benteen would be on Major Reno's left and would have the same instructions that he had. It is hardly necessary for us to linger to see how impossible this statement must be, for when he was asked where Benteen was at that time in order to receive instructions, Davern could not place him, and the whole testimony shows that Benteen had long before this been sent to the left and was already far out of sight.

I don't think anyone could have stated where Benteen was at that time, but for this to be a criticism of Davern or the orders he heard is ridiculous. It actually shows how important the orders were and the need for Reno's defense to disavow and discredit both the orders and Davern. The question is, why was Davern's statement of the orders Reno received so important that it needed to be rejected and Davern disparaged? Was it because Davern's answer indicated that Custer sent orders to Benteen at the time he issued his attack orders to Reno, and that Benteen was to join Reno in the valley attack? If Benteen and Reno had received such orders from Custer, then Reno should have been expecting Benteen to be his support from the rear and he shouldn't have left the valley. It would also indicate that an offense was underway. Why wasn't Davern asked if the orders indicated what Custer's part in the offense would be? Why wasn't Martin, Custer's orderly, asked about the orders Custer gave to Reno, and, at that time, if any were sent to Benteen?

According to Martin's account given to Colonel Graham years later, Custer's orders to Reno were: "The General told the Adjutant to order him [Reno] to go down and cross the river and attack the Indian village, and that he would support him with the whole regiment. He said he would go down to the other end and drive them, and that he would have Benteen hurry up and attack them in the center."

Previously in my writings, I thought this may have meant that Reno, after crossing the Little Big Horn, would have moved to the west in order to block the Indians from escaping to the south, and that Benteen would have moved closer to the river. However, after rereading Davern's account and taking note of the concern by Reno and his counsel, I realized that if Benteen had followed the path ordered by Custer when he divided his command, Benteen would have reached the Little Big Horn to the south and west of Reno's crossing at Ford A. The orders as stated by Davern were correct, in moving to support Reno, Benteen would have been on Reno's left or his western side. This, undoubtedly, is why Reno and his counsel were so intent on rejecting and downplaying Davern's remembrance of the orders given Reno.

The course of the Little Big Horn River and the other rivers, their location, confluences, etc. would have been known, and that knowledge was greater than indicated at the Reno Court. (Check W. Kent King's book showing the original maps of the Custer battle area.) Benteen's orders as expressed by both Davern and Martin had him crossing the Little Big Horn and moving in support of Reno. Benteen would then have been on Reno's left. Custer with his five companies would have attempted to encircle the Indians and drive them toward Reno and Benteen. Benteen, being on the left of Reno, could be construed to have been in the center of the encirclement. (Note map.)

This indicates several essential points: (1) Both Reno and Benteen received attack orders from Custer. (2) Benteen was to be the one supporting Reno from the rear. (3) Custer planned on encircling the Indians. (4) Reno and Benteen knew that an offense against the Indians was underway. (5) Both Reno and Benteen needed to cover-up such knowledge. (6) Lt. Hodgson had been killed, so an officer was needed to verify Reno's version of orders and events. The only officer that qualified and could be placed by Reno's side was the unattached Lt. Wallace.

The cover-up of orders created a battle scenario which belittled Custers actions, but was necessary to prevent Reno from being court-martialed and others indicted.

The linchpin in any analysis is recognizing that Custer at the Crow's Nest saw or accepted the scouts sighting of the Indian encampment, and that neither Benteen or Reno could admit to such knowledge since it would indicate that at the division of the command Custer formulated an initial plan to attack the Indian village. This was still Custer's plan when he issued his attack orders as he neared the Little Big Horn. Up to this time, the only way Custer would have changed his plan is if Benteen on his scout to the left had encountered Indians, or if he found additional camps to the south of the known camp. Custer, when nearing the Little Big Horn, saw Indians fleeing to what he assumed was the main camp. Custer, fearing the Indians would scatter, knew he had to launch his attack even though he had not heard from Benteen. He sent his attack orders to Reno by way of Adjutant Cooke, and sent the Sgt. Major to Benteen. He most likely had Lt. Hare assign the Ree scout Stabbed to go with the Sgt. Major. The orders to Reno, as heard and stated by the two orderlies, Davern and Martin, implied similar orders were sent to Benteen.

Map I

Map I Area Map

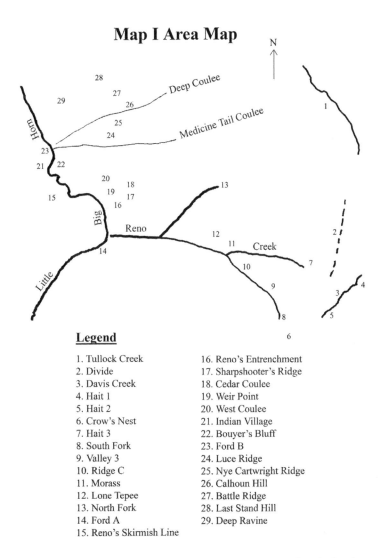

Legend

1. Tullock Creek	16. Reno's Entrenchment
2. Divide	17. Sharpshooter's Ridge
3. Davis Creek	18. Cedar Coulee
4. Hait 1	19. Weir Point
5. Hait 2	20. West Coulee
6. Crow's Nest	21. Indian Village
7. Hait 3	22. Bouyer's Bluff
8. South Fork	23. Ford B
9. Valley 3	24. Luce Ridge
10. Ridge C	25. Nye Cartwright Ridge
11. Morass	26. Calhoun Hill
12. Lone Tepee	27. Battle Ridge
13. North Fork	28. Last Stand Hill
14. Ford A	29. Deep Ravine
15. Reno's Skirmish Line	

Map I is an area map showing the named locations used in the book.

Map II

Map II

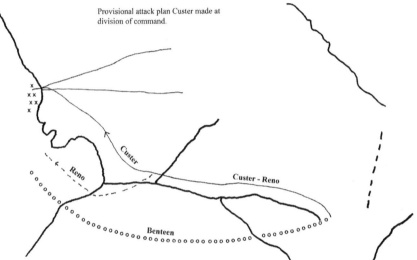

Provisional attack plan Custer made at division of command.

Map II shows Custer's initial plan at the division of the command. This was still his plan when he issued his attack orders to Reno and Benteen.

Map III

Map III

Deviation from Custer's provisional plan
because of Benteen's movement and
Custer's failure to attack at Ford B.

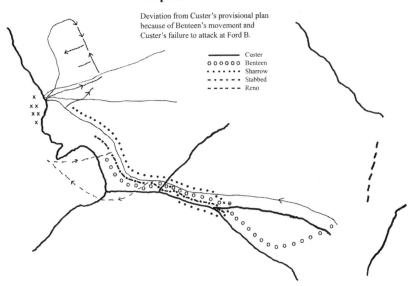

Map III shows the deviation from Custer's initial plan because of
Benteen's actual movement and Custer's failure to attack across Ford B.

1538529

Made in the USA